AN IMPERATIVE TO CURE

AN IMPERATIVE TO CURE

Principles and Practice of Q'eqchi' Maya Medicine in Belize

James B. Waldram

University of New Mexico Press | Albuquerque

First paperback edition 2022 | ISBN 978-0-8263-6444-9

Library of Congress Cataloging-in-Publication Data
Names: Waldram, James B. (James Burgess), author.
Title: An imperative to cure: principles and practice of Q'eqchi' Maya medicine in Belize / James B. Waldram.
Description: Albuquerque: University of New Mexico Press, 2020. | Includes bibliographical references and index.
Identifiers: LCCN 2020015343 (print) | LCCN 2020015344 (e-book) | ISBN 9780826361738 (cloth) | ISBN 9780826361745 (e-book)
Subjects: LCSH: Kekchi Indians—Medicine. | Kekchi Indians—Health and hygiene. | Traditional medicine—Belize.
Classification: LCC F1465.2. K5 W34 2020 (print) | LCC F1465.2. K5 (e-book) | DDC 615.8808997423—dc23
LC record available at https://lccn.loc.gov/2020015343
LC e-book record available at https://lccn.loc.gov/2020015344

Cover illustration: Itzamna, Maya god of medicine and science. Courtesy of Vexels.
Designed by Felicia Cedillos
Composed in Minion Pro 10.25/14.25

Contents

Illustrations

Maps

Figures

Tables

Acknowledgments

As I put the finishing touches on this manuscript before sending it to the publisher, I have just returned from southern Belize, one of several trips I make each year to keep in touch, strategize with my participants about next steps, and continue my research. I realize now that I have been working with Q'eqchi' medical practitioners, their patients, and interpreters for fifteen years! I have had the wonderful experience of watching their children be born and grow up, go off to school or get married, and start families of their own. Fifteen years is a long time. Some practitioners have passed on; others have become infirm. Medical problems have arisen as we all have aged. Some have been cured; others linger. Our relationships have grown stronger with each passing year. New technologies allow us to maintain more regular contact now, and I have learned about new apps that make it easier for practitioners to reach me at little or no expense. A beautiful young girl, named after my wife, Pamela, is about to enter high school. A little baby I just met is named after one of my graduate students who worked on the project two summers ago. I always tell my students that ethnography is fundamentally about relationships, yet I think they are still surprised at the joyful reaction I receive when I take them to Belize to meet these folks. Four students in particular have left such a positive legacy that our research continues to be welcome and anticipated: Andrew Hatala, Demi Vrettas, Krista Murray, and Michelle Gowan. My thanks to you all for your hard work, sincerity, and dedication to the people with whom we work.

At the very core of this research are the practitioners themselves: the late Albino Maquin, Francisco Caal, Emilio Kal, Manuel Choc, the late Lorenzo Choc, the late Manuel Baki, and Augustino Sho. This research was their idea, and they have continued to provide new insights and direction over all these years. The coordinator of their organization, Victor Cal, deserves great credit for facilitating this research, from the moment he first contacted me on behalf of the Maya Healers Association of Belize to my most recent trip in June 2019 when he inspired a new graduate student, bringing us both near tears as he declared her to be "a daughter of Toledo." As a Q'eqchi' cultural and community expert, he has guided me at every step, and he and his wife, Rosa, have kept an eye out for my students and ensured their welfare in the field. Simply put, without his vision and energy, this research would never have happened.

I have been fortunate to work with several Q'eqchi' cultural and language interpreters, including Pedro Maquin, Albino's grandson; his brother Rey; his wife, Fercia; and members of Francisco Caal's family, including Romulo, Federico, and Tomas Caal. They have worked closely with me to ensure that the knowledge of these medical practitioners is properly understood and communicated within proper Q'eqchi' ethical sensibilities and protocols. Tomas Caal has been especially invaluable and has worked with me on this manuscript to ensure accuracy. I count them all as friends.

My gratitude to Dr. Jamil Sawaya for the medical insights and assistance.

Funding for this research has come primarily through three successive research grants from the Social Sciences and Humanities Research Council of Canada (SSHRCC) and the 2017 SSHRCC Insight Award. Additional funding was provided by the University of Saskatchewan. A sabbatical in 2017–2018 afforded me the time needed to complete a draft of this book.

The Belize National Institute for Culture and History (NICH) has been very supportive of this research. I am especially grateful to Nigel Encalada and Rolando Cocom of NICH. It has been my honor to present some of this research at the annual conferences organized by NICH.

Maps, figures, and tables were prepared by the Social Sciences Research Laboratories (SSRL) at the University of Saskatchewan. The laboratories also provided statistical support for the data analysis.

I would like to thank Clark Whitehorn, former executive editor of the University of New Mexico Press, for his support of this work. Taking over for him as my liaison has been Sonia Dickey, who has been great. All the staff at the press who were involved in bringing the manuscript to fruition as a book deserve kudos as well. My gratitude is also extended to the anonymous reviewers of the manuscript. Reviewing is a huge task that takes time away from other work, and the reviewers provided important insights that allowed me to improve the book.

Finally, as always, there is the one who grounds me: my wife, Pamela Downe. A tremendous medical anthropologist, she has been my scholarly adviser (and unabashed critic!) in so many ways that I will never be able to repay her. As a life partner, she is all one could ask for. She has been amazingly supportive of my many trips to Belize and has provided untold logistical support during both adventures and misadventures. Her own work stands as a constant reminder of why what we do as anthropologists is important. When I need inspiration, I need to look no further than to her.

Prologue

A Ten-Minute Break

"Okay, Jim. Ten-minute break," announces Francisco as we drive through the village of Big Falls in southern Belize. Don Francisco Caal,[1] a Q'eqchi' *ilonel*, or medical practitioner, speaks only a little English, but his hand gesture, waving to the side of the road, makes it clear that I am to pull over. He climbs out, grabs his knapsack, and quickly scrambles up a hill toward a thatch house set far back from the road. The knapsack holds his medicines, and so it is clear to me that he is going to treat a patient. (Subsequently, I learn that the patient's mother had contacted him a week before to seek his services for her son.) I grab my own knapsack full of equipment and quickly follow, trying to catch up. Francisco, spry and athletic at middle age, beats me to the house, and as is the custom, I wait outside while he explains to the residents who I am and why I am accompanying him. A few moments pass. Then his head appears in the doorway and he waves me in.

I introduce myself to a late-twenty-ish man and a similarly aged woman I assume to be his wife. I explain, in English, the purpose of my presence. His wife, who speaks only Q'eqchi', seems wary, but she relaxes when I pull out my laptop and play a video of Victor Cal, coordinator for the Maya Healers Association of Belize, explaining in Q'eqchi' the nature of the research. As the video is playing, Francisco sets about his work, requesting that the young man bring him a bucket filled with water. Seated, he reaches into his knapsack and retrieves several packets of banana leaves wrapped tightly in vine. Opening them carefully, he selects a measure of leaves and places them in the water. With his hands he begins mixing, squeezing the plant mixture in the water and swishing it about. Hurriedly, I set up the video camera to record the treatment. Francisco moves quickly, and it has been a challenge in this research to be ready when he is. After only a few minutes, he signals for the young man to lie back in the nearby hammock. The treatment session is about to begin.

Up to this point, there has been very little conversation between the patient and the ilonel. The conversation they had while I waited outside was brief, less than a minute, and during a later interview, Francisco confirms that he was only explaining about me and was not asking any questions about the patient's disorder. Since my entrance, and until he motioned for the patient to lie in the hammock, he has not said a word other than requesting the bucket and water.

"In the name of the Father, the Son, and the Holy Spirit," Francisco utters in Q'eqchi', starting his opening treatment prayer known as *remeer.* As he does, he leans in to place his hands firmly on the patient's head, his left cupping the side above the ear and his right pressing on the forehead with fingers extended. Francisco's head is bowed, toward the patient's stomach, and his eyes show no engagement with the person in the hammock. The patient, in turn, looks blankly forward. There is no eye contact. They remain in this position, stationary, for almost ninety seconds while Francisco rapidly utters his prayer. Then, while still praying, he reaches down into the bucket, wets his hands, flicks off some of the plant material, and places his hands back on the head in the same position for another twenty-five seconds. "It is in the prayer that you ask for coolness of the plant medicine to treat the sickness," Francisco tells me later. During the prayer he "calls the name of the plant and places it on the patient's head."

Again, he reaches for the water and replaces his hands. Ten seconds later he breaks this position and, exhaling audibly as if blowing, runs his hands down both arms to the wrists before quickly repositioning them on the forehead and repeating the sweeping motion down the side of the face and across the chest. Hands return to the head, and this time he sweeps down past the chest to the upper thighs. Only when his hands return to the head a third time does he continue his prayer. Another thirty seconds pass as he speaks, hands in the original position as at the start. He twice repeats the motion, a procedure known as *jilok,* sweeping down the arms to the chest, quickly blowing in his hands between repetitions, and continuing to pray. The hands return to the forehead for another twenty seconds of prayer before Francisco reaches for the patient's wrists. With both hands, he places his thumbs on the artery of each wrist while curling the remaining fingers around the patient's hand to give him a firm grip. The praying continues while Francisco, hands still facing downward, reads the pulse, a procedure known as *xjilb'al xkik'el.* The clanging of pots and children's voices elsewhere in the house do not break his concentration for the forty or so seconds he's engaged in this procedure. "I am saying the prayer to the blood," he explains later, "telling or asking the blood and body fluids to calm down, because his whole body gets affected by the sickness."

Francisco blows on his hands as he rubs them together. He returns to the forehead, quickly sweeps down across the patient's arms, and then moves back to the chest and down to the upper leg before returning to the wrists. Only a moment passes before Francisco breaks his concentration, leans back, and directs the patient to stretch his legs out in the hammock. This is the first communication between them since the treatment commenced some four minutes before.

The patient does as directed, and Francisco quickly grasps both feet in his hands, placing his thumbs on the arteries at the top of the feet, and recommences his prayer. This moment is brief, and less than ten seconds later, Francisco reaches up to the top of the arms and twice sweeps down to the feet, exhaling and praying as he does. After the second pass he leans back, passes his hand in front of his body in a partial cross-like motion, and announces "*us*" (good).

This part of the treatment session is over after roughly four and one-half minutes. Now making eye contact with the patient for the first time since the treatment began, Francisco directs him to use the medicine water. The patient reaches in and takes a handful of the wet plants and squeezes the water out. As he does, Francisco sits down across the room in the only chair available and begins to extract plant medicines from his bag. Both are focused on their tasks and there is little dialogue. The patient finishes scooping out all the plant material into a bowl while chatting with his mother. Francisco explains about the plants he will leave behind and how to prepare and use them. The patient's wife asks a few questions and takes the plants. The three of them chat idly for a few minutes while the patient continues to retrieve the plant material from the water. Stepping just outside the doorway, the patient reaches into the bucket with his hand and splashes water over the top of his head. After more than a dozen repetitions, his hair is drenched and water is dripping off. "It is necessary to bathe his entire body," notes Francisco later, "but he is having the pain in his head, so that is why he has to take care of that first. The next time he makes the medicine, he will bathe his entire body with it."

The treatment is now complete.

"Headache," explains the patient when I ask about the problem. Francisco later confirms the diagnosis of *taqenaq tiqwal jolomb'ej* (headache or high head pressure). "When I am out in the hot sun," the patient adds, "I feel like my head is spinning around." Francisco suggests later that more than simply the hot sun is causing the problem: the patient has been dousing himself with cold water to cool down, and the rapid change in body temperature has caused the headaches. This problem of thermal regulation is purely physiological; there are no evil spirits, bad air, or other forces involved. These headaches have been plaguing him for quite some time, leading him to ask Francisco for help. The patient discloses during our brief interview that sometimes his vision is blurry as well but that he is not photophobic. He has been to the hospital in the nearby regional town of Punta Gorda, but they have given him only acetaminophen. "It doesn't help."

"Did you understand what Mr. Francisco was saying when he was doing the treatment?" I ask. "No," he shakes his head. "It's a different language." But he did understand the instructions regarding the medicine, and his reference to a "different language" is a comment on the technical medical and spiritual language Francisco uses, as they both speak Q'eqchi'. He will take it for two days, whereupon Francisco will come back to check on him. "I told him that he was to do a follow-up treatment the next day," confirms Francisco. "The sickness that he has needs to be treated with pure water; no chlorine. Either rainwater or water from a spring should be used. At three a.m. this water is taken outside to get cold from the dew, then it is used in the morning for the treatment. His problem is caused by coldness, so the treatment has to be the same."

There is nothing unusual about this case. "I have many patients who suffer from this problem," says Francisco. "I hear of the symptoms, and I already know what is the problem." If the patient does not get better, "then I will change my approach to treatment," he responds matter-of-factly.

CHAPTER 1

Empiricism, Materialism, and Indigenous Medicine

We may say even that these peoples practice an art of medicine which is in some respects more rational than our own, in that its modes of diagnosis and treatment follow more directly from their ideas concerning the causation of disease.

—W. H. R. RIVERS, 1924

Romanticism in anthropology and sociology leads to an overvaluation of the skills of traditional healers.

—LEON EISENBERG AND ARTHUR KLEINMAN, 1981

I OPENED THIS book in the prologue the way many modern ethnographic monographs do, with a story. As you read this, I imagine you asked yourself, What is going on here? Is this a religious ritual? Shamanic performance? Traditional healing? "Primitive" medicine? Prescientific medicine? Folk medicine? Folk healing? Symbolic healing? The anthropological literature has described similar activities in just these terms. Frustratingly, rarely have these terms been clearly defined, and not only are they still loosely applied, it is not uncommon to find such a vignette described as "healing," "medicine," and "religion" even in the same article.

My interest in such epistemological issues began some years back when I raised two fundamental questions about Indigenous mental health research in Canada and the United States: What do we think we know, and on what basis do we think we know it (Waldram 2004)? As I documented in *Revenge of the Windigo*, what we thought we knew was constructed on a wonky methodology typically underscored by antiquated, stereotypical, and often racist assumptions about Indigenous people. We were creating more so than uncovering mental disorders and their treatments in the Indigenous community. I felt very nervous about my ability to answer the most fundamental of questions, put to me many years ago by a Cree elder on a trapline in northern Manitoba: "What do you know . . . [pause for effect] for sure?"

The study of "healing" in all its dimensions has been central to my scholarship since graduate school, and my attention has been focused on Indigenous and, to a lesser extent, non-Indigenous Canadians. I thought I had come to "know . . . for sure" what Indigenous[1] healing looked like, based on my work in Canada. What I thought, and why I thought it, was not only the product of my own research efforts but also influenced by trends within and beyond my discipline of medical anthropology. My myopia was challenged, even shattered, when I traveled to southern Belize to study the knowledge and practices of a group of Q'eqchi' Maya *iloneleb'*, medical practitioners or "seers." The case described in the prologue comes from that research. Struggling to understand "what was going on," I was initially hamstrung by the biases I had internalized concerning Canadian Indigenous healing. It took some time, and a great deal of patience from the iloneleb', for me to come to understand just how different was Q'eqchi' therapeutic knowledge and practice from what I had seen, documented, and experienced in Canada. And this led me to rethink the concept of healing.

"Healing" and "Medicine" in Medical Anthropology

Since its inception, medical anthropology has grappled with how to characterize the therapeutic approaches of non-Western peoples. The field has waffled between questions of religion, belief, and symbolism versus empiricism, knowledge, and materialism; between immateriality and materiality; between irrationality and rationality. Over time there is both a discursive and an ethnographic shift in scholarship in which what was initially thought of as Indigenous "medicine" (fueled by voluminous historical documents such as traders' journals) becomes Indigenous "healing." Although I cannot provide a precise date, the idea of Indigenous "medicine" simply starts to disappear. This is not just a change in terminology or a refinement of these two concepts. Rather, there is a deeper meaning to this shift, one that springs from several influences, including critical anthropological engagement with bioscience and biomedicine, and symbolic and interpretive turns in which the focus moves from ethnographic description to interpretive meaning in ethnographic studies. These influences in the discipline subtly change the nature of Indigenous therapeutic practice as discursively rendered in scholarship. The result is that today what is seen as legitimate Indigenous therapeutics involves an emphasis on transformative rather than restorative practice—or "healing" rather than "curing"—which in turn marginalizes it as inherently symbolic and psychosocial in orientation and sidesteps questions of the nature of Indigenous medical empiricism (Waldram 2013). This shift opened the possibility of Indigenous medicine being accepted to some extent by the dominant biomedical system, since if defined as "healing" it is not then directly a challenge, but only by being restricted to the delivery of culture-based psychotherapeutics to culturally "distinct" Indigenous populations, particularly in areas underserved by formal, state-sanctioned biomedical systems.

Much anthropological engagement with Indigenous medicine in the early twentieth century was predicated on the notion that medical practice was largely an element of religious practice and ideology, and the only practitioners of interest to the early ethnographers were shamans (Morley 1978; Young 1982; Atkinson 1992; Lock and Scheper-Hughes 1996). Yet these early scholars fully referenced the idea of Indigenous medical practice as part of the broader magico-religious complexes in which they were mostly interested. This may have something to do with the fact that many early commentators had medical training, especially in psychiatry. Psychiatrist and anthropologist W. H. R. Rivers (2001 [1924]), for instance, defines medicine as an approach that "regards disease as a phenomenon subject to natural laws"; medicine then differs from magic and religion in how disease is conceptualized and in the role the supernatural might play (2001 [1924]:4). Medicine as practice, then, involves efforts "to direct and control a specific group of natural phenomena" that negatively impact the individual's "physical and social function" (4). Like many of his generation, he was influenced by the "natural/supernatural" ontological dichotomy, in which Indigenous medical knowledge was characterized as religious "belief" as much as or more than empirical knowledge, and treatment success was understood as mostly due to "faith and suggestion," an idea that would later fluoresce with the concepts of symbolic healing and placebo. Nonetheless, he allows that within the context of a belief system there is an inherent rationality in that "modes of diagnosis and treatment follow more directly from their ideas concerning the causation of disease" (48).

Another early influence of relevance here is E. E. Evans-Pritchard (1976 [1937]), who engages with the idea that there is a material dimension to Azande sickness as well as a supernatural one. Every Azande disease diagnosed has its own treatment, he notes, "which in some cases has evidently been built up on experience and in other cases, though it is probably quite ineffectual, shows a logico-experimental element" (196). His characterization of the empirical nature of Azande medicine, however, emphasizes "trial-and-error . . . if one [medicine] does not alleviate pain they try another," as if this is random and there is no empirical tradition informing the process of differential diagnosis and the selection of medicines to be used (196). Indeed, he defines "empirical behaviour" as based essentially on "common-sense" (229), although this is not defined. Following suit, other scholars also often reduce the nature of Indigenous empiricism to crass "trial and error." But both Rivers and Evans-Pritchard were willing to engage with Indigenous knowledge as not based simply on belief and supernaturalism but also on "empirical elements" that have "real therapeutic value" (Evans-Pritchard (1976 [1937]:196). At some point beyond this, scholars begin to lose sight of these "empirical elements."

The ambiguity regarding the nature of Indigenous therapeutics exhibited in the work of Rivers and Evans-Pritchard came to characterize most of the subsequent work in the pre-interpretive period in anthropology; is it a belief system or an empirical system? Scholars grapple with fundamental epistemological and ontological issues, and even consistent, basic terminology eludes them. Paramount among these is Erwin Ackerknecht, a historian and ethnologist whose productive writings on "primitive medicine" dominated the field for decades. Ackerknecht's (1942, 1943, 1945, 1946, 2016 [1968]) main interest in shamanism led him to consider the parallels between Indigenous medicine, psychiatric disorder, and associated psychotherapy, augmented by a functionalist interpretation that emphasized "primitive" medicine's "social role . . . and holistic or unitarian character which [bio]medicine has lost in our society" (Ackerknecht 1946:468). This interpretation—bolstered later by psychologist Jerome Frank's seminal work *Persuasion and Healing* (1961)—set the field down a path that has continued to this day, a path that highlights somewhat romantic and utopian views of non-Western societies—a kind of "primitivist" thinking (Lucas and Barrett 1995) that I would argue results in scholars largely missing the empirical basis of much Indigenous medicine.

Ackerknecht (1946:467) allows that "primitive people" understood "naturally caused diseases" and that they were both "rational" and "logical" in their medical thinking, based in part on "empirical premises." Indeed, he even offers that the magical element of their thinking and medical practice could "cloak . . . a fundamentally rational therapeutic method" (1946:474). But the meaning of empiricism for Ackerknecht is unclear, as he notes that among the Masai, "the tradition-bound attitude of primitive medicine is in general unfavorable to the use of trial and error methods" (1946:477). Building from Evans-Pritchard's (1976 [1937]:200) notion that the Azande "do not think very much about" how their medicines work, Ackerknecht (1946) uses the concept of "tradition" to account for "habitual knowledge" that determines "almost automatic acts" in which people "operate below the threshold of full consciousness" in identifying and treating sickness; such patterned responses to known disorders and situations simply do not require much deep reflection. Ackerknecht ultimately challenges the "myth of primitive empiricism" (1942:504) and "the myth of the overwhelmingly rational primitive medicine" (1946:481) created by scholars "putting aside consciously every magic and religious element" (1942:504). He sees primitive medicine as fundamentally based on magic and not as an "objective" (by which I assume he means scientific) acquisition of knowledge. He declares that "primitives actually know [little] about those diseases and treatments which might be regarded as natural and rational," in part because their "medical beliefs [have] important social, if not medical, functions" (1946:486). Ackerknecht (489) concludes that while "primitive medicine" may be rational and logical within the context of a magico-religious system, it is not science because it lacks both experimentation and skepticism. "The primitive specialist," he determines, "is trained for preservation of existing lore, not for new discoveries" (490). But we are left to wonder: Where does the "existing lore" come from, and is it hermetically sealed and incapable of expanding with new knowledge over time?

Ackerknecht's (1945:428) influence was profound, especially in supporting the exploration by anthropologists of psychopathology. "Modern ethnographers," he lamented, "are very often afraid of publishing observations and descriptions of purely pathological or therapeutical facts," in part because of the complexity of the phenomena, and in part because their training does not lend them authority to comment on medical matters. Instead he encourages the exploration of "a host of sociological and psychological data in the field of primitive medicine." While these fundamental ideas were not solely those of Ackerknecht, he certainly became their champion. Ari Kiev, a psychiatrist writing in 1962, shows, like many others, the influence of psychologist Jerome Frank (1961), which was making inroads in anthropology and other disciplines in the early 1960s. Kiev's focus is on the psychotherapeutic aspects of "primitive medicine," and while acknowledging the existence of a "medical system," he argues that "there is little systematic organization of theories and practices" in most "food-gathering" societies (1962:25). Like Ackerknecht, Kiev accepts that "much of the success of 'primitive medicine' is attributable to the psychotherapeutic aspects."

There are those who caution that a focus on psychotherapeutics may be selling Indigenous medicine short. Norman Scotch (1963) questions the common assumption that the "medicine of non-literate peoples" is closely similar to Western psychiatry, adding that proving the efficacy of the latter is itself highly problematic (1963:48). Horacio Fabrega Jr. (1971), another psychiatrist, writes that "in ethnomedical descriptions of illness features and illness classification, the moral, social, and interpersonal dimensions tend to be given principal emphasis" (1971:179), adding that the relationship between psychiatry and anthropology has colored the latter's focus in "ethnomedical" studies. This has led to viewing medical problems primarily in terms of "culturally patterned sociopsychological happenings," which has "tended to obscure the influences that biological components have on (culturally defined) illnesses" (1971:186).

A few other contrasting voices in this era resist the idea of Indigenous medicine as inherently psychotherapeutic and nonempirical. J. M. Cooper (1935:370), for instance, argues that "primitive culture" is largely based on rational, even scientific thinking. Sol Tax (1950) equates rational thinking found in Indigenous societies with the scientific method and the elicitation of truth about the natural world. Charles Erasmus (1952) argues that "folk beliefs" could be based at least in part on processes of inductive reasoning, the essence of empiricism, and that the "curer's . . . results are an empirical demonstration that his methods, as well as the theories and explanations on which they are based, are in general valid though not infallible" (424). William Laughlin (1963:116) writes that "primitive medicine contains a storehouse of empirical knowledge. Embedded in its variegated corpus of techniques, procedures and beliefs," he explains, "are many strands of pragmatic approaches, comparative tests and effective treatments for the restoration and maintenance of well-being in the human organism." Other scholars, such as Robin Horton (1967a, 1967b), Peter Morley (1978), George Foster (1976, 1984a), and George Peter Murdock (1980), allow that Indigenous knowledge and medicine have an empirical, rational, even science-like aspect that recognizes the role of the "natural" world. As Murdock (1980:3) argues, "primitive medicine . . . [has a] substantial component of sound, pragmatic knowledge."

But the emergence of the defined field of ethnomedicine within anthropology shifts the emphasis away from the "natural," material, and physiological aspects of sickness, priming the field for the emergence of symbolic approaches. Charles Hughes (1968:99), for instance, defines the field as "those beliefs and practices which are the products of indigenous cultural development and are not explicitly derived from the conceptual framework of modern medicine," a definition still being circulated decades later (e.g., Rubel and Haas 1996). Ethnomedicine "treats illness and illness behavior as a cultural category" (Colson and Selby 1974:246), emphasizing beliefs about sickness, etiology, and treatment rather than empirical knowledge, with the focus squarely on "ethnopsychiatry and non-western psychotherapeutic procedures" (248). Rubel and Haas (1996:117) point out that researchers tend to avoid studying scourges such as infant diarrhea or schistosomiasis in favor of "concepts, prevention, and curing of folk diseases or diseases with psychiatric implications."

The tenacious hold of the psychotherapeutic paradigm leads ultimately to the development of symbolic healing as a framework to understand what is going on in Indigenous therapeutics. While the early scholars sought to understand in what ways Indigenous medicine was or was not logical, rational, and empirical, especially in comparison to science, the symbolic and interpretive turns result in a dramatic shift toward meaning as experientially and subjectively understood, with little engagement with the material and empirical aspects of medical knowledge systems among Indigenous peoples. Victor Turner (1975:159), a scholarly pioneer in this area, suggests that "tribal" medicine involves "the mobilization of efficacy through symbolic action for restoring internal integrity to the patient and order to his community . . . here, health represents a restoration of wholeness both to the person and group" (159). Conceptualizing Indigenous medical treatment as a "rite," Turner places it firmly within the sphere of the symbolic and sidesteps issues of empiricism and pragmatism in the understanding of effectiveness.

Daniel Moerman (1983) and James Dow (1986) subsequently emerge as the central figures in the anthropology of symbolic healing. Both seem to start from the premise that there is nothing "real" going in Indigenous medical treatment in the material or physiological sense separate from the patient's symbolic mobilization toward efficacy as Turner (1975) details it. Moerman (1979, 1983:157) focuses his exploration on the idea of "general medical therapy," otherwise known as placebo, to argue that "the form of medical treatment as well as its content can be effective." "Meaning mends," he argues. "Study meaning and we learn about mending" (165). Further, "the construction of healing symbols *is* healing" (1979:66; emphasis in original). Dow (1986), like Moerman (and both were influenced by Jerome Frank), works from the premise that there are important and similar psychological processes common to Western psychotherapy and religious and shamanic healing; therefore, he logically focuses on understanding the psychological mechanisms by which these forms of treatment work to improve the lot of the patient. "Symbols affect the mind," he argues, "which in turn affects the body" (59). Neither Moerman nor Dow pays significant attention to the medical, physiological, or material aspects of sickness, and even the admission that, for instance, "native American" treatment includes "rational techniques" such as pharmacologically active drugs from plants, as Moerman

(1979:60) suggests, does not change the interpretation that in Indigenous medicine, "It seems equally clear . . . that neither native practitioners nor patients saw drugs as a more vital (life-sustaining) portion of the healing process than song and dance."

Certainly, Moerman and Dow are not alone in their focus on therapeutic symbols and their role in psychotherapeutic-like forms of healing (e.g., Harwood 1987 [1977]; Glik 1988; Sullivan 1993). In my own work on the therapeutic uses of Indigenous spirituality in Canadian federal penitentiaries (Waldram 1997), I too invoke the psychotherapeutic value of symbolic healing, and like the others, I cite processes such as meaning-making, suggestion, and catharsis to explain its effectiveness. The issue is not if there are symbolic aspects to therapeutic processes; of course there are. The issue is: Have we, as scholars of the therapeutic process, been blinded to those aspects that invoke a rational, logical, empirical engagement with the world—especially one in which "supernatural" as well as "natural" forces are active—in favor of "song and dance?"

Mark Nichter (1991) castigates the field of ethnomedicine for its simplistic characterizations and assumptions designed largely to force a distinction with biomedicine, a critique that holds also for symbolic healing. These problematic characterizations include "that traditional systems of ethnomedicine are circular in their reasoning; are consensual and complacent; rely little on experimentation; and entail no critical thinking," whereas "biomedicine, in contrast, is presented as logical and self-correcting through the deployment of standardized replicable procedures which test for the falsification of hypotheses" (Nichter 1991:139). Nichter (1991) further suggests that the impetus for this simplistic understanding of Indigenous medicine is to define an alternative utopian medical system that positively accentuates those aspects highlighted by critics as unfavorable characteristics of biomedicine, including the idea that in ethnomedicine there is a rich, meaningful relationship between practitioner and patient, with excellent communication, all couched within shared cultural models, despite little anthropological evidence in support. The idea that within ethnomedical systems some problems are actually medicalized, or that within biomedicine "cultural sensitivity" and open communication are indeed possible, simply is not entertained in much of the research.

Several leading scholars are identified at the core of the interpretive or phenomenological turn in medical anthropology, including Allan Young (1976a, 1976b, 1981, 1982, 1983), Arthur Kleinman (1980), and Byron Good (1994). Unlike many others writing at the time, Young is willing to entertain the idea of Indigenous empiricism in medicine, a fact that is somewhat lost by his continued referral to Indigenous medical knowledge as "beliefs." Whether Indigenous peoples can be seen to have a "medical belief system" (Young 1976b) or a "traditional medical culture" (Young 1983), approaches that emphasize cultural and symbolic aspects, as opposed to simply a "medical system," which references local epistemological and ontological understanding, remains unclear from his work. Young does not explain what he means by "beliefs," unfortunately, but his willingness to admit that there is empiricism to Indigenous medicine suggests that he thinks "beliefs," rather than being "false" in the scientific sense, are really knowledge taken at face value to be true by virtue of tradition rather than personal experience. Plausibility, rather than scientific-like proof, is the standard for evaluation. Traditional medical systems "make plausible explanations when they are needed," he explains, and "provide empirical proofs in support of these explanations" (Young 1976a:12). While such thinking is certainly teleological, it provides the mechanism that integrates knowledge and experience into a "medical system."

Young's work is one of the best developments of the issues of efficacy or effectiveness of traditional forms of medicine, including the acceptance of phenomenological proofs (1976b). He writes, for instance, that "people maintain their medical traditions because they affect undesirable biological states in expected ways, and because they are effective ways for dealing with disruptive events that cannot be allowed to persist" (1976a:5). Here Young is straddling the line between the symbologists, who tend to see Indigenous medicine in terms of repairing ruptures in social relations, and the approach that I take here, that Indigenous medicine must be understood to also engage with biological or physiological processes regardless of how these are understood.

Arthur Kleinman (1980) emphasizes the role of interpretation of sickness by both practitioner and patient, and, like others before him, reinforces stereotypes regarding Indigenous medicine as holistic and meaning-centered, with practitioners sharing the same worldview (among themselves and with their patients) and focused on treating "illness," in contrast to biomedicine's singular and reductionist goal to cure disease (Kleinman and Sung 1979). Indigenous medicine in this framework remains largely symbolic and cultural: "The indigenous practitioner usually (but not always) is exceptionally well poised to maximize psychosocial and cultural treatment of the illness," Kleinman and Sung (1979:24) determine, and "contrariwise, he may not be competent to effectively control severe, acute diseases." Byron Good (1994), in turn, presents a strong critique of viewing cultural others' medical knowledge as "beliefs" in need of correcting when they are seemingly irrational or contradicted by science; such beliefs, he suggests, often seen as closely linked to religion, tend to be interpreted symbolically rather than empirically. "In medical anthropology," he writes, "analysis of 'beliefs' is most prominent in cultural accounts of those disorders (such as infectious diseases) for which biological theories have greatest authority, and least prominent for those forms of illness (for example, psychotherapy) for which biological explanations are most open to challenge" (20). Good rails against the use of biomedical science and its related nosological system and practices as standards for comparison with traditional knowledge, yet surprisingly, he adds that some people "have mistaken notions about disease," suggesting that a comparative standard external to those knowledge systems (that is, science) is in play. The challenge for scholars, he declares, is "to fashion an epistemologically coherent position, one which makes sense of the claims of human biology and medicine and still acknowledges the validity of local knowledge in matters of sickness and suffering" (1994:63). We can do so, he says importantly, if we focus on "the formative practices of health care systems, rather than on beliefs and behaviors associated with given diseases" (175). However, we cannot entertain such practices until we understand the broader local medical knowledge system through understanding the local knowledge of diseases (or disorders or pathology). As Good suggests (176), within medical anthropology, "symbolic forms and interpretive practices" are typically the focus of analyses of medical knowledge, whereas the "empirical world," understood as "found within human experience," is more elusive.

The shift toward an interpretive or meaning-centered perspective of Indigenous medicine does little more than pay lip service to material and empirical knowledge, yet again presenting a view of Indigenous medicine, knowledge, and peoples more generally as cultural and symbolic essentialists, holistic, and nondualists, in contradistinction to Westerners and their science. "Not for them the seductive Cartesian division between body and mind," declares Charles Hughes (1996:136). But it is the thesis of the holistic Indigenous medical system that proves to be seductive. Critical-interpretive medical anthropology (Lock and Scheper-Hughes 1996; Scheper-Hughes and Lock 1987), an offshoot of the work of scholars like Kleinman and Good, while contributing significantly to cultural analyses of biomedicine, characterizes non-Western societies and their knowledges in problematic ways, in part because of their focus on critiquing biomedicine itself (which is also essentialized in this critique; see Montgomery 2006) and, by extension, using the knowledges of traditional or non-Western peoples as a straw system comparator. Such critiques argue that biomedicine and science are not the standards by which things Indigenous should be assessed, and yet very frequently a generalized, stereotyped, and essentialized Indigenous knowledge is presented, sometimes subtly and other times not, to hammer away at biomedicine.

The target of the critical-interpretive critique is typically those who suggest that scientific medicine is a culture-free knowledge system built upon a rational understanding of the material world generated by an infallible methodology. This is especially evident in Lock and Scheper-Hughes's discussion of Cartesian or mind–body dualism, which they suggest contributes to the materialist thinking characteristic of scientific progress. In "some non-Western civilizations," they suggest, there are "alternative epistemologies" (presumably alternative to "Western"?) that view the relations "among mind, body, culture, nature, and society" as "monistic" and "holistic," rather that dualistic. This means, for instance, that there is a conception of "harmonious wholes in which everything from the cosmos down to the individual organs of the human body is understood as a single unit" and where thinking is based on "complementary (not opposing) dualities" (Lock and Scheper-Hughes 1996:50). Many "ethnomedical systems do not logically distinguish body, mind, and self, and therefore illness cannot be situated in mind or body alone" (58). "The body," they assert, "is not understood as a complex machine but rather as a microcosm of the universe" (59). Granted, they are borrowing such ideas from scholars such as Fabrega, but they are doing so uncritically; the "critical" part of the "critical-interpretive" approach does not seem to include deep exploration into the stereotypes constructed about Indigenous peoples, even though they argue the need to go beyond "culturally sensitive presentations" (68). Indeed, they endorse the surprising assertion that "non-western and nonindustrialized people are 'called upon to think the world with their bodies'" (O'Neill 1985:151, cited in Lock and Scheper-Hughes 1996:60). *They* think with their bodies, but Westerners use their minds? Further, the primary reference in support of their argument is to broad, formalized non-Western knowledge systems such as that of traditional Chinese medicine, and this is even more problematic if that argument is then uncritically applied to less formalized Indigenous systems like that of the Q'eqchi'.

The use of Indigenous medicine and other traditional forms of knowledge as the comparator for studies of biomedicine remains strong despite criticism (e.g., Eisenberg and Kleinman 1981; Singer and Baer 1995), and over the years it has worked both ways. For a while, science and biomedicine were taken as the standard against which traditional knowledge and Indigenous medicine were evaluated, with the latter coming across as "primitive." But then the roles reversed, with Indigenous knowledge and Indigenous medicine appearing to be the more civilized, and biomedicine characterized as the big evil. Lucas and Barrett (1995) characterize these contrasting and oscillating perspectives as the Arcadian (utopian) and Barbaric ("primitive") traditions, a concept I elsewhere apply to North American Indigenous mental health (Waldram 2004).

The power of such caricatures is self-evident in a volume such as *An Anthropology of Biomedicine* by Margaret Lock and Vinh-Kim Nguyen (2010), which contains significant discussion of these Indigenous systems. The way in which they are characterized, in contradistinction to biomedicine, suffers the kinds of problems that befall any generalized comparisons. So, while there is an admission that there is value to the "experiential knowledge" of traditional healers, that traditional medical systems "are neither static nor lacking in innovation" (63) and that they are proving to be quite adaptive to globalizing influences, there remains the notion that they have a "personal approach to patients" that contrasts with the "decontextualized objectivity characteristic of biomedicine" (65). Further, Lock and Nguyen identify "perhaps the most crucial distinction" between biomedicine and other forms of medical practice as biomedicine's "insistence that bodies can best be understood as standardized entities," in contrast to these other medical traditions, "which pay careful attention to contingency when accounting for misfortune, often locating affliction in the chains of previous events, local environments, the vicissitudes of various non-human actors including the spirit world, or an imbalance between individual bodies and the cosmos." "For biomedicine," they continue, "the laws of biology dispense with the need to search for local particularity" (56). The "internalizing discourse" of biomedicine, they argue, decontextualizes disease; in contrast, the "externalizing discourse" of other medical systems "emphasizes familial, social, political, and environmental contributions to ill health" (43). Like many other aspects of Indigenous medicine scholarship, a persistent focus on the idea of "balance" as integral to health, while important, can lead to absurd essentialist statements. Medical historian Roy Porter (1997:39), for instance, suggests that in traditional medicine, preventing imbalance is "more important than curing"!

Lock and Nguyen (2010) are a reflection of a long-standing trend to use Indigenous and other traditional knowledge systems as a comparator to critique biomedicine and the social aspects of health care delivery in Western societies (e.g., Gaines and Davis-Floyd 2004). This is the essence of primitivist discourse, using an essentialized, often romanticized portrait of an Indigenous "other" to lament modernity and globalization. Contemporary attempts to define biomedicine in contradistinction to Indigenous medicine underscore this issue, and this seriously distorts our understanding of Indigenous medical systems.

Overall, then, two major interpretive tacks serve to influence how Indigenous medicine is understood through scholarly time. First, the strong influence of medical—and in particular psychiatric and psychological—scholars skews the research toward favoring a psychosocial and symbolic interpretation of these therapeutic systems. Second, the emerging Western compulsion to critique aspects of Western society by reference to non-Westerners creates essentialized, stereotyped caricatures of the latter that fail to reflect their complex ontologies and epistemologies. The portrait that emerges from all this commentary, dating back to, and even beyond, Rivers and Evans-Pritchard, can be summed up quite tidily. Indigenous medicine is not really "medicine," and the knowledge of medical disorders—including physiological and anatomical knowledge of the body as well as disease entities—while often rational and logical within the local cultural context, is nonetheless often "wrong" or at the very least rather simplistic. The fact that it is not really "medicine" is contradictorily suggestive of its primitiveness (hence it should be dismissed because it is not scientific) or its value (hence should be emulated because it deeply connects with the psychosocial aspects of sickness), depending on your perspective. Generally, it is understood that within these Indigenous medical systems, actual (scientific) knowledge of the material aspects of the world, including sickness and its treatment, is largely absent, its place taken by "beliefs" placing sickness and treatment in broader environmental and social contexts, including the spiritual realm, and beyond the organic. The mind-body-spirit is one entity; there are no meaningful distinctions in Indigenous medicine. The practitioner, sharing the same "mythic world" (Dow 1986) or cultural context with the patient, intrinsically understands the patient and offers a warm, supportive clinical environment. The "healing techniques . . . of folk healers," asserts Erickson (2008:7), "often involve a more holistic approach that restores social, environmental, and spiritual harmony as well as alleviation of illness for the individual." Evidence that Indigenous medicine "works" is largely based on what Young (1979) refers to as "symbolic" and "empirical" proofs, understood in the context of what practitioners and patients hope for or expect. In this framework, Indigenous medicine is, at its roots, a cultural and symbolic system, something that can just as easily be placed within the context of religion as within medicine. While older literature typically refers to Indigenous medicine's practitioners as "doctors" or "physicians," seeking to "cure" their patients, through time we see a movement away from these ideas as practitioners are rewritten to become "healers" seeking to "heal," an approach to treatment more in common with psychiatry than with biomedicine, as imaginary problems of the psyche, symbolic misalignment, or the embodied tensions inherent in society, and not disease, become the focus. Healing, then, comes to be characterized as fundamentally about well-being, and only marginally related to bodily health—the focus is on making life better, or making the social body better. "Medicine" is about the health or optimum physical operation of the body. The focus is on making the physical body better. The Q'eqchi' therapeutic system I encounter looks more like "medicine" than "healing."

Materialism, Animism, Ontology, and the Meta/Material

I believe that much anthropological research and theorizing has taken us too far down an epistemological and ontological path in which things Indigenous, such as medicine, have been too narrowly understood primarily in symbolic and spiritual terms—as essentially immaterial—and less so in material and what I call meta/material terms. (I detail what I mean by this below.) Is it possible to talk about Indigenous medicine without making symbols and spirits the central focus? What does it look like if we restrict reference to the idea of "beliefs" and instead discuss "knowledge"? How does our understanding change if we talk about "medicine" instead of "healing" and medical procedures instead of ceremony and ritual? What do we gain or lose if we shift our thinking about Indigenous therapeutic intervention away from "healing" discourse and toward (or back to) that of the empirical practice of medicine? Can we reclaim the concept of "medicine" from science and return it to the other knowledge systems of the world?

To be more precise, I argue that what my Q'eqchi' interlocutors do is a form of medicine, as understood by them, and their knowledge constitutes an empirically sound medical system. It is not scientific medicine or biomedicine; nor is it some form of "prescientific medicine." I will not even bother to explain why it is not "primitive medicine." And it is not reflective of a literary tradition with textbooks. Rather, what these individuals do is practice a form of Indigenous medicine, a dynamic, empirical, experience-based, phronetic, and gnostic approach to understanding and applying knowledge of the world to identify, prevent, and cure sickness.[2] Indigenous medicine springs from and reinforces cognitive, affective, and spiritual connections to place in the broadest material, geophysical, existential, and metaphysical senses. It is dynamic in so far as it does not have precise, rigid boundaries and is not temporally limited to a historic period; rather, it has proven adaptive and flexible in the face of colonization and globalization by, for instance, incorporating knowledge and techniques from historical and contemporary colonizers/settlers. The goal of Q'eqchi' medical practitioners is to alleviate sickness and make their patients better, and they are open to new information, new technology, and new techniques that may assist them.[3]

My main assumption in this book is that people strive to understand the properties of the universe as they are affected by them, "a speculative organization and exploitation of the sensible world in sensible terms," as Claude Lévi-Strauss (1966:16) writes. I diverge from the views of this great anthropologist, however, in suggesting that such people are not at all content to sidestep the question of causality (which he feels is the domain of Western science). I contend that people's knowledge systems, in part, reflect a hope to achieve some measure of control over the forces that affect them, in part as a component of humanity's sentient existential quest. For the Q'eqchi', "all things, whether animate or inanimate, are imbued with unseen power," explains Pedro Kukul (2013:571). Qaawa', he continues, the "Supreme Being . . . created a series of powerful supernatural forces including lightning, the sun, fire, wind, clouds, and water, which have a direct bearing on Q'eqchi' life." It is this understanding of the forces of the universe that the Q'eqchi' seek to uncover, understand, and manage.

Q'eqchi' medicine, then, is composed of elements that meet the test of empiricism, but an empiricism understood to extend beyond a kind of random stimulus-response or "trial and error." It is inductive—or better, abductive—intentional knowledge, not accidental. This notion of empiricism accommodates animistic thinking—that many "things" (Ingold 2014)[4] in the world have spirits or souls, or a kind of personhood—by using both empirical, material proofs and broader symbolic proofs (cf. Young 1979) of the existence of other-than-human persons and forces (cf. Hallowell 1955, 1960) to establish a degree of certainty about the veracity of that knowledge. Key here is that these properties of the universe are both material and something else, something often referred to as "supernatural" or "spiritual," two terms that remain exceedingly disagreeable because of their dualistic bracketing. Not all elements of the nonhuman world are inherently spiritual; some, rather, exist as invisible forces that physically affect humans by consequence, as gravity does. This aspect of Indigenous knowledge is often ignored in favor of animistic metaphor, analogy, and symbolism.

Let me start with materialism, an idea that few scholars seem to want to engage with when it comes to Indigenous knowledge. Materialism, in philosophy, is the very old idea (sometimes also known as physicalism) "that everything that exists is material" (Robinson 1998)—that is, it consists of matter. As Stack (1998) explains, "In general, the metaphysical theory of materialism entails the denial of the reality of spiritual beings, consciousness and mental or psychic states or processes, as ontologically distinct from, or independent of, material changes or processes." But rather than seeing spiritual beings and forces as products of mental processes, if we think through a decolonizing lens we can understand that these may be elements of a society's materialist philosophy, that they are "real" and coexist with but are independent of humans. My concern here is with the idea of a materialist empiricism, the quest for knowledge about the salient properties, processes, and forces of the world that affect humans. To broaden the idea of materialism to include what appear to be other-than-material entities may seem contradictory. What I am proposing is that we consider all those entities that lack a physical form and that exhibit some degree of agency or animation, or an ability to affect humans by their action, presence, or mere existence, or that exist in some kind of relationship to human beings, to be ontologically part of the material-like world from the perspective of many of the world's peoples, and especially Indigenous peoples. I call this meta/materialism.

"Meta," from Greek, means "beyond," "after," or "of a higher kind" (Shivola 2007). By meta/materialism, then, I mean to include those aspects of human existence that transcend corporeality—the physicality of the human body—and that are ontologically understood to be "real" even if invisible to the senses. The existence of the meta/material is often known by the consequences of its existence, through both empirical and symbolic evidence, such as when sickness happens. Meta/materialism is a materialism "of a higher kind."

The idea of the meta/material has a life in several other disciplines. In engineering, "metamaterial" was originally conceived of as a reference to manufactured compounds that "display properties that are not found in nature" (Shivola 2009:90). "Nature," in this sense, is understood materially in Cartesian terms. Metamaterials are human-made entities, combining elements of the known to create something now knowable. When combined, these materials create something very real. This idea is readily applied to the ideological, where what is materially known about the universe and its effects on people is combined to offer a parallel, abductive, material understanding of what would otherwise be the "unknown." In its totality, this represents Maya "cosmovision," a worldview "composed of the sky, the ground, and the inner earth that, although separate, are conceptualized as an interrelated whole where cosmology blends space and time" (Cabarrús 1979; Astor-Aguilera 2010:225–26).[5] Ideology and symbolism, both human creations, are intimately intertwined with ontology and present an aspect of worldview usually deemed "supernatural" in older anthropological literature. I seek to rescue ontology from this deep hole by accentuating its material aspects.

In art, metamaterialism refers to the use of virtual rather than physical materials, inspired by Gilles Deleuze's idea of virtuality (Si-Qin 2011). The "virtual," according to Deleuze (2004:260; see also Deleuze 1991:96–97) "is opposed not to the real but to the actual. The virtual is fully real in so far as it is virtual." "The virtual," he continues, "must be defined as strictly a part of the real object." Boellstorff (2008:19) (citing the *Oxford English Dictionary*) describes the virtual as something "that is so in essence or effect." Shields (2003) suggests that the virtual is really in opposition to the material rather than "actual." Shields (2006:284) subsequently clarifies that "the Virtual designates objects and states that exist but are not tangible, not 'concrete.' The Virtual is known only indirectly by its effects." The virtual and the actual/material inhabit the same worldspace for the Q'eqchi' medical practitioners who are the center of this study; for them it is not so much "a reconfiguration of the binarism between nature and culture," as Boellstorf (2008:19) suggests, but rather a different ontology entirely, one that sees more of a gradation between, and a necessary relationship among, the material and the virtual forces of the universe as these affect humans. For the Q'eqchi' iloneleb', the "virtual" is "real" in both essence and effect, even as they understand the distinction between the material—the tangible, the concrete—and the "intangible" elements of the universe. In other words, material and virtually material forces—what I call meta/material—have material consequences for humans.[6]

The "new materialism" also provides some important insights, a "move away from anthropocentrism," where "things are not reducible to symbolic representation, nor are they merely passive data for phenomenological perception" (Hazard 2013:64, 69). Here the ideas of Deleuze and Guattari (2004) and DeLanda (2006) have been influential, especially the notion of "assemblage." Assemblages are contingent and contextual associations of things, human and otherwise, visible and invisible, permanent and fleeting, that have material effects for humans yet also exist in relation to each other separate from human cognition or agency. Fitting within the ideas of the new materialism, the emphasis here is on a material world that exists independent of humans and thus opens to the idea of deliberate human effort to understand that world not simply in a phenomenological sense—where we end up back at metaphor and symbol—but in a tangible, indeed material way.

The challenge in anthropology has long been to find a way to study and reference cultural phenomena that have been characterized as "religious" or "spiritual," as opposed to "real" in the crass material, and largely scientific, sense, so that these phenomena can be taken seriously as more than "beliefs" characteristic of unsophisticated minds, waiting to be supplanted by the liberating arrival of scientific truth (Holbraad and Pedersen 2017). Worsley (1982:327) touched briefly on the notion of the "metamedical" context of all forms of medicine, explaining that "medical conceptions of illness and its cure are always embedded within wider frameworks which supply cognitive, normative, and conative ideas (concepts, values, models, and projects), ultimately within some explicit metaphysic or implicit metaphysical pathos." The idea of meta/materialism—rather than metamedical—allows us to appreciate that gnostic phenomena are most certainly real and have properties and characteristics that emulate those of the material world as locally understood. The existence of these forces is rational insofar as people see consistency in the cause/effect relationship (Young 1981).

One of the founders of anthropology, E. B. Tylor (1913 [1871]), argues that both religion and science are inherently materialist and seek to explain the world. We need a space for the material that encompasses this human drive to understand how the world affects us, and how we shape that understanding in a way that is logical and makes sense to us, by combining what we can see/touch/feel with what we know to be "virtually" there as evidenced by different kinds of proofs. This is definitely a rejection of a Cartesian model of the world in which dualisms reign, where nature/culture, material/ideal, natural/supernatural have strictly guided Western thinking (Morrison 2014), in spite of evidence that many peoples in the world do not think this way (Hallowell 1960). Even the World Health Organization (1984) has succumbed to the power of such dichotomies, making a clean distinction between the material and the spiritual.

Meta/materialism forces us to think not in terms of such strict dichotomies and categories but rather in a more integrated way. Tylor recognizes that "souls" and spirits are understood as material beings by many peoples (1913 [1871]), even if he saw the materialisms of religion and science as fundamentally clashing and the existence of "souls" to mark the divide between animism and materialism (Tylor 1913 [1871]; Segal 2014). Hallowell's (1960) classic study of the Ojibwa (Anishnabe) did not specifically allude to the material dimensions of their ontology, but these can be inferred from his references to "other-than-human persons" to explain how Ojibwa worldview is seen through the lens of personhood, which must always have a material dimension. Entities such as stones are treated analogically "as if" they are persons and not "things," "without inferring that objects of this class are, for the Ojibwa, necessarily conceptualized as persons" (Hallowell 1960:26). Not persons, not things, yet somehow "real" at least because a stone can be seen, touched, and manipulated despite any animated agency it might seem to have. Of course, the Ojibwa would know that a stone also has a status as an inanimate entity, because Hallowell's participants noted that not all stones are imbued with an "other-than-human" personhood. This has been argued with respect to the Maya as well (Astor-Aguilera 2010:114), and Wilson (1995:143–44) specifically states that the Q'eqchi' do not view all matter as inherently having spirits. So we must avoid overextending the notion of "personhood" to the nonhuman realm or reducing it to one of "barely differentiated humans, non-human personas, [and] material objects," as Rival (2014:99) cautions. Perhaps the Ojibwa also harbor a notion of "brute materiality" (Tilley 2007) alongside animistic reasoning. Nonetheless, that the Q'eqchi' are understood to "imbue material items with the spirit of the individual owner" (Kahn 2006:117) suggests a dynamic system in which the material and the spiritual intertwine if not merge. This intertwining is fundamentally relational in the sense that, while not all objects are seen to be alive, person-like, or essentially with-spirit, Q'eqchi', like other animists, "see the potential of subjective life in *all* objects" (Permanto 2015:23), with this life force becoming animated through establishment of relationships (material or ideological) between people and specific material elements in their universe.

Work on the "new animism" (Harvey 2006, 2014) continues to show a struggle with the idea of materialism and the role it plays in societies typically characterized as animistic. Morrison (2014:39), for instance, suggests that Nurit Bird-David's (1999) extension of Hallowell's work leads to the conclusion that "indigenous life is organized around the existence of persons, human and otherwise, rather than around materiality, functionality, and abstraction." Further, Morrison suggests that there is an "ontological similarity between humans and animals," which "means that indigenous peoples do not recognize nature, culture and the supernatural at all, let alone as separate cosmological domains" (43). I find this a problematic assertion, if at least since it implies a kind of simplistic, even primitive, cognitive ability. The persistence of "reductive materialism," according to Plumwood (2014:449), excludes meaningful inclusion of animistic thought. She argues instead for an "enriched" or "animist" materialism that reimagines "materiality in richer terms that escape the spirit/matter and mind/matter dualisms." I could not agree more. But rather than "animist materiality," a term that conjures up notions of primitive thinking ascribed to Indigenous peoples as evidenced in much early anthropology, "meta/materiality" keeps the focus on both the "actual" and the "virtual" material construction of the world as they exist in relational ontologies and epistemologies (Bird-David 1999). I am not suggesting that people are unaware or unable to discern the difference between a living human and a spirit, or the spirit of a tree and the soul of a person. The focus here is on both the things that can be seen/touched/felt and those things that can be "virtually" seen/touched/felt or otherwise be known to exist. It is an effort to approach the relationship between "materials" and "forces" (Deleuze and Guattari 2004:377) in an integrated manner, but that acknowledges that the whole idea of materiality is a human construct, one that "is comprehended, appropriated and involved in human projects" (Pollard 2004:48, cited in Ingold 2014:219). In this vein, Ingold (2014:220) defines "not a material world but a world of materials, or matter in flux." As he eloquently elaborates, in terms reminiscent of the notion of metamaterials in engineering and art, "It is about the way in which materials of all sorts, with various and variable properties, and enlivened by the forces of the cosmos, mix and meld with one another in the generation of things" (213). The material world is not passive, then, as "it provokes and resists human action" (Sillar 2009:370).

But as importantly, even the "new" animism—a rejection of the dualist notion of nature and culture as distinct (Harvey 2006)—is somewhat static and complacent, focused on establishing relational parity of ways of knowing but much less concerned with how knowledge is acquired and how what is known remains open to scrutiny and amendment. An emphasis on relational epistemology (Bird-David 1999) obscures the idea that not all entities and forces in the material and meta/material world are relatable to humans, that not all are open to relationships (which does not mean they cannot be understood). Contrary to Ingold (2007:12), in animist societies, sometimes objects are just objects; to imply otherwise is to take a too literal interpretation of general, often metaphorical pronouncements by Indigenous informants.

As Herman Konrad (1991) notes, the Maya in general do not make a distinction between the secular and the sacred. This provides fertile insight for appreciating the Maya view of the world, in which the material and the meta/material are inherently equal and interrelated ways of knowing the world (and are not fundamentally opposed) and are both substantially empirically based. It allows us to appreciate a "nonvisible reality" (Berlin and Berlin 1966:52); to "take spirits seriously" (Erazo and Jarrett 2017:2); to appreciate the Maya view of their "living landscape," which is "spiritually alive and connected to them" (Hinojosa 2015); to avoid "assuming from the outset that animist peoples do not reason in terms of ecological properties" (Rival 2014:94); and to consider how forests might "think" (Kohn 2013) or glaciers "listen" (Cruikshank 2006), both metaphorically material capacities. Further, meta/materialism allows us to move beyond an animist understanding of a world dichotomously consisting of humans and other-than-human persons, to include the full range of forces that impinge on humans and that stand in some kind of relationship to them (and those that do not), and that humans continuously seek to understand. That said, it differentiates what is known from what is knowable; the unknown is not necessarily ontologically unknowable mystery but rather the product of an epistemological technology that conceives of the currently unknown as theoretically capable of being known in some way at some point. Hence the unknown sits well within a meta/material framework and inspires humans to explore it, its properties, its form, its role in the universe, its materiality. It may well be a human "conceit" to think that the "world can be held to account" (Ingold 2006:18) because the world "goes its own way, regardless." But humans still strive to understand how it works, how the world going "its own way" affects them. Maybe this is more of a practical curiosity than a conceit. If "physical presence is how Q'eqchi' people understand, gain knowledge, desire, and feel pleasure" (Kahn 2006:120), then conceptualizing "physical presence" as a theoretically or empirically inductive construct provides the lens we need to understand meta/materiality: things are known because of their tangible presence but also through the consequences of those things acting on humans even when not visible. They are theorized to exist because the consequences of their existence are visible and impactful. One need not "see" electricity to understand what happens when you flip the light switch.

While the challenge to existing knowledge and paradigms within such Indigenous knowledge systems is not typically as bold, deliberate, or expeditious as it is within science, it does exist; existing knowledge is constantly being tested with new experiences. Even within the domain of "religion," where much of the animistic work especially in the past has been anchored, people are not content to simply accept received wisdom and unthinkingly re-create belief systems, and colonial processes have shown that a change in very fundamental aspects of belief systems happens (albeit for a variety of reasons, including forced assimilation). The Maya, for instance, are well-known to have experienced religious syncretism, melding colonial Catholic and Indigenous elements into a new Maya spiritual complex (Wilson 1993). But the search for "authentic," precontact Maya spiritual or cultural elements among contemporary peoples—reflective of a "continuity thesis" of Maya culture (Cook 2000)—risks denying them their modernity. In this research it matters not where an idea came from but rather that it exists today. The notion of a single, dominant "God" among the Maya is clearly a post-colonial development, and while in subsequent chapters I allude to newer ideas integrating with those thought to be precolonial, I do so for purposes of ontological and epistemological explanation and not as a means of arguing for cultural authenticity, continuity, or change. While decades ago Young (1976a:5) explained that a "people's medical beliefs and practices persist because they answer instrumental and moral imperatives and they are empirically effective," if we shift our gaze from trying to understand persistence or continuity to that of understanding empiricism, and from beliefs to knowledge-based practices, we generate the potential for new revelations about the dynamic nature of these medical systems.

Indigenous Knowledge and Science

Indigenous medicine is a form of Indigenous knowledge, and this discussion of animism and materiality blends necessarily into one on Indigenous knowledge and tradition, both concepts thrown about with considerable recklessness by scholars and others seeking scholarly and/or political positionality (Lanzano 2013). "Indigenous knowledge" often defies definition, yet it is a ubiquitous concept that shapes much scholarly discourse. Oguamanam (2006) provides an excellent overview of the various perspectives taken, noting, among other features, that Indigenous knowledge tends to be learned through practical experience and observation, transmitted orally, and "checked, validated and revised on regular or seasonal basis" (17). But perhaps what distinguishes it from other, similar types of knowledge—that is, what makes it "indigenous"—is not simply that we are talking about an Indigenous group, understood as precolonial occupants of a territory, but that their knowledge stems from a long history of occupation of that territory and that the method by which that knowledge was attained and transmitted, and what is actually known, predates in part the arrival of colonial influences while nonetheless demonstrating adaptation to, and incorporation of, endogenously new and externally introduced ideas. My interest in understanding Q'eqchi' Maya medicine here is with what is known—a kind of epistemological snapshot of a dynamic knowledge tradition—but also with *ways of knowing*, how people come to know something as "an achievement of work, experience and time" (Harris 2007:1).

Indigenous knowledge is invariably contrasted with science, of course. Sillitoe (1998:226) offers that "their [Indigenous] practices and knowledge relate, we assume, to the same natural world 'out there' albeit expressed in quite different idioms revealing concerns for somewhat different issues." Whether one accepts that Indigenous knowledge *is* science depends on one's own definition of "science." E. N. Anderson (2000), in a discussion of Maya biological knowledge, usefully identifies several ways in which "science" is understood, including the process by which knowledge is uncovered and "truth" validated. This methodological approach, centered on a particular process of knowledge generation, is identified with Western societies and a particular historical moment in human intellectual development. If, however, one accepts an alternative view, that science represents "the activities of people who want to know something about the world, beyond what intuition and received wisdom tell them" (134), then pretty much any knowledge tradition can be seen as "science," rendering the concept rather useless. I privilege method rather than intent and so do not view Q'eqchi' knowledge as science (and neither do they). This does not mean that it lacks any kind of objective "truth" about the world, of course, for it is fundamentally an empirical tradition, and empiricism stands as perhaps the original means of knowing over the course of human development. This perspective only floats if one accepts the validity of both material and gnostic or "immaterial" knowledge, the latter an idea antithetical to science that has nevertheless attracted so much attention by anthropologists and others that the empirical nature of these knowledge systems has been ignored. If we refrain from privileging one way of knowing over any others, Q'eqchi' knowledge can triangulate with science to enhance human knowledge about the world. How and to what extent multiple ways of knowing ultimately point to the same truth, or to different truths, strikes me as a fascinating epistemological question (cf. Agrawal 1995), as it does the Q'eqchi' iloneleb' with whom I work.

Is Q'eqchi' medical knowledge systematic? Medical *traditions*, according to Young (1983:1206), "are distinctive combinations of ideas, practices, skills, apparatuses and materia medica." Are these "distinctive combinations" systems or simply aggregates? Even the current definition of "traditional medicine" by the World Health Organization implies the lack of a system, referring to the "sum total of the knowledge, skill, and practices" (WHO 2013:15). There is no mention of organized, integrated knowledge or systematic empiricism here. Nor does this definition easily accommodate the attainment of new knowledge within the tradition (as opposed to introduced knowledge).

We know that the actual situation is far more complex and nuanced than this. So, for me, an Indigenous medical system like that of the Q'eqchi' has three components: integrated ideas about health, sickness, and treatment that emerged in the precolonial context of place and an associated appeal to "tradition" as the authoritative means of validation;[7] a means to test existing knowledge and to acquire new knowledge; *and* an organizational structure to categorize this knowledge and associated practices, in part to ensure its transmission to future practitioners. Explicating the organizational structure of Q'eqchi' medicine is one goal of this book. But suggesting that a system has an organizational, epistemological structure is in no way to suggest homogeneity in knowledge content or practice, or even that the system is understood the same way by all. The localized, situated context by which such knowledge is manifest ensures its "hybrid and contested nature" (Lauer 2012:177).

The appeal to tradition adds legitimacy to Indigenous knowledge by implying a degree of empiricism ("if it's been around a long time, it must be true"). Young (1979), however, notes that there are many reasons why such medical knowledge persists through time, beyond evidence that the knowledge and associated practices are beneficial in a medical sense. Hence the durability of knowledge alone cannot be evidence of empiricism if we narrowly define empiricism as active (not necessarily scientific) investigation into the validity of specific existing knowledge. Rather, if we take the broader view that empiricism refers to knowledge gained by experience, we better accommodate a broader range of phronetic and gnostic criteria by which to understand how ideas of apparent long-standing can remain salient in changing contexts.

Restorative and Transformative Processes

My own thinking on healing was originally largely influenced by symbolic and meaning-centered approaches, described earlier in this chapter, where the focus on phenomenological matters detracted from an examination of the material. Not surprisingly, within this popular anthropological tradition, discussions of treatment efficacy (from a scientific way of knowing) or effectiveness (from experiential ways of knowing) tend to be vague when offered at all; anthropologists seem to want to avoid judging whether something did or did not actually "work." Hence the attention on rituals and symbols, which has provided some rich ethnographic descriptions that have stood the test of time. But therapeutic engagement, and the knowledge and practices entailed therein, cannot be properly understood without a reference to outcome. Therapeutic process is essentially teleological, and to understand it, one must understand the intended endpoint or goal. I have begun to think of therapeutic process in terms of outcome by employing a simple dichotomous scheme that distinguishes transformative from restorative processes.

Transformative processes refer to treatment interventions that define the patient's problem in largely psychological, social, symbolic, metaphorical, and existential terms. Transformative treatment typically references a form of suffering linked to a patient's psychosocial situation, often deeply embedded in historical contexts, which is not easily escapable. The return to a pre-suffering normality is not typically possible or necessarily a desired option; the patient must move forward rather than backward. In a word, they must transform to achieve a healthy state of mind and/or body, perhaps to adopt a new existentialism, a new way of being in the world. This tends to be a long-term proposition, consisting more of "small turns," often imperceptible to self and others, than dramatic, sudden changes (Kirmayer 1993:176) (although epiphanies may spark the process). It is a process heavily laden with symbolism and metaphor, especially of travel and transportation: one is on the "road" or "path" to recovery. Yet this is often characterized as a journey without a precise destination; it is a journey that never ends, so "healing" becomes a lifelong process of therapeutic maintenance, where the patient, transforming into an adherent of a new way of life (sometimes as a member of a group of adherents), continues to be confronted with challenges and threats. In this therapeutic model, one is never really "cured."

Restorative processes refer to treatment interventions that define the patient's problem in largely material or meta/material terms, often with physiological or biological components. These processes identify a specific pathology, its cause and its course, its signs and symptoms, and offer a fairly defined notion of therapeutic success. Simply put, "cure" is the goal of restorative processes—that is, to eliminate the pathology and return the patient, as much as possible, to the pre-sickness state. Treatment tends to be focused and temporally defined; unlike with transformative processes, here the relationship between the practitioner and the patient reaches an intended conclusion, and the patient does not venture forth dependent upon the practitioner or a group of other cured individuals. Further, treatment tends to focus on an aspect of the patient, not the "whole" patient as is commonly suggested with transformative processes. I argue in this book that, while much Indigenous "healing" has been seen as largely transformative, especially in recent decades, Q'eqchi' therapeutics are more properly thought of as "medicine," wherein the focus on restorative processes is central.

Why does it matter that we understand the difference between "healing" and "medicine"? The interpretations often given to these terms serve to isolate and marginalize therapeutic practice. In the Canadian Indigenous context, "healing" has come to refer to a transformational psychosocial process that makes little reference to specific bodily or physiological dysfunction and identifiable diseases or disorders. Certainly, there was a time when medicine was practiced, and some practitioners still use plant medicines in their treatments, but the space that historically has been made available to Indigenous medicine in Canada (and the United States) has been in the "soft" areas adjacent to scientific medicine, particularly psychological issues involving interpersonal problems, addiction, and trauma responses (Waldram 2012a). Much of the medical knowledge of Canadian Indigenous peoples as it existed in precontact times and up to the mid–twentieth century has fallen out of living consciousness, the result of centuries of assimilative pressures and programs (by government and churches) and expanding biomedical services. Hence "healing" has emerged as a response largely to the effects of colonialism and these assimilationist policies, which were executed often in brutally effective fashion (for instance, in residential schools), and it found a place in programs that are inherently transformative in nature and typically sanctioned by government (and, more silently, a vigilant biomedicine). The idea that "traditional culture heals" (e.g., Brady 1995) is an example, a therapeutic approach that has taken on great importance in recent years; culture, as an essentialized therapeutic modality, is closely linked to "traditional" spirituality in such programs. But should an Indigenous person announce that he or she is practicing "medicine," the government/legal response would be less charitable. In Canada and Belize, as is common throughout the world, "medicine" is the domain of biomedicine and, more specifically, those trained in biomedical programs and recognized postsecondary institutions and who subsequently meet defined standards of knowledge and competence, being certified practitioners. Typically, the parameters of medical practice are reinforced by legal systems and criminal codes.

To say that the Q'eqchi' with whom I have worked "practice medicine" is to say that they are doing something very different than what I have observed in Canada. The terms "healing" and "healer" are frequently seen in the context of their activities, and the term they use for themselves, *iloneleb'* ("seers" or "those who see," as in the ability to discern or diagnose sickness), is glossed as "healers" when translated into English. Yet they are less engaged in transformative processes and more in restorative processes. In this book I refer to them as either *iloneleb'* (or, in the singular form, *ilonel*) or medical practitioners, and not healers. Whereas Indigenous healers in Canada often do not typically speak of "cure" in their practice, in Belize "cure" is precisely the goal: you had a disorder, you have been treated, now it is gone. This, in a nutshell, defines Q'eqchi' medicine. Iloneleb' have an imperative to cure.

Moving Forward

The plan for the remains of the book may appear to some as though I am simply mimicking biomedical epistemological structure. I suggest, however, that this structure makes some sense to the iloneleb', even though they do not typically think in such a manner about their practice. I begin in the next chapter by situating the research and myself as researcher, examining broader Maya medical ethnography in the context of the critique offered in this first chapter and describing the collaborative methodology employed to dig into Q'eqchi' medical ontology and epistemology. This is followed by chapters on the general principles of Q'eqchi' medicine, sickness etiology and nosology, diagnosis, and treatment. I conclude with some key observations about the principles and practice of Q'eqchi' medicine and detail why it matters—to the Q'eqchi' and to us—that approaches to therapeutic intervention by Indigenous peoples be reconsidered as inherently medical as well as psychotherapeutic, not always "healing" but sometimes "medicine."

CHAPTER 2

Maya Medicine, Medical Ethnography, and the Research Context

THE ISSUES IDENTIFIED in chapter 1 regarding medical anthropology's engagement with traditional and Indigenous medicine are also visible in Maya ethnography and understandings of Maya medicine, not surprising since some of the key ethnographers of the Maya, such as George Foster and Horacio Fabrega Jr., were also influential figures in the field of medical anthropology in much of the twentieth century. These issues coalesce around one central question: Are Maya therapeutics a form of "medicine" comparable to biomedicine or are they something else, be it belief, religion, healing, or whatever? Before I move on to the detailed presentation of the Q'eqchi' medical system, in this chapter I detail some of the major works on Maya medicine and position them within the critique of medical anthropology offered previously. I follow that with a discussion of the ethnographic context and then the collaborative methodological approach used in the research to counter the erroneous generalizations and misconceptions that have blanketed understanding of Maya medical knowledge and to provide a more nuanced understanding of a local Q'eqchi' medical system in southern Belize.

Ethnographic Conceptualizations of Maya Medicine

Maya ethnography is vast, so here I focus my attention on some of the most influential scholars whose work has characterized Maya medicine over the years. Let me begin with the studies of Robert Redfield and his colleagues. Throughout much of this work, and like many of his contemporaries, he uses the term "primitive," typically presented in quotation marks, to describe the ideas and practices of the Maya, and he speaks of "folk medicine" and "folk curers," a reflection of his deep interest in defining and describing "folk" societies. Redfield and Alfonso Villa Rojas published their classic ethnography on the rural village of Chan Kom in 1934; Redfield followed up with a restudy in 1950, and Redfield and Margaret Park Redfield issued a report on medicine in Dzitas in 1940. Redfield and Rojas (1934) argue that most sicknesses, and especially serious ones, are externalized, exerted through "supernatural" means "not characteristically thought of as operating on the sick person through mechanical or chemical means" (160) and are much less likely due to "functional disturbances or lesions within the sufferer's natural organism" (160). The one exception to this is "a sort of physiological principle" based on the hot/cold dichotomy of humoral medicine (161). They acknowledge the great many herbal remedies used, yet they also state that the "great body of remedies and therapeutic practices" are largely ritual based (171). However, they also conclude pessimistically: "It would be a misrepresentation to assert any detailed consistency or system or rules governing native thinking on these matters." In the restudy, no explanation is offered for how the healers, or "h-men," continue to practice, "curing sickness" despite the lack of a system of knowledge and despite competition from emerging biomedical services (Redfield 1950:122).

In Dzitas, a more urban community, local Maya avail themselves of "the arts of the traditional curer" while also accessing biomedical services (Redfield and Redfield 1940:55). One healer even has a clinic where, "as in more sophisticated medicine, [she] listens to the patient's story, makes a diagnosis and prognosis, often gives a treatment then and there, and finally instructs the patient as to what to do at home to continue the course of healing" (57). Redfield and Redfield (1940:71) characterize the "professional knowledge of the curer" as based "partly upon the ritual and somewhat mystic knowledge she has derived from the esoteric lore of the shaman-priests of the villages, and partly on her mastery of therapeutic techniques." Could such references to "mystic knowledge" and "esoteric lore" actually refer to an empiricism shrouded in the problematic paradigmatic discourse of the era? They admit that "there is a fairly coherent and widely recognized body of medical lore"; the question, which remains unanswered, is how such coherence has developed and is maintained given the manner in which the curer is understood to learn and practice. The curer is represented as a kind of "general practitioner," with knowledge of herbal and ritual medicines and spiritual rites. Despite the latter, however, the authors argue that this "folk medicine" is "largely detached from the religious and moral life" of the village; it is, rather, "the medical and secular part of the village tradition . . . without the sanction of religion" (78).

Horacio Fabrega Jr., and his colleagues, also worked extensively on Maya healing in the 1960s and 1970s. Fabrega, Metzger, and Williams (1970), focusing on the psychiatric aspects of Tenejapa medical practice in Chiapas, employ the common term "primitive medicine" or "so-called primitive medicine" (622) while also offering up similarly common and contradictory details. They refer to both "healers" and "curers," for instance, without making a distinction. More importantly, they refer to the Tenejapa "medical system," in which signs, symptoms, and cause are well detailed, noting that "almost all of these include elements . . . [that make] reference to the body almost exclusively" (615). Yet they also state that "the knowledge that underlies disease diagnosis and cure does not appear to depend in any significant way on an articulated set of native ideas about the structure and function of the body, what could be termed ethnophysiology or ethnoanatomy" (621), and that etiology is mostly understood as located external to the body, with the exception in both cases being traumatic injuries. Echoing the broader approach of that era to link Indigenous medicine to religion, within a structuralist-functionalist tradition, these authors highlight the role of sickness and "curing" "in the articulation between social and personality systems," with the "curer's social power" coming largely from his ability to affect psychological processes (622).

Metzger and Williams (1963), in a separate, earlier publication, also use the term "curer" to describe the Tenejapa medical practitioner. They note that while non-curers have access to the key prayers that are used during curing, and likely know some plant medicines, the curer's ability includes specialized diagnostic procedures, especially pulsing, and the ability to combine prayer, diagnostics, and medicinal plants to greatly enhance the likelihood of successful treatment. Some of this knowledge can be learned by simply watching the curers at work, since treatment is usually public (at least in the context of the household), and plant knowledge is often widely distributed. Curers demonstrate considerable variability in knowledge, skills, and specializations as well, and they tend also to be ranked as "master" and "junior" curers, suggesting the importance of learning through both apprenticeship and clinical experience.

In research on medicine in Zinacantan, Fabrega and Daniel Silver (1973; see also Fabrega 1970) continue to demonstrate some confusing insights. While lamenting the "psychiatric bias" of much contemporary research, they exhibit a clear affinity for the ideas of Jerome Frank (see also Holland and Tharp 1964), arguing that "folk healing" is successful because of the "psychosocial factors" grounded in the strength of the relationship between practitioner and patient, especially the former's ability to "emotionally arouse others" (8). "Clinical judgement," here, refers to the ability of the practitioner to recognize in the patient only those disorders amenable to this form of psychosocial treatment, although they acknowledge that "some general appreciation of bodily function, a general understanding of illness behaviors, and an intuitive knowledge of the relationship between both of these" is evident (8). They muddle things a little when they suggest that "systematic ideas about the structure and function of the body are not important in Zinacanteco medical knowledge" (87) and further that the body is not viewed as "units composed of elements that can be differentiated in mechanism and function but harmoniously interact" (90); in other words, the body is not viewed as an "interrelated system" (211). Despite the statement that there is "a somewhat elaborate and systematic body of knowledge regarding illnesses" (87), the Zinacanteco medical system is said to view the body "as a holistic, integrated aspect of both the person and his social relations" (218). They do lament that most research into Indigenous medicine fails to explore aspects of sickness that involve biological functioning, or how "medical judgements" are made by "folk practitioners" (8). Yet they, like many contemporaries, focus on the *h'iloletik*, or shamans, who employ "curing ceremonies" and spiritual knowledge to treat sicknesses caused by "imbalance or lack of harmony" in the patient's "psychosocial and moral state" (92). They note some variability in the knowledge held by practitioners and that there might be an empirical dimension to this knowledge based on practice, what they refer to as "trial-and-error testing" (211). Elsewhere, Fabrega (1970:398) characterizes this knowledge as "recipe knowledge or truncated explanations that specify ways of dealing with illness and symptoms." And much of medical practice, in particular the ceremonies, is understood to come from the gods (167). Reflecting the emerging critique of biomedicine within the social sciences, here Fabrega and Silver (1973:220) provide an elaborate comparison that, among other things, contrasts the "distance" and "coolness" of the "western" practitioner with the "warmth" and "informality" of the h'iloletik.

Several other insightful articles appear in this same era and offer somewhat contradictory views. Francisco Guerra (1964), writing about "Maya medicine" in general, refers to the practitioners as "physicians" and notes that the general parts and functions of the body, "gastric, pulmonary, and renal," were well-known and named (39). Indeed, he references a Spanish text from 1746 by Father Pedro Beltran containing 150 anatomical terms and more than two hundred "organic syndromes" (39). Clinical syndromes for mental disease were also elaborate (39), he notes, and the Maya understood the mechanism of infection (39). Guerra describes this medical knowledge as "science," involving medicinal plants (34), but he also states that disease was "always related to religious and ethical concepts" (38). Similarly, James Tenzel (1970), exploring Cakchiquel speakers in Guatemala, suggests that shamanic treatment of *susto* and witchcraft does not actually resemble psychotherapy—these are not mental illnesses as psychiatry understands them—but rather the practitioner is treating physical diseases through "curing ceremonies." However, while he suggests that these might well lower anxiety, he concludes disparagingly that "their ability to alter significantly the outcome of these diseases is doubtful" (378).

Botanists Elios Berlin and Brent Berlin (1966) also take the position that Maya "traditional medicine" is "scientific" and that the "ethnobiological knowledge of traditional peoples conforms in many respects to basic scientific principles" (3). Their emphasis is on the use of plant medicines linked to "an astute understanding of the signs and symptoms of common disease disorders" (4). They acknowledge the existence of both a "natural, usually visible reality that follows physical norms," what I am referring to as the material world, "and a frequently nonvisible reality that relates to extranatural phenomena" (52), my meta/material world, one that also follows a set of "norms." Health disorders stemming from the natural world are subject to empirical determination, they write, whereas in the case of the "extranatural," the diagnosis is based on analysis and identification of an "etiological agent" (52). They refer to Maya medical practitioners alternately as "healers" and "curers" without clarification. They also decry the research focus on the "cosmological aspects of Maya healing" that has deemphasized their medical ethnobiological knowledge, and they critique the work of scholars like Fabrega and Silver, especially the ideas that the Maya have limited knowledge of anatomy or physiological processes and that their medicine focuses on psychosocial issues (53). They argue instead that the Maya "have a remarkably complex ethnomedical understanding of anatomy, physiology, and the symptomology of particular health disorders" (53). Ultimately they refer to Maya knowledge as an "*ethno*scientific system of *traditional* knowledge" instead of a scientific one, adding that it is "based on astute and accurate observation that could only have been elaborated on the basis of many years of explicit empirical experimentation with the effects of herbal remedies on bodily functions" (53; italics mine). The implication is that Maya knowledge is science-like, especially in its empiricism, but not science in the Western sense.

These somewhat positive views can be contrasted with the dismissive ideas presented by William Holland and Roland Tharp (1964), whose work on highland Maya psychotherapy, inspired by Jerome Frank, suggests that the Maya "have only vague and elementary knowledge of the human body and the illnesses to which it is subject" (44), with a poor understanding of the structure and function of bodily organs. The Maya have largely "magico-religious interpretations," which they suggest "usually predominate where little rational, empirically-derived knowledge of the physical and organic basis of disease is accessible" (41). Even the pharmacopeia of the highland Maya is dismissed as "extensive but very ineffective" (44), although the bases for any of these assertions is unclear. The "curers," rather, work through "curing rituals . . . toward reconstructing the patient's proper relationship with his social and supernatural universe" (50). They conclude that "Tzotzil curing is psychotherapy as Frank (1961) defines it" (51).

While "modern medicine . . . leaves out the active cooperation of the patient . . . folk medicine places special emphasis on such cooperation," according to June Nash (1967:132). Her study of Tzo-ontahal in Chiapas seeks to detail the "logic" of medical practices while also referring to "systems of belief." She identifies the existence of a "native taxonomic hierarchy of disease," which provides a "checklist" used by practitioners in diagnosis. While social relationships are suggested as the primary cause of sickness, environmental disorders such as temperature, wind, or precipitation "provide disorders favorable to the entry of disease" (139). But individuals also have predisposing disorders or states that affect vulnerability to sickness, age being one example.

George Foster uses Maya research to advance many of his ideas about ethnomedicine. In a set of articles on how to "get well" and "stay well" in Tzintzuntzan (Foster 1984b, 1985), Foster suggests that while practitioners seek to "cure" their patients, Maya knowledge of the body's organs is limited mostly to the realm of folklore rather than accurate anatomy, and curing techniques focus mostly on humoral principles. Most illnesses are attributed to natural causes, an idea not always compatible with other research cited here, and the use of "empirical remedies" is common among the citizenry, who self-diagnose and then consult practitioners if self-treatment is unsuccessful (1985:810). "Through such deductive processes," he writes, "symptoms are fitted into a theoretical framework of cause and effect that villagers view as rational" (811). Therapies are usually but not always "theoretically consistent," he notes (816). He continues:

> How can we account for such juxtaposition of theoretical consistencies and inconsistencies? The answer appears to lie in empiricism. Like people everywhere, when faced with a problem Tzintzuntzeños are first pragmatic and only secondarily theoretical. . . . Their first concern is to apply the treatment judged most likely to work, not the treatment that conforms most closely to humoral demands. (817)

He does argue, however, that the approach used to treat patients, presumably one involving ceremony, masks the "underlying therapeutic system" based on these humoral principles (1985:807). Foster was a good advocate for the idea that medical knowledge was not randomly scattered about but rather part of "a remarkably coherent and logical medical system" (807). For Foster, this system is constituted by introduced classical elements of the humoral system from Europe during colonization, in combination with

Indigenous knowledge, which he frames as "empirical treatments . . . [that] most people know about, agree upon, and utilize without thought as to theoretical consistency" and that are memorized by the people (817). This is a form of "protoscientific medicine" (807) with Old World origins. So, while there is a system, Foster's view is that at least as it is found at the time of his research, it is one heavily influenced by non-Indigenous ideas. While this suggests that the Maya medical system is open to new ideas and striving toward syncretism, which I will show persists to this day, not everyone agrees with Foster's "diffusionist hypothesis" on the offshore origin of the humoral system (Chevalier and Sánchez Bain 2003).

Barbara Tedlock (1987) argues that the hot/cold aspect of the humoral system, which is central to Maya medicine, is in fact nearly universal. Frankly, however, for my purposes it matters not what is the origin of the humoral system. Rather, her emphasis on syncretism and the fusion of Indigenous and colonial elements makes more sense insofar as the people themselves pay little attention to the origins of particular ideas. And Tedlock, along with some others (e.g., Young 1978), suggests that the hot/cold distinction is less important than many have thought and may even be an artifact of anthropological research because the metaphorical symbolism involved attracts interest. Tedlock references Quiché empiricism in the use of plant medicines in "curing" (she also uses "healing" interchangeably with "curing"), "based on generations of experimentation" (1987:1076). However, Sandra Orellana (1987:28), exploring documentary sources from the early colonial period for highland Guatemala, suggests that while there was use of "medicines discovered empirically," there is no evidence for an "all-embracing theory or mechanism of illness" prior to the sixteenth-century introduction of the humoral system (here she is clearly in the Foster camp), even though she references "the aboriginal medical system" as one "developed by trial and error over a long period of time" that may have involved "experimental research" (259). Practitioners of various kinds, who learned primarily through apprenticeship, employed empirical knowledge of plant medicines along with "curing rituals" (61).

Sheila Cosminsky and Mary Scrimshaw (1980; see also Pedersen and Barufatti 1985; Watanabe 1992) also highlight the open and pragmatic nature of the Maya medical system. In their research in Guatemala, they identify the serial and simultaneous use by patients of various medical alternatives until they feel better, a kind of "empirical and pragmatic behavior" that is reflected in the Maya medical system itself (275). The Maya "folk practitioners . . . are eclectic and adopt whatever is useful and available to them from various systems," including Western or cosmopolitan medicine. As Karin Eder and Maria Manuela Garcia Pu′ (2002:21) argue, "there is not a 'pure' indigenous Maya medicine," and "the predominating indigenous Maya medical practice is dynamic and often plural, and is steered by daily life." While my research supports this view of Maya medicine as dynamic and plural, this should not suggest that such flexibility means that there is no coherent medical system. Such a view simply privileges a kind of rigidity that seems characteristic of no other medical system. Indeed, a fundamental characteristic of Maya medical systems is their openness to change.

Eder and Pu′ (2002) think of Maya medicine more in cultural than biological or physiological terms, and their work represents a more contemporary reading of the work of the symbologists. Arguing that the Maya worldview is holistic, they suggest that Maya medicine in Guatemala is "a system that sustains the principles of the Maya worldview" (112) and "a specific manifestation of the social organization of this culture" (108), that disease is located at the conjunction of "natural and social phenomena" (65), and that treatment requires "culturally accepted procedures" (65). The implication of this cultural argument is that Maya medicine is not suitable for non-Maya or those Maya who lack knowledge of the "mythic world" and its symbols, a fundamental prerequisite for symbolic healing (Dow 1986; Waldram 1997). Yet the Q'eqchi' iloneleb' in this study treat any and all regardless of cultural factors.

Maya medicine in Yucatan is characterized by its openness to new ideas and the "curer's" willingness to "experiment" by combining the old with the new, according to Marianna Kunow (2003:41), which in part explains its resilience in the colonial and post-colonial eras. Yet she also argues, importantly, that "contemporary Yucatecan curing reflects a unified regional oral tradition" (2), despite the somewhat individualized knowledge (medical and spiritual) of the curers, an idea that helps to explain the existence of a medical system in the absence of formal educational institutions or regulated training programs. Empiricism, as well as spirituality, is an important element of Maya medicine, she adds, although her own work seems to focus mostly on what is known, especially with respect to plant use, rather than how it is known. This is evident in her characterization of the learning process of practitioners, involving either dreams or apprenticeship; the role of experimentation in the development of new knowledge is not articulated. Kunow accepts the idea that the curer and patient must have "faith" in the system and that the treatment will work, which echoes Eder and Pu′'s dependence on the symbolic rather than the material as the explanation for effective treatment, and therefore for the psychosocial over the physiological.

Jacques Chevalier and Andrés Sánchez Bain (2003) also highlight the pluralistic nature of contemporary Maya medicine while arguing not only against Foster's diffusion thesis but also forcefully in favor of the resilience of traditional Maya knowledge of health and sickness. Although they use the term "folk healing" throughout, they also refer to "native medical systems" (xv) and spend considerable time grappling with the idea of empiricism. Their critique of Foster on this issue is compelling: They argue that Foster confuses "experience," the building blocks of empiricism, with "mechanical remembering" and "cultural filtering." Their examples highlight the important distinction among "we've tried this poultice and it works," "we've been told that this poultice works," and "this poultice works because we believe that . . ." (13). I would suggest that they are actually defining the process through which latent empiricism is constructed as a content-laden system consisting of knowledge derived from practice and shared laterally and intergenerationally (Waldram and Hatala 2015); indeed, they are describing the interrelated processes of learning by practice and learning from the experiences of others. Their definition of empiricism is better than many: They too refer to it as "learning by trial and testing" (13), with "testing" implying a more deliberative and intentional approach than the more common "error" in "trial and error" implies, but they question how important empiricism is to the development of medical knowledge. "Why should empirically minded people," they query, "hold on to beliefs and practices that can be shown by experience to be useless or even dangerous to their health?" (13). Allan Young (1979) and Robert Edgerton (1992) both answer this question; the key issue here is the incorrect assumption by scholars that all current medical knowledge and practices would be unambiguously therapeutically sound and that empiricism is fail-safe, standards that no medical system meets. And, of course, there are many reasons why particular knowledge remains extant in human populations, since such knowledge is never restricted to one, narrowly defined domain.

There have been a few voices attempting to shift the ethnographic lens away from the focus on symbolism, the supernatural, and personalistic etiology that has obscured our ability to recognize the more material aspects of Maya medicine. Kevin Groark (2005:768) prefers to explore the "quotidian illness experiences and the preventative, therapeutic, and health maintenance functions" of what he terms "lay healing," that form of therapeutics within the expertise of nonspecialists. Working among Tzeltal and Tzotzil peoples in Guatemala, Groark argues that these lay practices, what he refers to in places as "curative medicine," are actually the "bedrock" of therapeutic intervention (786). Using the steam bath as an example, he identifies what I would call a medical system—that is, "a unified conceptual and therapeutic framework for maintaining and restoring health" (793). But Groark (2008) also acknowledges, along the lines of Jerome Frank, that with respect to trained practitioners (not laypersons), the quality of the therapeutic relationship, what he calls "empathic knowing," is crucial to success and that the "medical is not clearly segregated from the moral, religious, or political" (441). In effect, with respect to medical practitioners, their domain is personalistic etiology, as curers create a narrative that links one's suffering to another's actions (442), although I suspect that the practitioners here also harbor notions of "natural" etiology and disorders they typically treat. Certainly, the existence of both "lay" and practitioner "ethnomedical theories" (786) speaks to the complexity and dynamic nature of the overall medical system of which they are a part.

In sum, there is little consistency in the ethnographic treatment of Maya therapeutics. Certainly there are optimistic references to ideas of cure, system, empiricism, and medicine—I am certainly not the first to suggest these as core—but often alongside somewhat contradictory interpretations. Are Maya therapeutics fundamentally "trial and error" at best? Are they essentially a form of religious practice? Are they holistic or reductionist? Are they examples of culturally grounded symbolic healing, or empirical knowledge of the body and sickness that has developed outside a scientific paradigm? Is the goal healing or curing? In what ways are there local as opposed to regional or pan-Maya medical systems? My research in Belize was designed to address these questions in the context of one group of Q'eqchi' iloneleb'.

The Q'eqchi' Homeland in Belize

Belize (Map 1) is a small Central American country on the Atlantic side, with fewer than twenty-three thousand square kilometers and a population (albeit growing quickly) in the 340,000 range. It is also tremendously diverse. In addition to the Maya peoples (11 percent), the country boasts substantial Mestizo (Maya and Spanish heritage; 49 percent), Creole (English and African heritage; 21 percent), Garinagu or Garifuna populations (descendants of African slaves and Carib Indians; 5 percent), and many other European and Asian immigrant groups, including British, Chinese, East Indians, and Mennonites (Government of Belize 2014). More recently, Belize has become a popular retirement destination for both US and Canadian citizens.

Although the Spanish conquistadores traveled throughout the area that would one day become Belize, they demonstrated a general lack of interest due to the poorer resources found there in comparison to other territories. English and Scottish laborers eventually arrived, attracted by a nascent logwood industry, and in 1862 the territory was claimed as a British crown colony and named British Honduras (Bolland 2003). English, of course, was the working language of the colony. In 1981, when the colony gained its independence and was renamed Belize, English was made the official language. Guatemala continues to dispute the southern and western borders, and occasional skirmishes between the Guatemalan army and the Belize Defense Force, or between nationals of each country, still occur.

"Maya" is an externally generated appellation, based primarily on similar archaeological and linguistic criteria (Astor-Aguilera 2010). The Q'eqchi' are one of three Maya groups found in contemporary Belize, along with the Mopan and the Yucatec. The Yucatec, who fled south from Mexico to escape the Caste War in the 1840s, are found in the northerly areas. The Mopan are considered to be indigenous to Belizean territory, although throughout their colonial history they have been forced back and forth across the Guatemala border. The Q'eqchi' are understood to have originated in Guatemala and

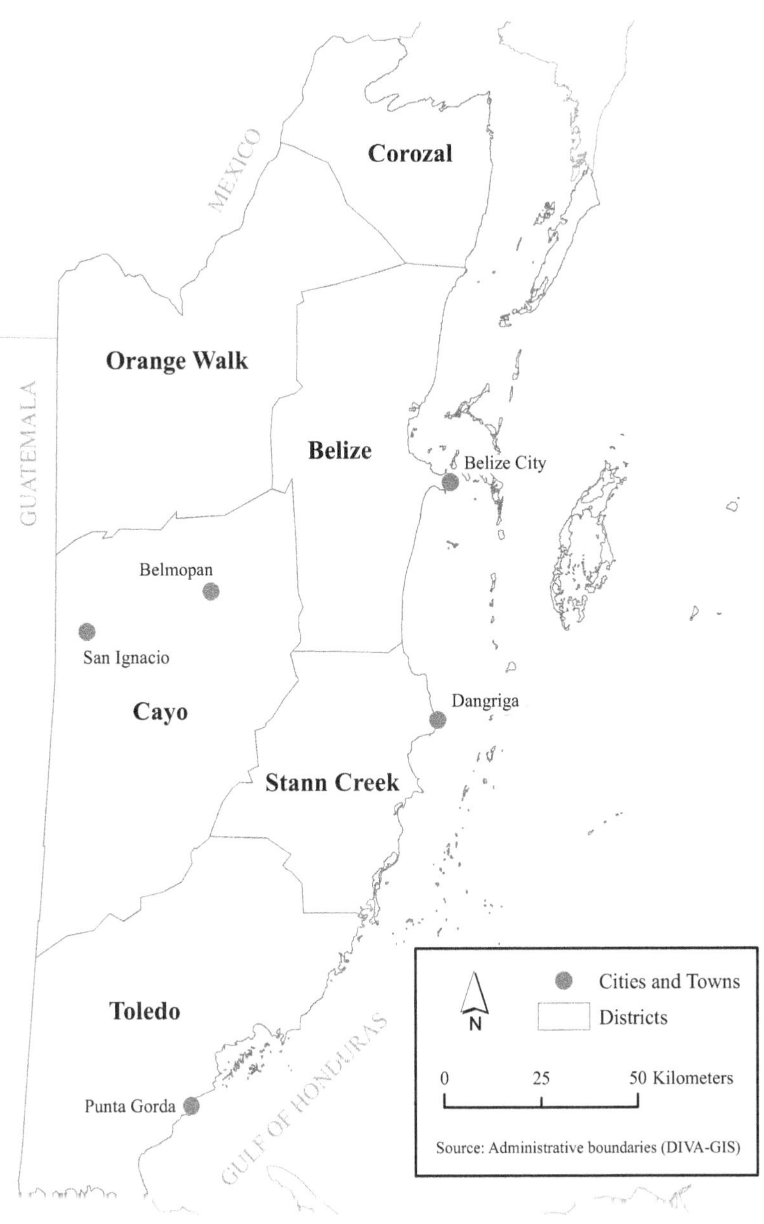
MEXICO
GUATEMALA
Corozal
Orange Walk
Belize
Belize City
Belmopan
San Ignacio
Cayo
Dangriga
Stann Creek
Toledo
Punta Gorda
GULF OF HONDURAS
N
Cities and Towns
Districts
0
25
50 Kilometers
Source: Administrative boundaries (DIVA-GIS)

MAP 1. Belize.

have moved into Belize on and off in response to oppression in Guatemala. Only recently have the Q'eqchi' been accorded Indigenous rights in Belize, and many still remain undocumented in Belize and retain their Guatemalan citizenship (Wilk 1997). The Mopan and Q'eqchi' territories are mostly in the southern and southwestern parts of the country, and people have many relatives who remain on the Guatemala side of the border.

Together the Maya total about thirty-six thousand people (Statistical Institute of Belize 2013). All my research has been undertaken in the southern Toledo District (Map 2), which stretches from the Bay of Honduras west and south to Guatemala. Overall, Toledo is a rural and somewhat remote area, with the lowest overall population (in 2017, about thirty-one thousand) and population density in the country. Throughout Toledo there are many Q'eqchi' and Mopan villages, where milpa agriculture (mostly corn, beans, and rice) provides the economic backbone. A complex, and in many cases rough, road network links the villages inland to the main administrative center of the district, the coastal town of Punta Gorda, with a population of about seven thousand people. My research was undertaken in villages stretching west along this road network from Punta Gorda to Jalacte and San Vicente, along the Guatemala border. The Southern Highway, which was constructed in the 1960s to link Toledo with Belize City, afforded many Q'eqchi' the opportunity to expand their village networks (Wilk 1997:70), and villages such as Big Falls and Indian Creek were established. These villages are also central to this research.

The name Q'eqchi' was originally a reference to a language spoken by one of several Maya groups in this region of Central America, and identity was usually anchored to communities rather than a pan-Maya or pan-Q'eqchi' notion of nationhood (Wilson 1993). By the time of my research, a clear collective Q'eqchi' identity had emerged alongside community identity, fueled by the independence of Belize and the emerging need to secure rights to village and farming lands. The Q'eqchi', numbering some fifteen thousand people, are the largest "ethnic" group in Toledo identified by the 2010 census. The Mopan number slightly more than five thousand, and fewer than one hundred identify as Yucatec. The overall poverty of the Toledo District, and the Q'eqchi' in particular, is evident from the usual statistical indicators: low levels of literacy, high unemployment, poor sanitation and housing, highest

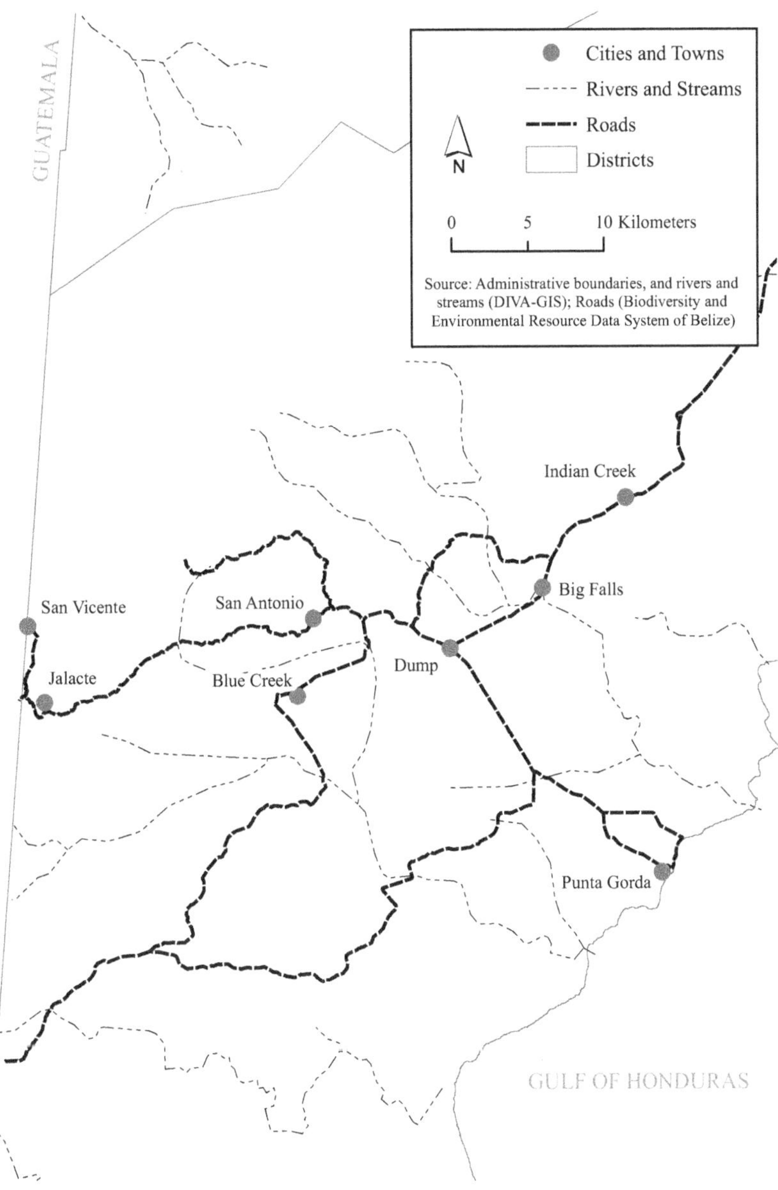

MAP 2. Toledo District and Study Area.

mortality and morbidity, and so on. The only hospital in the Toledo District is in Punta Gorda, although many villages have a variety of small medical or nursing outposts and polyclinics that are irregularly staffed with medical professionals.

Methodology

The research presented here represents the fruits of a fifteen-year collaborative relationship with a group of Q'eqchi' Maya healers in southern Belize, starting in 2004. The year prior I received a communication from Victor Cal, the coordinator for a group of Q'eqchi' who had come together in 1999 to form an association, known initially as the Q'eqchi' Healers Association and subsequently as the Maya Healers Association of Belize (in response to the inclusion of Mopan practitioners; hereafter MHAB). At the time, many Q'eqchi' people were concerned about the loss of language and traditions among their people, a common concern (e.g., Permanto 2015). Europeans had brought many centuries of cultural change to the people of Central America, and in recent years, many US-based evangelical churches had been established in Belize. Younger people were not learning the Q'eqchi' language as much as in the past and were not interested in becoming iloneleb'. While formal education in schools is considered important, many older Q'eqchi' believe it is also important that young people retain their identities as Q'eqchi'. The practitioners in the MHAB were interested in having someone study the cultural aspects of their medical knowledge and practice, and were particularly interested in appealing to Westerners, scientists, and policy makers. The desire—even need—to translate Indigenous medical knowledge to a broader world is one that Indigenous groups themselves are increasingly identifying—a recognition of the brute power imbalance in global health and medicine—and one in which medical anthropologists are now playing an important role (e.g., Craig 2012).

Membership in the MHAB has fluctuated over the years, with ten to fifteen active members at various times. As my work unfolded with them, I found it best to narrow my focus on a smaller number of practitioners, those who seemed both most keen and most knowledgeable. I have worked most closely with six of them:

- Don Albino Maquin (also spelled Makin), now deceased, is considered the founder of the association. Albino was born in the department of Alta Verapaz in Guatemala and came to Belize sometime in the 1950s, living first in San Benito before moving to the Indian Creek area in Toledo. As a young man he began learning medicine from his father and uncle, and for much of his life he was content to simply provide medical care for his family. Only in his later years did his expertise draw attention more broadly. It was his idea to bring a group of iloneleb' together, and he traveled about the region consulting and gauging interest. As the eldest member of the group, his knowledge was respected, even revered, and when he spoke, the others always listened carefully. He was spry for an elderly man; the last time I visited with him in 2006, less than a year before his death in his nineties, he was hauling large logs by himself as he directed the construction of his new thatch house.
- Don Manuel Baki passed away in spring of 2018, well into his eighties. He was born in Cha'al, Guatemala, and came to the Toledo District when he was thirty years old, settling in Big Falls. He began to learn Q'eqchi' medicine around age thirty while still in Guatemala, completing his training just before he moved to Toledo. He decided to study medicine when his wife fell ill and was not effectively treated by a local ilonel. He wished to be of more service to his family. So, a week after his wife's sickness, "I went to ask someone to teach me. I studied with this person for six months." When he moved to Belize, he continued his training for another year, studying with his godson, who was already a practicing ilonel. Manuel's practice was local, in the Big Falls and Indian Creek areas. In the latter years of our work together, as a result of his advanced age, he rarely traveled outside his home, so patients visited him.
- Don Lorenzo Choc was in his mid-seventies when he passed away a few years ago, after living in the Indian Creek area of Toledo for several decades. Originally from Chacalté in Guatemala, his family moved to southern Belize when he was small. He lost two of his brothers to sickness when he was young, and he himself experienced a serious sickness: He collapsed, was unable to speak, and felt he was going

to die. There were no medical doctors to be found anywhere, so his father took him to an ilonel, who helped him to get better. Lorenzo, by that time, had already shown an interest in plant medicines, so he treated himself as well, and his sickness led him to think about becoming a practitioner. Eventually he engaged in an apprenticeship with his father, and he began his work as an ilonel at age twenty-two. Throughout his life, his medical practice was primarily local.

- Don Manuel Choc is in his late-seventies now. He was born in Cha'al, Guatemala, and moved to Belize when he was young. When his father died, his mother remarried and moved back to Guatemala. Around age fifteen, he returned to Belize, and he now resides in the Indian Creek area. Growing up, he knew of iloneleb' in his community and began to learn about plant medicines. His stepfather, it turns out, was an ilonel, and Manuel began to learn about medicine from him when he was only twelve. "I was interested in being a ilonel," Manuel recalls. "My stepfather told me that it would help me in my life. It would also help my family whenever someone gets ill. He also told me that, whenever he was to die, I would continue his work." After his stepfather passed, his thoughts drifted away from medicine for several years before he took up with another master. Today his practice is primarily focused in the Indian Creek area.
- Don Francisco Caal is approaching sixty now and has been working as an ilonel since age eighteen. He was born in Chacalté, in Guatemala, and came to the Toledo District around age twenty-three. His home community in Guatemala was close to the Belize border, and when he saw that his children might have better educational opportunities in Toledo, he emigrated, settling in the village of Jalacte. Francisco decided to become an ilonel after his first wife became ill and died while they were living in Guatemala. His first child with her also died. While there were iloneleb' from whom he could have sought assistance, he did not find them satisfactory. Like many other practitioners, then, he was encouraged to learn medicine in the first instance to help his family. "I was really hurt by that experience," he says. "It made me think that if I am to be married again, it is better to know how to take care of the family through traditional healing." He turned to his uncle,

an ilonel, and asked him to become his first master. Today Francisco lives in Punta Gorda and is a well-known ilonel in Belize and Guatemala; he is often called to treat patients long distances away. He is considered one of the most knowledgeable iloneleb' in the MHAB, and with his younger brother, Emilio, is also designated as a Guia Espiritual Maya (Maya spiritual guide). This appellation signifies an elevated status as an individual with deeper spiritual knowledge, including knowledge of the role of the spiritual in sickness and curing.

- Don Emilio (José) Kal, Francisco's younger brother, is in his fifties. He was born in San Benito Poite, in Belize, and currently lives in the village of Jalacte. There was much sickness in his village when he was growing up. Many people suffered, and some problems, such as snakebites, were often fatal. There were no medical services available to his people at that time. "A father is responsible for the health care of his family," Emilio explains, "and when they got sick sometimes it was difficult to find an ilonel." He decided to undergo the rigorous training required to acquire the knowledge and skills to help his family, and others, in times of sickness. Emilio has had several teachers in Guatemala and Belize over the years, including Francisco, with whom he often works collaboratively. As a renowned medical practitioner and Guia Espiritual Maya, he is often called to attend to patients throughout the two countries and lead, or participate in, Maya spiritual ceremonies. He and Francisco are the only iloneleb' in the group who regularly use the complex Maya calendar in diagnosis and treatment, Emilio more so than his brother.
- Don Victor Cal, although not an ilonel, has functioned as the coordinator for the group since its inception. Like many others, Victor came from Guatemala and settled in the Toledo District. A community organizer and teacher, he worked at Tumul K'in School in Blue Creek for many years, one of the few truly public schools in Toledo, where he directed the program in Maya culture and languages. Victor has deep knowledge of Q'eqchi' culture and medical practices, and has served as both a research participant and coresearcher throughout this project.

In recent years I have also started to work with a Mopan practitioner,

FIGURE 1. Members of the Maya Healers Association of Belize. Left to right: Francisco Caal, Manuel Baki, Lorenzo Choc, Emilio Kal, Victor Cal, Manuel Choc, Tomas Caal. Itzamma Medicinal Garden (Indian Creek), 2012. Photo by Andrew Hatala.

Augustino Sho, a recent member of the MHAB. He lives in the same village as did Manuel Baki, one of several mixed Q'eqchi' and Mopan villages in the Toledo District. Augustino is fluent in English and works as a schoolteacher, and we have done our work together in English (with the exception of a documentary film, to be discussed below, where he spoke Mopan). His approach to medical practice is very similar to that of the Q'eqchi' members of the group; however, to avoid ethnographic complications, I have chosen to not use any direct data from him in this book but rather to use his insights as confirmatory data where appropriate.

All the iloneleb' who are members of the MHAB and are cited in this research have asked that their real names be used. As with many Indigenous peoples, among the Q'eqchi', what a person knows and their right to impart that knowledge is linked to who they are as named individuals and community members. The idea of anonymity or use of pseudonyms would be nonsensical to these iloneleb'.

There are no female members of the MHAB. The group is by no means exclusionary, and they have reached out to known female practitioners, most of whom work officially as midwives. Occasional joint meetings have been held, but as yet no women have ventured to publicly join, in part because they do not wish to jeopardize their government employment. Nonetheless, these women do use Q'eqchi' medical knowledge and techniques in their work, alongside their biomedical training. De Gezelle (2014) reports the widespread belief in Toledo that there are no Q'eqchi' women medical practitioners, but my work suggests this may be a semantic issue as well as a matter of disguising one's practice. In other words, there are women who practice aspects of Q'eqchi' medicine, in the domestic sphere for instance, but not necessarily women who act publicly as iloneleb'. The men I have worked with agree that there is no gender-based limitation to the training and practice of their medicine, often stressing that there are Q'eqchi' women practicing in Guatemala. Watanabe (1992:190) details a "tacit division of labor" between women and men practitioners among the Mam in Guatemala, and Kunow (2003) in her Yucatan work suggests that there are a few areas of medical practice that are gender-specific. Both suggest that women are more likely to concentrate on treatments involving botanicals and on midwifery. There is no doubt that the lack of women practitioners in this research is an important limitation, and suggestions that their knowledge and specializations would vary from those of the men are noteworthy. The question of the extent of that variation and its implications for my analysis simply cannot be addressed at this time.

The research certainly posed many challenges for me. I had never worked in Central America and did not initially speak Spanish (many Q'eqchi' do) and especially Q'eqchi'. My initial approach was to build the research collaboratively and learn along the way. I began immediately to take Spanish language training at my home institution, and the practitioners and their families patiently taught me Q'eqchi' to the point where I had a solid Q'eqchi' medical vocabulary and the ability to speak informally in social settings and follow conversations (often through the use of both Spanish and Q'eqchi').

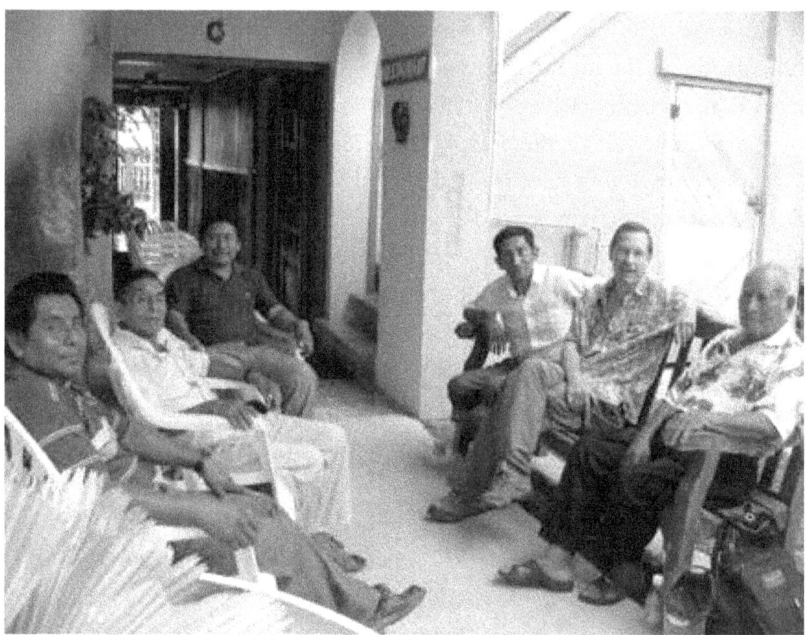

FIGURE 2. Research meeting. Left to right: Augustino Sho, Manuel Choc, Tomas Caal, Francisco Caal, author, Manuel Baki. Punta Gorda, 2012. Photo by author.

We began with meetings about research goals and methods. The practitioners told me what they wanted studied and why, and I presented them with some methodological options. They understood research to a certain extent and had been visited by researchers in the past. Most importantly for me, they had formed a strong relationship with University of Ottawa botanist John Thor Arnason, with whom they were working to identify specific plant medicines. The positive experience they continued to have with Arnason and his team clearly paved the way for me; they were not afraid of research and indeed encouraged it. It was important to them that the world come to appreciate their knowledge.

Those early meetings were pivotal in establishing how I would undertake the research. I presented them with my "Cadillac" methodological model, explaining the options for data collection and analysis that I thought would best meet their goals. They were more than willing to accept my advice, even

FIGURE 3. Author interviewing Albino Maquin. Indian Creek, 2006. Photo by author.

after my detailed explanations of the tasks that would be required of them and the ethical issues that creating a database and doing the work might entail. First off, I suggested that the best way to collect information in a manner that would create the legacy they hoped for was to digitally record interviews and treatment sessions using both audio and video. They quickly appreciated the value of such an approach to create an archive, despite the intrusiveness. While they became pros at being interviewed on camera, other family members and especially children, who were almost always present, found the video to be especially entertaining. I spent many hours filming the children just so they could see themselves on "television" (that is, my computer monitor).

Overall, we have held more than two dozen group meetings. Almost all meetings were recorded, and frequently these ongoing planning sessions provided important research insights as well as direction for each new phase of the project. However, most of the data ultimately came from individual interviews and treatment sessions. The practitioners are spread throughout the Toledo District. At the time I started, the Southern Highway had not been fully completed, and the fifteen-kilometer stretch from the village of Big Falls to Indian Creek was slow and bone-jarring. The gravel road to Jalacte in the west was worse, and when it was passable, the fifty-kilometer trip typically took up to three hours each way by vehicle. The practitioners did not have phones—and the single village phones did not pan out as a means of effective communication—so contacting the practitioners in advance to set up interviews was next to impossible. I would sometimes send word with other villagers that I encountered, but this too was a frustratingly imperfect means to make contact. So the only real option was to travel out to the practitioners' homes, in hopes of finding them home and available to talk. This hit-and-miss approach, augmented by only a periodic bus service on the main roads (I subsequently acquired a truck!), led to many hours of zero productivity. Things have changed dramatically since I first started, with paved roads and cell phones now common throughout much of my research area.

I usually interviewed each practitioner for sixty to ninety minutes, typically in the mornings and often followed by lunch. Most interviews were undertaken in the homes of iloneleb' or at Itzamma, their medicinal plant garden north of Indian Creek, named after Itzam Na (or Itzamna), the pan-Maya creator and god of medicine (Thompson 1970). The early interviews were rather global as I sought out the scope of the project and often followed whatever topical opportunity presented itself. These open-ended, unscripted interviews allowed me to better understand what I was dealing with, to appreciate the depth of the knowledge I was seeking to tap, and to learn the most salient issues from the ilonel's perspective. As we moved further into the research and as I assessed new insights in an ongoing fashion, I shifted to more focused interviews built around themes and more scripted questions to ensure similar coverage of topics with each practitioner. "Diagnosis," "natural sicknesses," "use of alcohol," "psychiatric disorders," "infection and contagion," are examples of themes. Then, even further into the research, the foci became even tighter—"epilepsy," for instance, or "pulse diagnosis." At each interview, I made a point of manually recording in my notebook key Q'eqchi'-language terms for disorders, anatomy, techniques, and so on. These were often recorded initially phonetically, while I was learning elements of the language, to be corrected later with language experts.

Beginning with the first interviews in 2006, overall I conducted 134 formal interviews with the Q'eqchi' practitioners. Rather than seek a broad base of knowledge, I chose to work only with active and interested members of the association, striving for depth of knowledge. And deep it is! I am aware that I have not managed to reach the level of knowledge of the practitioner of Q'eqchi' medicine. They did offer to train me, but I have no desire to abandon my ethnographer's position to pose as the shaman-ethnographer that some have done in similar research. Instrumentally this also aided my work, as I was able to explain to concerned family members, political operatives, and other villagers who were suspicious of the research work that I was not positioning myself to "steal" practical knowledge that I could sell. What I was learning, and the very untraditional manner in which I was learning, ensured that I would never gain the knowledge the practitioners have so I could launch my own Q'eqchi' medical career. (They had heard of a non-Maya individual in northern Belize who they believed had done just that.) Research knowledge is very different from practical knowledge.

Any researcher who has worked with the same community or group for many years will appreciate the problem of participant fatigue. While the practitioners were always keen to be interviewed, over time, I sensed some degree of boredom with the format. Therefore I turned to additional, timeworn ethnographic techniques: diagnostic tests, pile sorts, and photovoice. At the outset, I was uncertain how well these would work, and I was pleasantly surprised by their robustness.

Given that the practitioners did not read any language, the use of index cards with written text certainly presented a challenge. The diagnostic tests involved signs and symptoms written on cards, which I compiled in groups to reflect known Q'eqchi', biomedical, and psychological/psychiatric disorders; participants were asked to diagnose any known disorder based on the sign/symptom set. For the pile sorts, I wrote out the Q'eqchi' and the English words of sicknesses, and the practitioners were asked to sort first by similarity (without further prompting) and then by cause, seriousness, treatment, prayers used, and plants used. Afterward, I interviewed each about the contents of the piles and why they were constructed as they were. The

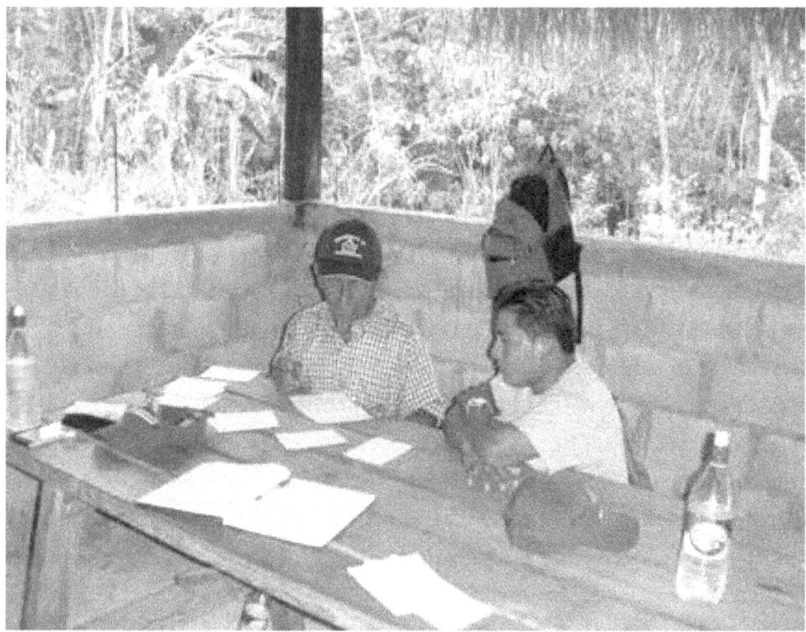

FIGURE 4. Francisco Caal undertaking pile sort. Itzamma, 2008. Photo by author.

practitioners proved adept at remembering what was on each card as they sorted and created their piles and determined their diagnoses, and I always confirmed their understanding of the cards by reading them back. Frequently they would pick up actual cards and look at the text as well, no doubt creating a mnemonic from the written shapes they saw.

For the photovoice project, each practitioner was given a disposable analog camera with twenty-eight exposures and shown how to use it. (In some cases, they simply passed the technical task on to one of their children or grandchildren, who shot whatever they indicated.) This technique was a variation of one proposed by them: They requested that I give them video cameras so they could shoot for themselves what they felt was important. I had only one video camera, and given the technological aspects of operating the camera, the difficult environmental conditions in which the camera would be kept, and the fact that it would never be meaningfully secure, I felt that the use of still cameras made more sense. I took a photo of each ilonel at the outset, to identify photographic sets. They were provided with one charge: "What do you want to tell the world about your work as an ilonel?" Not surprisingly, when the film was developed, there were many shots of both family (they wanted the prints!) and medicinal plants, but there were also many shots of medical technology and paraphernalia, other objects, and some of patients. Almost all photographs came out sufficiently to allow for the interviews to take place. For these, a variety of questions were posed (for example, What did you want the world to know about this photo? What is it a picture of? Why did you take it? What does it have to do with your work as a medical practitioner?). Of course, there were a few instances when a practitioner could not recall why a photo had been taken or even what it was (in part, I suspect, because others had accessed the cameras).

I was also able to videotape forty treatment sessions (subsequently, several graduate students working under my supervision made many more recordings), observing roughly one hundred in total. For the most part, patients were agreeable to video and audio recording and were often intrigued to watch the playback of the session. The practitioners move quickly, and it was often a challenge to get the camera set up properly before they started the treatment. Only Q'eqchi' was spoken during these sessions, or occasionally some Spanish, and especially with the former, I was able to follow only the basics of what was happening. Although I was with an interpreter, it would have been inappropriate for him to speak during the treatment, explaining what was being said and done. So subsequent to each treatment, I met with the practitioner to watch the playback of the session on my computer and discuss what was happening and why. Immediately following each treatment session, I also interviewed the patient. I asked about their understanding of their problem and what the practitioner said and did. These tended to be short interviews, ten minutes or so; some patients seemed reluctant to talk in detail about the treatment or, in many cases, simply had no real idea what had happened, as the practitioner made little effort to communicate. I did not deliberately follow up with any patients to see how they were doing and so cannot speak to the issue of the long-term effectiveness of the treatments they received. However, many patients encountered after treatment reported improvement.

Skilled interpreters were essential to the research, and with only a few exceptions, I used them in my work. The exceptions occurred primarily in treatment sessions where the patient spoke English or when there was no interpreter available (in which case we all communicated in bits of Q'eqchi', Spanish, and English). The interpreters were highly knowledgeable, and most had prior experience interpreting for researchers and government officials. In most cases, they also had detailed knowledge of Q'eqchi' medicine and cosmovision; in fact, most were children or grandchildren of practitioners in the Maya Healers Association: Romulo Caal, Tomas Caal, Federico Caal, Pedro Maquin, and Rehinalio Maquin. Each had the ability to write the Q'eqchi' language as well, although there was much individual variation in spelling. The Q'eqchi' words and expressions used in this book are those offered by Tomas Caal, whose language proficiency is unparalleled and who has served as a language instructor and interpreter for many NGOs. The Q'eqchi' spoken in the villages of Toledo is a localized variant of that in Guatemala. It often contains elements of Spanish, English, and expressions more commonly heard in Guatemalan villages, but there are also local expressions and short forms unique to Toledo, and even to specific villages, that differ from some of the Q'eqchi' language dictionaries produced in Guatemala. Local expressions are used in this book.

In many ways, the interpreters served as cocreators along with the practitioners of the knowledge being captured. They did not simply translate—and those who have worked with interpreters know full well that there is nothing simple about it; they also worked with me and the practitioners to make questions and answers as mutually intelligible as possible. They often engaged in lengthy discussions with iloneleb' about the questions being asked and how to frame the answers in a meaningful way. Readers must keep in mind that, as is frequently the case in anthropological research, we often ask questions about issues to which our respondents have never given much thought; scholarly "knowledge" is often produced on the spot in response to such questions. The interpreters worked with me and the practitioners and patients in a collaborative manner to generate such knowledge.

I used a double translation approach in my work, which allows me to access more fully the discussions. The interpreter was charged to interpret on the spot, of course, and while we always discussed the session topic and the questions in advance, my flexible approach to interviewing was no doubt

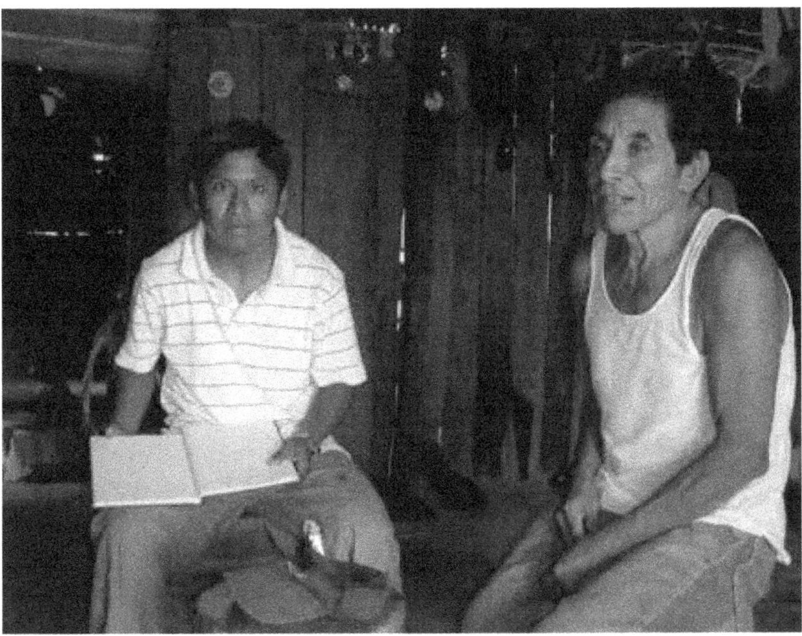

FIGURE 5. Interview with Manuel Choc (right); interpreter and research assistant Federico Caal is on the left. Indian Creek, 2007. Photo by author.

a challenge for them. It is impossible for an interpreter to live-capture all that is being said, so the digital recordings of the interviews were translated and transcribed post-interview by a different individual. This double translation approach allowed me to carefully document all that was said, to create full, complete, and accurate transcripts of interviews. This resulted in considerably more insight. I could see how my questions were actually interpreted as delivered to the ilonel, allowing me to judge the accuracy of the question. Similarly, I was able to see the full response as uttered and not the necessarily truncated response of the on-site interpreter. I could tap into conversations between the interpreter and the practitioner or patient as well, where a whole variety of issues were often discussed (including comments about me and speculations as to why I was asking certain questions). And I was able to distinguish insights offered by participants from those offered by interpreters. Thus I was able to get as accurate an understanding as possible without being solely reliant on the ability of the interpreter to both recall long answers (and sometimes questions) and translate them. Many anthropologists are familiar with research situations where a long answer offered by a participant in another language is frustratingly translated into simply, "He says no." The double translation approach works around this problem.

The transcribers were provided with digital recorders and headphones so they could undertake the work in a manner that allowed for both audio clarity and privacy. In the early years, all transcripts were handwritten in notebooks in Belize and typed once they were received in Canada. Over the years, as more people obtained laptops, sometimes provided by me, some transcriptions were entered directly into Microsoft Word files, but technical issues always lurked about, and resort to the notebooks was frequent. Needless to say, notebooks were sometimes lost, digital files corrupted, USBs infected, and equipment lost, stolen, or broken. Since I always made and protected several copies of all data no matter its form, no data were ever compromised.

The interpreters also served as valuable sources of knowledge about Q'eqchi' medicine and related aspects of Q'eqchi' life. The transcripts clearly show that they often added their own insights to the answers offered by the practitioners, easily identifiable in the double translation approach. Keeping in mind that they all had close family members who were practitioners, and in some cases had undertaken training themselves, the additional knowledge they provided was clearly value-added; it was as if they were being interviewed simultaneously with the practitioner. They also served as valuable experts on Q'eqchi' ethics and social protocol. They ensured that questions were asked appropriately and that sensitive topics were approached humbly and with care. They helped gain the consent of patients to be videotaped and interviewed. (I also carried a prerecorded video message from Victor that explained the research and why the MHAB was having it done. I would show this to patients as part of the consent process.) And they worked with me and the practitioners to ensure that there were no violations of the unwritten Q'eqchi' ethical code regarding what could be filmed and what could be discussed.

The quoted passages from the practitioners and their patients as they appear in this book are the product of the translation and editing processes.

All the interpreters and translators speak English as their second (at least) language, and so in addition to the usual problems in translating one language into a very different one, we must be mindful that competency in the second one is quite variable. I have edited all the passages to some extent to improve their readability without tampering with their meaning, but as minimally as possible to better reflect the tone of the fieldwork experience. So, if the English passages seem a little rough or simplistic, I encourage the reader to consider this process. It is most certainly not a reflection of the intellectual competence of translators or participants.

It is also crucial to appreciate that, for the most part, I was asking practitioners and their patients questions they had never been asked before and requesting that they explain things they had never had to explain before. Q'eqchi' traditional learning, like that of many Indigenous peoples, is experience-based, not dialogical. The practitioners, who are the main subject of this book, did not sit through lectures or read textbooks to gain their knowledge. They often struggled to articulate verbally what they knew, or what they were doing and why. This is reflected in the analysis to follow, especially in terms of ambiguity, lack of clarity, and apparent contradiction, all of which I attempt to rectify with recourse to the broader data set (where they often spoke about the same thing more than once).

What ultimately became the first phase of the project that commenced in 2004 concluded in 2011. In 2007 I spent four months in Belize working with the practitioners and their patients. It was necessary to be on site for a longer period to intersect with the rhythms of the group, so that I could be available on a minute's notice when an ilonel was heading out to treat a patient. Prior to that, my research activity was restricted to trips to Belize two or three times a year for shorter periods. The interviews from this phase amounted to almost fifteen hundred transcript pages. A further 190 pages of field notes augmented the data set, usually my observations about the interviews or treatments, as well as other aspects of the domestic lives of practitioners. I was able to videotape the treatment sessions in this phase. Between 2007 and 2011, several more research trips were undertaken each year.

In 2011, at the request of the practitioners, I turned my attention to the production of the documentary *Kawil Poyanam, Chaab'il Yu'am: Laj lilonel re B'elis* (Healthy People, Beautiful Life: Maya Healers of Belize) (Waldram

FIGURE 6. Interviewing for the documentary. Left to right: author, research assistant Tomas Caal, Francisco Caal. Punta Gorda, 2013. Photo by author.

2015a). This involved more interviewing as we worked together to flesh out the script. The data from the production of this film are included in this book. The years between 2011 and 2015 were largely dedicated to the film project, and I traveled several times each year to work with the practitioners and interpreter Tomas Caal to refine the script, shoot the necessary interviews and "B roll" footage, record the audio narration in both Q'eqchi' and English, and workshop rough cuts with the practitioners. The final cut was premiered for the practitioners and their families in 2015 and is now available on Vimeo, YouTube, and Anthro*In*Sight on Facebook, and from Anthro*In*-Sight Productions.[1]

While I returned to the field annually between 2016 and 2019 to undertake more thematic interviews, including seeking clarification or confirmation for interpretations in this book, it is important to note that several graduate students also became involved in the project, beginning in 2011. I have always been concerned that practitioners are not overwhelmed by researchers, so during the period 2011 to 2015, outside of work on the film, I did not undertake many new interviews. Readers will note that the book contains several references to articles coauthored with Andrew Hatala, then a PhD student working with me; this has been a fruitful collaboration that has led to several refinements to some of my germinating theoretical ideas. However, unless by direct reference to these publications, the data presented here stem entirely from my own research and interviews undertaken by me.

The research has ensued through the lens of three ethical protocols. The Behavioural Research Ethics Board at the University of Saskatchewan has approved three related research projects, each tied to a grant from the Social Sciences and Humanities Research Council of Canada, and in adherence to the Tri-Council Policy Statement on Ethical Conduct for Research Involving Humans. Securing institutional ethics is at times a frustrating process, as board members rarely have the expertise to understand ethnographic research despite their good intentions. I am pleased that with each submission, fewer and fewer concerns were raised about the emergent nature of this kind of work. I also received ethics approval from the government of Belize through the National Institute of Culture and History's Institute for Social and Cultural Research, and who licensed each field season. The third ethics protocol, and the most important one for ethnographers, is that of the participants themselves. Q'eqchi' ethics are not codified, although there have been efforts by the MHAB to generate standards to apply to researchers. Further, "research" per se is not seen as distinct from broader Q'eqchi' ethics of how to be a proper person. Q'eqchi' ethics are also situational, contextual, and in some ways individualistic. They are a site for constant discussion and negotiation. Over the life of this research, many meetings were held with the MHAB to discuss the research and to seek guidance on what was or was not an appropriate topic to explore and the method to do so. The collaborative nature of the work was crucial to this process, as the practitioners often suggested areas for further investigation. The interpreters were also crucial here, as they acted as ethics brokers, helping me understand the ethical aspects of studying Q'eqchi' medicine and helping the practitioners and their patients understand the ethical aspects of research and complex ideas such as data ownership and publication. At all times, Victor Cal provided the guidance needed from the broader perspective of the cultural and political ramifications of the work.

In sum, the data presented in this book relate to the work I have done with this very specific group of Q'eqchi' iloneleb', their patients, interpreters and translators, and key interlocutors. What I document here is an expression of a local medical and cultural tradition as understood and articulated by these individuals and mediated through the research process. Although there are many similarities with knowledge acquired by other researchers working with Q'eqchi' and other Maya peoples, as a discipline, anthropology has long since passed a point where we could talk of *the* Q'eqchi' in overarching generalizations. What I present here is what I have learned from those with whom I have worked for these fifteen years.

Defining an Audience

Research such as this, especially of long duration, depends entirely on the strength of the relationships formed. My professional inclination to collaborate in my research has been rewarded by the practitioners and their families with rich data and even richer experiences. Always believing that social science research should be of value to the research participants, I and my students have worked closely with them to identify priorities and outcomes, to plan, to share, and to work collectively toward their goal of promoting their activities and knowledge as medical practitioners.

Anthropologists are aware of two often contradictory forces that have dogged the discipline since its earliest formation. On one hand, anthropologists seek to understand, on their own terms, cultural phenomena, an idea referenced within the discipline as cultural relativism. On the other hand, anthropology has always been in part a translational discipline, seeking to understand such cultural phenomena but also to find a way to compare and explain them to a broader audience, typically individuals who have no familiarity with the phenomena in question. Certainly, the postmodern moment in the discipline has represented challenges to both relativism and translationism, peaking in what became known as the "crisis of representation" (Clifford and Marcus 1986; Marcus and Fisher 1986). When the audience for ethnographic works expanded beyond the literate Westerners initially targeted—especially to those of whom we wrote—anthropologists were confronted by an often-angry Indigenous readership that resented the cultural characterizations being presented. One response to this issue has been the emergence of more collaborative models of research, wherein we no longer study people but work with them to identify the issues of study that have salience to them; this often includes bringing them into the analysis and writing phases of research. But at the end of the day, the question remains in any ethnographic work: Who is your audience?

My audience in this book is not the Q'eqchi' medical practitioners with whom I have worked. They do not speak English and lack the formal education to meaningfully engage with the ideas here. As part of my research I have constantly consulted with and produced products for them, including a small book and the documentary film, both done in their language and under their guidance. Here I wish to address a larger audience, and I do so at the behest of those practitioners. They have charged me to, in effect, speak on their behalf to certain audiences they cannot reach. They want the world to know about their medicine, and this world extends beyond their own villages. To be specific, the Q'eqchi' practitioners have asked that I produce research that speaks to key non-Q'eqchi' people, such as government administrators, biomedical practitioners, and scholars. Their goal is to have their medical knowledge and practice recognized as valuable in both their own country and beyond. They also wish to counteract the destructive influence of the evangelical churches, almost all based in the United States, that aggressively use their power and wealth to turn the Q'eqchi' people away from their culture and traditions.

What all this means for my presentation is that I will use Western scholarly conventions in writing and sometimes biomedicine as a comparator. A common translational language is needed if the research presented here is to positively impact the audience intended by the Q'eqchi' practitioners (cf. Craig 2012:259). Anthropologists appreciate that we can never fully translate across ontologies, that often all we can hope for is a surface-level understanding of other's worldviews. But the potential for a translational perspective within the broader "ontological turn" is well exemplified by Herrera (2018:9), who argues that "there are [different] modes of reasoning that can grant access to the same conclusions." I remain mindful of the need to convince an audience much larger, and more influential to the Q'eqchi', than ontological theorists. It you want to create a space for other ontologies, you cannot ignore the hegemony of scientific ontology, as it underpins policy and politics, arenas necessary to engage even in postcolonial contexts. The simple fact that the unique, situated worldview of people like the Q'eqchi' is not easily equated to anything in Western thought or the English language renders translation a cautionary, yet necessary, exercise.

Conclusion

The ethnographic understanding of Maya medicine has—quite logically—been influenced by broader scholarly trends in the field of medical anthropology over the years. It is my argument that the combined effect of this knowledge and these trends has been to short the empirical and systemic nature of Q'eqchi' medicine, grounded in a material and a virtual, or meta/material, understanding of the world. Approaching the topic collaboratively and abductively, I seek to understand Q'eqchi' medical ontology and epistemology on its own terms. But in turn I endeavor to explain it to those with no understanding of the Q'eqchi' and those who perhaps are hostile to the very idea that the Q'eqchi' might "know" something about medicine. This is the challenge to which I turn in the next chapter.

CHAPTER 3

General Principles of Q'eqchi' Medicine

NOTIONS OF WHAT constitutes a "medical system" focus on the integration of knowledge and practices in reference to standardized, even official, epistemology and ontology. This presupposes a means of systematizing the training of practitioners and the communication of that knowledge, and this is reinforced by regulated means for testing the compatibility of practitioner knowledge with that officially sanctioned and recognized as "truth" or at least "best practice," including certification and licensing of practitioners, legislated consequences for straying from the official knowledge, and legal sanctions for engaging in medical practice without adherence to these regulations. Q'eqchi' medicine, however, like much Indigenous medicine, is largely an orally and experientially transmitted system of knowledge, and practitioners are typically trained as apprentice individuals in relationship with a master. Rather than learning broad theory of the body, or its systems, as an initial entrée into medicine, practitioners typically learn one sickness at a time; knowledge of the body's systems, and Q'eqchi' medical theory, is built implicitly rather than explicitly. There is no textbook or official, group-sanctioned knowledge, and while practitioners are typically validated by community support (or at least some kind of social support), knowledge and skills are only one aspect that is considered in assessing competence (family and social relations, for instance, are also important), and it is not uncommon for there to be divergences of opinion among the citizenry about who is a competent practitioner and what those competencies might entail (cf. Garro 1990). There is not a single, unified medical system of knowledge, then, but a dynamic set of systems that typically share common features and yet are also divergent and somewhat idiosyncratic. Unlike biomedicine, which is heavily regulated, Q'eqchi' medicine accommodates this diversity as a core characteristic. This idea goes beyond the suggestion of Good (1994:178) and others that there exist "local worlds of medical knowledge." A virtual system is created in the moment through the overlay of knowledges of any particular configuration of practitioners who share broader cultural or experiential characteristics, such as language, grounded in notions of history and commonality of place. Change any element of the configuration—for instance, add in or remove a practitioner—and the dynamic nature of the system becomes evident as there is a shift in the sum total of all that knowledge. Too often have Indigenous medical systems been understood as static; often they are anything but!

In the previous two chapters I discussed some understandings of "medicine" as both epistemology and practice extant in the (primarily) medical anthropology literature and in Maya medical ethnography. It is essential that we conceptualize this key concept in a manner that unhinges from science or biomedicine if this inquiry is to be meaningful. So I propose to use the following. "Medicine" as a field pertains to indications (subjective, objective) of deviation from either the individual's normal, usual, or desired psychological or physiological state, processes, or function, or from a broader normative standard held by a social group to be the optimal psychological or physiological order or functioning of a human being, and to the practices designed to avoid or address these deviations. This definition puts the individual at the center of the analysis while also interpreting the individual within historical, social, and cultural context. The desire of the individual (or significant others) to return to the normative state, to ease the suffering or temper the worry, is core if the deviation is troubling, uncomfortable, problematic, painful, disfiguring, stigmatizing, or morally challenging for the individual—now the patient—and/or possibly others. The practice of medicine, then, references restorative processes and is therefore different from healing, which focuses on transformative processes (Waldram 2013). When sick, people want to get better; they do not necessarily want to change.

Following the model outlined by Kleinman (1980:72), then, "disease" references a "malfunctioning of biological and/or psychological processes"; to unhinge it from biomedicine, however, I am inclined to use the term "disorder." "Curing," according to Kleinman, is "the establishment of effective control" of those malfunctioning or disordered processes (82). (As I will show,

Q'eqchi' practitioners accept "control" but typically strive for complete elimination of the pathology and a return to the normal state.) "Illness" refers to "secondary personal and social responses" to the malfunctioning, the "reshaping of disease into experience and behavior" (82). Young (1982:270), largely accepting these articulations, rejects "sickness" as a term simply referencing disease and illness combined but rather defines sickness as "the process through which worrisome behavioral and biological signs, particularly ones originating in disease, are given socially recognizable meanings, i.e., they are made into symptoms and socially significant outcomes." In other words, for Young, "sickness" refers to the social identity of the person suffering from the problem. These definitions resonate well with the Q'eqchi' medical system, and I use "disorder" and "sickness" in particular throughout. However, I diverge from any argument that "curing" be linked to standards of efficacy found only in biomedicine, as Young (1983:1208) suggests; nor do I accept the assertion that "the traditional practitioner's strength is in healing patients rather than curing them." Indeed, I show in this book how the notion of curing is core to Q'eqchi' medicine, and I argue that appropriate standards for "cure" are meaningfully invoked.

Young (1983:1206) also provides a useful articulation of how a practitioner gains knowledge that speaks to the concept of a system. A practitioner's knowledge, he states, is a product of both clinical experiences and access to the clinical knowledge of other practitioners, including the ancestors. More specifically, this knowledge is based on four factors: "whether he gets to examine and treat a relatively large number of patients who fall into a single diagnostic domain (e.g., common infectious diseases); his ability to learn outcomes of the cases he treats; his technical means for recording and communicating his clinical findings; and his opportunities for pooling and comparing his findings with those of other practitioners." These factors represent the dimensions of what I have referred to as latent and manifest empiricism—that is, knowledge available to the practitioner through the long-term development and maintenance of a body of knowledge based on cumulative individual practices, and knowledge gained by the individual through clinical practice (Waldram and Hatala 2015). The first of Young's two factors are easily documented in Q'eqchi' medicine; the latter two, however, clearly privilege certain medical traditions over others, in particular those with written rather than oral traditions, and those with some form of professionalization. Young suggests that systems such as those typically found in Indigenous medicine are unlikely to meet these tests. However, with some flexibility in interpretation to make Young's framework more cross-cultural in utility and less biased toward biomedicine, I think the latter two factors especially can also be seen to operate within Q'eqchi' medicine, and Indigenous medicine more generally, similar to the first two. What Young is speaking to is the development and maintenance of a system of knowledge and practice that transcends individual practice, which is understood as too isolated and insulated, too idiosyncratic, for a system to emerge. However, to "see" the system in such cases, one needs to look more closely. Q'eqchi' medicine may appear to be idiosyncratic, but this is not the case. Further, in response to broader national and global influences, the Q'eqchi' iloneleb' with whom I work have in fact professionalized to some extent, in part to better share knowledge, as I discuss later in this book.

Q'eqchi' Medical Cosmovision

At its essence, a medical theory is an explanation that works at both the level of the individual patient, in the context of diagnosis and treatment, and at the broader epistemological and ontological levels framing the knowledge of the disease or disorder, its cause, and its treatment, based on existing evidence or knowledge (Thagard 2005). A medical system can be seen to consist of multiple theories, perhaps tagged to very specific diseases or disorders, with the possibility that together they constitute a more or less integrated paradigm, worldview, or episteme. For the Q'eqchi', the accepted term for such a paradigm is "cosmovision," a term possibly introduced by the Spanish that has been adopted and applied by Maya and other Central American peoples (e.g., Tedlock 1987; Kukul 2013; Consejo Mayor de Médicos Maya'ob' por Nacimiento 2016) to articulate material and meta/material principles of the universe in relation to human existence, which likely predate colonialism. To understand any Q'eqchi' medical paradigm, one must understand at least the basics of cosmovision.

For the Q'eqchi', the world is an integrated system of material and meta/material forces and entities, known through both phronesis and gnosis, that provide an overarching explanation for how the world works. This knowledge meets indigenous standards for empirical and subjective proofs of validity and reliability (Waldram 2013), two concepts that, while typically associated with science, really speak to the extent to which people can trust in what they think they know. The broad details of this paradigm have been presented elsewhere in the many ethnographies written about Maya and other Central American peoples that I have referred to already in this book. My concern here is to focus on the key elements that help us understand my Q'eqchi' participants' perspective on Q'eqchi' medicine in the context of the Q'eqchi' world; this is where the logic and rationality of their system is evident.

The material and the meta/material are not easily teased apart in Q'eqchi' cosmovision, and this is an artificial and somewhat heuristic exercise. As discussed in the introduction, "meta/material" refers to a kind of "virtual" world, where entities and forces are taken to be real even where they do not meet a universal standard of materialism. I am referencing, in the first instance of course, the spiritual world, a world that has a very direct impact on the lives of Q'eqchi' people. But there are many other meta/material forces within Q'eqchi' cosmovision. The integrated nature of this world is evident in the emphasis on the interrelationships and mutuality of the entities found therein, and the importance of maintaining those relationships. As Ingold (2014) explains, an animistic view often maps human sociality onto the world, as a means of relating to it in a known, logical manner, where humans and other-than-human beings can hope to understand one another. In this, human beings are the primary agents, as the other entities tend to act in response to human actions or inactions but rarely on their own volition. And some forces are not infused with spirit at all and exist beyond any relational potential.

The Q'eqchi' iloneleb' in this study acknowledge a hierarchy of meta/material entities, with Qaawa', or God/Creator, at the top as "supreme being." (Sometimes iloneleb' use the Spanish term *Dios* and the English term "God" as well.) Quite likely the notion of God in the singular is post-colonial, as there is little evidence that a supreme God among gods was known prior. Iloneleb' not only make reference to "the Father, Son, and Holy Spirit," they also often cite Jesus Christ and make a version of the sign of the cross as part of their treatment prayers. (See Astor-Aguilera 2010 for a detailed discussion of this.) Qaawa' is the god of all people on the earth and is the same entity no matter one's religion. Qaawa' created the earth, including the mountains (Tzuul) and valleys (Taq'a) that figure centrally in the Q'eqchi' paradigm. The supreme character of Qaawa' is evident in the fact that the iloneleb' directly communicate with him (he is gendered male by these practitioners; Kahn [2006] indicates both male and female in her study of Q'eqchi' in Guatemala) in all curing activities; Qaawa' has the power to both create problems such as sickness (yajel) and to facilitate the cure of patients. Within the Q'eqchi' humoral system, he is neither hot nor cold, unlike other spiritual entities, but rather neutral.

Technical humility exists as a basic principle of Q'eqchi' medicine. The Q'eqchi' iloneleb' use the term *b'anok* to mean "cure" as I am employing the term here, although this is often translated into English as "heal." This may be a reflection of Catholic influence. The iloneleb' relate that they cannot cure without the involvement of Qaawa', who actually works through them; they act as intermediaries. Francisco explains, "It is in the name of God the Father that I'm curing this problem, and in the name of God the Father that the plant medicines help to cure the sickness." "I'm praying to God," confirms Lorenzo, explaining an aspect of his treatment,

> so that God will help to cure the person. That is why I ask for the miracle of blessings from Jesus Christ. . . . I ask God for help and blessings that I will be helping this individual to get over his sickness. [I would say] "I don't have power to cure, but you [Qaawa'], you have the power. Heavenly Father please give me strength and help me to cure this individual." These are the things you need to say; then you start the next prayers to heal.

One day after another treatment session, Lorenzo explains further: "It is God's words of healing that I am calling upon her [the patient]. Whatever is affecting her . . . is only clear to God. God will be helping the patient. I am only relating his healing."

Essentially, there is a partnership between Qaawa' and iloneleb'; "they work hand in hand," explains Manuel Choc. The iloneleb' cannot successfully cure without Qaawa', and this partnership, like any, requires ongoing work to maintain. Qaawa' also looks after the iloneleb' in many ways, according to Manuel. Since it is not appropriate to request payment from a patient for services rendered, Qaawa' provides other opportunities of good fortune. Manuel also explains that Qaawa' looks after the health and safety of those who show respect by seeking his blessing, allowing them to work and travel without fear. In return iloneleb' pay appropriate respect to Qaawa' through prayer and respectful actions. Humans are to avoid actions that are understood as a transgression of the relationship between humans and Qaawa'. According to Francisco, "We sin because we usually make a mistake by forgetting God or we no longer think of him or pray to him; as a result we often get into accidents and get sick."

Prayer (a problematic term that I critique later) is dialogical; iloneleb' use prayer to "talk to" Qaawa' about the patient's sickness. They may use aids to facilitate this, such as burning *pom*, or resin from the copal tree, with the thick, black, pungent smoke carrying prayers to Qaawa'. Francisco tends to open all curing sessions with a prayer to Qaawa' called *yoob'tasinel*, the "God prayer." But a great many prayers may be used—some general ones like this, others specific to the particular sickness, often used in various combinations depending on the knowledge of the ilonel. Francisco and Emilio know dozens of different prayers, for instance, whereas Lorenzo knows fewer and tends to use those for a broader range of disorders. Further, prayers can be distinguished in terms of the degree of difficulty in curing a sickness; Albino Maquin refers to this distinction as "major" versus "small" prayers. The most senior of the iloneleb', Albino knew five major prayers. The genesis of the prayers is with Qaawa'. "You have to ask God's name because those are the words of God," explains Lorenzo. "He gave them; we did not invent them ourselves." Qaawa' does not directly answer the iloneleb'; nor do they expect a response per se, for he "is far away" in heaven, but Qaawa' does respond in other ways, and his powers are brought to bear on the problem. The proof of his work is found in the response of the patient to the treatment.

Qaawa' works to protect humans from sickness and other dangers. "God is the giver and helper," explains Manuel Choc. "If you ask his name with your whole heart and soul, that sickness will go away. God will only send his spirits to heal." Francisco adds, "When we go out [into the countryside], we would usually pray to God to ask that nothing would happen to us, because he is guarding us. When a person does not believe in God, he would be easily affected."

Some people may petition Qaawa' to engage with humans in witchcraft, according to some iloneleb', a misunderstanding of Qaawa's relationship to humans and an activity eschewed by iloneleb' in this study as contrary to their ethos as medical practitioners. And asking for help in engaging in witchcraft is not the same as getting it, but is rather an acknowledgement of the supreme and omnipotent power of Qaawa'. Manual Choc characterized Qaawa' in the more typical way as mostly charitable: "God is the giver and helper. If you ask his name with your whole heart and soul, that sickness will go away. God will only send his spirits to heal."

The relationship between Qaawa' and the spirits of the mountains and valleys is complex. Qaawa' is all-powerful, and the Tzuul and Taq'a—often referenced together as a single entity, Tzuultaq'a—in a sense work under him. Qaawa's "place" is in "heaven," but the Tzuultaq'a are understood to be of the material world, spiritual forces that dwell in the geophysical places important to the Q'eqchi' people and that have control over all nonhuman elements found therein. They are "exemplars of morality-in-action" (Kahn 20006:53), which explains their significant role in the causation of sickness due to moral breaches. And they watch humans. "They know what we are doing," relates Lorenzo. Indeed, along with Qaawa', a kind of panoptic surveillance of humans is engendered; you cannot hide from these entities, so respect and propitiation are essential.

Qaawa' and the Tzuultaq'a are sometimes indistinguishable in prayer due to their mutuality (Wilson 1995; Kahn 2006), yet they have separate functions. While Qaawa' created the earth—including the Tzuultaq'a—he left its stewardship to the Tzuultaq'a, who in turn expect cooperation from humans. The Tzuultaq'a are alive, and more humanlike than Qaawa'.[1] There is much disagreement over the number of Tzuultaq'a across the Maya world, with some suggestion that the Q'eqchi' recognize thirteen (Kahn 2006:55). They are assumed to look like humans but are never seen. They are known to do humanlike activities, such as making pottery. They even assemble to have "meetings," according to some iloneleb'. One must "introduce" oneself to them before venturing into their territory; the Tzuultaq'a will create problems for anyone they do not know who travels into the mountains, such as by stoning or otherwise harassing them. Their presence can be felt out in the countryside, but their existence is more evident from the consequences of being maligned or poorly treated. They certainly have a range of humanlike emotions. They demand respect and must be "fed" (Kahn 2006:55). They anger easily if they are ignored or treated dismissively. They expect humans to follow certain rules, and iloneleb' even more so. They will "teach you a lesson," says Manuel Baki, or "give you a lashing," contributes Francisco, such as ensuring that your crops do not grow, sending a snake to bite you, or causing sickness. But they also exist to serve humans and Qaawa' in a beneficial way. Says Albino, "The mountain spirit cares about us." They provide water and air, and breezes that cool the body.

Emilio explains that Tzuultaq'a have names; an important local one is Kojaj (cf. Tedlock 1992). Francisco explains their central role in human health, in part as therapeutic places:

> That huge, big place, very healthy mountains, green and very natural; that is really a healthy place, and that healthy place gives us a healthy way of life where you can go and you can charge your energy and feel healthy. And this is why we say that a healthy environment, to have a healthy place, is to have a healthy spirit and healthy way of life.

Francisco and Emilio often retreat to the mountains, usually on a specific day in the Maya calendar (more on the calendar later), to undertake a ceremony "to keep in contact with the mountain spirit" and ensure health and safety.

The integrated nature of the environment—*sutam* in Q'eqchi'—is important to health, Francisco says, "because from the plants [we get] life to us. . . . We share to them carbon dioxide, and plants give off oxygen for us to live and breathe. We have to share life with each other." While Qaawa' created the plants and animals for humans to use, the Tzuultaq'a are responsible for them. Like humans, most nonhuman material elements of the world also have spirits, although these are different from and inferior to those of humans. The existence of these spirits is known both empirically and intuitively; the spirits of the trees are "visible" in the way the branches sway, and the spirits of rocks are "visible" as the mist that clings low along the ground.

They are also known in consequence: Failed crops, bad luck, loss of a spouse, and sickness are just some of the calamities that can befall a human who disrespects these spirits and their guardian. As environmental stewards, the Tzuultaq'a are especially important to the iloneleb' because of the need for medicinal plants. Francisco emphasizes the relationship, saying, "The plants will be very close to you as if they are your wife." Victor Cal, interpreting, adds, "You will get all the medicine and resources from the mountain, and that becomes your shadow, a part of yourself." Francisco explains this principle of connectivity (sometimes referred to as a relational epistemology; Bird-David 1999):

> [Everything] is connected and everything has life, and when we touch something, we have an effect. When we destroy something [by removing plants, for example], we have effects. We are the same [plants and humans], made from God. That means we are connected to everything. When we do not ask permission [to remove plants], we lose this sensitivity, we lose the feelings or respect to all creatures. . . . If you destroy, you have to inform the spirits of the mountains; that is, you go into the mountain to pray and to ask permission. . . . We are close to the spirits of the mountains because they breathe, and we also breathe, and as a result they live because we make them live, and we live because they make us live.

Medicinal and food plants cannot simply be picked and used; they belong to the Tzuultaq'a, after all, who must be properly entreated to release them without harm to the human and to ensure their full potency. This can be done in several ways: through prayer, ceremony, or sacrifice. As part of his training, Francisco undertook a ceremony on a mountain to request support of the Tzuultaq'a. When I asked how he knew whether he had gained their support, he explained that a strong feeling of calmness and confidence came over him, a feeling "that I will learn everything very quickly."

While the Tzuultaq'a have both a human and a spiritual form of agency, and act deliberately to affect human lives in one way or another, their simple presence represents a strong enough force that an unsuspecting human, and especially one who is "weak" in some manner, can become sick if they enter an area soon after Tzuultaq'a have passed. Sickness can also result by being "seen" by the Tzuultaq'a.

The mountains are also home to the *maa'us aj musiq'ej*, or evil spirits. Indeed, the notion of evil spirits looms large in the traditional Q'eqchi' worldview, but the influence of Christianity is also evident in terms like "devil," *diablo*, and *satanas*, which are sometimes used. And many sickness terms have *maa'us* as a root; the iloneleb' in this research often use this root instead of the full term as a short form to refer to evil spirit–related sicknesses, which tend to be the most serious. And despite their mountain home, these evil spirits can be found anywhere, although they are known to be particularly active in some places, at certain times of day, and even on specific days. Abandoned locales, such as old houses and sheds, are common locations. Being in their vicinity or passing a place where the evil has also recently passed is enough to cause sickness in a vulnerable person. In some cases, the spirit literally "hits" the individual (like someone throwing stones, says Manuel Choc), may knock them down (which can lead to fright-related sickness), and may even enter the body. Manual explains about one patient's sickness:

> These spirits use small creatures which pass in the water, or [they] sat on the rock at noon. That is how you contact the sickness. Or it can be on trees, sticks, and so on. This is how it works. I'm not sure if that's the way it happens in your country, Jim. Maybe only here we have these problems. You can find it at your corn shed, and other places. You can't see them. Probably they rested there.

Riverbanks are especially dangerous places. "They like to rest there, just like we do," adds Manuel.

Unlike Qaawa' and Tzuultaq'a, there is no upside to the maa'us aj musiq'ej. They do not serve humans. They are to be avoided as much as possible by being aware of their likely haunts. Individuals can offer prayers to Qaawa' and Tzuultaq'a to ask for protection and can undertake preventive measures to strengthen their blood and bodies in case they encounter them. When spirits do make humans sick, it is often said that they are demanding to "be fed." Feeding can take the form of animal sacrifices or tortillas, but sometimes also a small amount of blood extracted from the patient at the forehead and taken to the place where the spirit is believed to dwell.

There is some ambiguity regarding the concepts of "soul" and "spirit" among the Q'eqchi', with different terms and meanings sometimes being noted in the literature. (Kahn provides different explanations, for instance, 2006:113.) In this research, the medical practitioners explain that humans have a spirit, *musiq'ej* (or *mu*), the function of which can be understood in part by its homonyms, "breath" and "breathing" in the Q'eqchi' language. This spirit is not the same as *ch'oolej*, or "soul." The term *ch'oolej* is also used to mean heart. Practitioners state that the soul remains with the body until death, when it goes to heaven (or possibly some other locale, such as the mountains or the cemetery, as Hinojosa [2015:65] suggests for the Kaqchikel). The spirit is much more mobile and can exit the body, due to a fright, for instance, necessitating a treatment to return it. Quite possibly the concept of soul was added to Q'eqchi' cosmovision via Catholicism, to coexist with the preexisting notion of spirit; animals and other elements of the meta/material world, such as trees and rocks, may have spirits but never souls.

According to Emilio, the body has seven spirits: mind, blood, heart, sight, hearing, smelling, and finally the entire body. Each spirit can act separately and be affected through sickness. Most iloneleb' do not have such detailed knowledge as Emilio, however, and think primarily in terms of a single spirit inhabiting the body. It has considerable agency and exists in harmony with the body. Iloneleb' may communicate directly with the spirit while it is still in the body, in effect bypassing the human, and engage in a dialogue with it. But it is also capable of exiting, a circumstance that leads to sickness. The spirit can also be frightened out of the body, to be found roaming about, usually near the place where the fright occurred. Although often implicated in sickness, according to Manuel Choc, the spirit itself cannot become sick; only the material body is subject to sickness.

There is also a conception of an entity called a *nawal*, which Francisco explains is a kind of "gifted energy," linked to one's spirit, which a person acquires at conception.[2] The character of the nawal is determined by the specific day in the Maya calendar when a person is conceived or born, and Emilio and Francisco in particular use the calendar to diagnose and treat, a kind of patient-centered approach. The nawal grows and develops over the life course, and it requires some effort to maintain, typically through prayer and ceremony, and this can help prevent sickness. Nawal predicts to a considerable extent the kind of life one will have—it references ideas of gift, destiny, and luck, what the iloneleb' refer to as *maatan*. According to Francisco, "Yes, you have to develop it [nawal] because if your spirit is strong, you are strong. Your nawal is your shadow, your mirror. If you keep yourself very quiet, your spirit is quiet. Treat good your nawal, keep in a good contact with it, build a good energy through ceremony." People generally are unaware of what their destiny holds, though, and few understand the complex Maya calendar, so often they learn their maatan only after they have fallen sick or experienced misfortune, and subsequently consulted with an ilonel or a religious specialist trained in the calendar's use.

One's nawal and maatan can explain particular vulnerability to sickness in general, and even to specific kinds of sicknesses, so understanding both and acting to counteract them as much as possible is a form of preventive medicine. Maatan is not without some malleability; one's destiny is not necessarily out of one's hands. As Emilio put it, in a clear expression of human agency, you can "befriend your destiny" and work with it to improve your life. Through proper ceremony, one can even "borrow" another day in the calendar that is more suitable to one's goals. However, there remain limits to such acts of human agency, and the iloneleb' are not all in agreement. Some aspects of maatan are beyond influence. Emilio explains somewhat pessimistically that "it depends on when the person is born, whether the destiny is to live happy or healthy. At times a person's destiny might not to be healthy and happy. It does not matter how much he tries." Adds Lorenzo, "One does not change his maatan. No way to change one's life. What is yours is yours. What is your gift, or where you are given a gift, you are given. It is yours. No way to find out if you will get sick or not. It is the person's body that would be able to fight any sickness. If the body wants sickness, then he would be sick."

The number 4 is considered an essential element of the Q'eqchi' world. The earth has four cardinal points to which the iloneleb' pray during diagnosis and treatment (Kukul 2013). The human body also has four cardinal points, or "corners"—head, two hands separately, and two feet together as one—which are seen as essential pathways through which sickness will leave the body. Similarly, there are four components to the earth—sunrise, sunset, water, and wind—each of which corresponds to a color and an aspect of the human body. The symmetrical symbolic system (compatible with previous research, such as Thompson 1970) is as follows:

East—sun/sunrise—red—blood
West—night/sunset—black—hair
South—water—yellow—flesh
North—wind/air—white—bones

In addition, green represents the environment or forest, and blue the sky. Together, these six colors are those of the candles used in treatment ceremonies to assist in praying.

The systemic nature of the Q'eqchi' worldview focuses on how all elements external to the human body are integrated such that there is always the risk of reverberations and consequences if any part is inappropriately treated. The Q'eqchi' world is a personified one, with the agentive elements, such as Qaawa', Tzuultaq'a, and the various spirits, anthropomorphized to varying extents such that their behavior is understandable and predictable in human terms. With both beneficent and benign elements, a certain reciprocity is invoked; it must be carefully honored, for these gods and spirits are sensitive and jealous. They exert and carefully guard their ownership, control, or claim over aspects of the environment that directly affect humans and therefore must be compensated in some way by humans who wish to trespass or access resources. Hence the system revolves around the concept of permission (Thompson 1970); it must be sought to travel, pick medicinal plants, plant corn, and so on. Otherwise, the consequences range from a poor harvest to snakebite, sickness, and even death. Permission is requested through prayer, offerings, and sometimes animal sacrifice, and when things go wrong as a result of a breach of the reciprocal relationship, specialists such as iloneleb' are called in to mediate and correct the problem. Other spirits and forces are just plain malicious, to be avoided, but prayers to Qaawa' or Tzuultaq'a can help strengthen the body and protect one from the consequences of encountering an evil spirit or other malign force. As I have noted, the human body is also infused with a spirit, which can engage in independent actions that create problems for the person. As

Francisco suggested above, maintaining control of one's spirit, keeping it "calm," is essential to the maintenance of health.

The Thermal Principle

The Q'eqchi' iloneleb' employ a simple form of the humoral system in which the focus is on environmental and bodily as well as metaphoric temperature. Since the "humors" of the classical version of humoral theory seem absent (Chevalier and Bain 2003:12), it probably would make sense to refer to this aspect of Q'eqchi' medicine as the thermal principle; others have referred to it as the "equilibrium model" (Foster 1985), the "temperate equilibrium" model (Chevalier and Bain 2003), and the "vital warmth idiom" (Groark 2005), among others. The idea of "temperate equilibrium" in the body is central, and a healthy body is one that is neither too hot nor too cold. "Our body gets affected by the hot and cold, because we're living flesh," explains Manuel Choc. Sicknesses and the plant medicines to treat them are often categorized according to thermal properties. Unlike the principle of sympathetic medicine, however, iloneleb' apply the opposite when treating patients. Knowledge of the thermal properties of plants is learned by iloneleb' from their masters as part of their training. But it is crucial to note that some scholars have emphasized that the hot/cold distinction is but one means of categorizing Maya sicknesses and that there has been an overemphasis of this aspect (Young 1978). As Chevalier and Bain (2003) argue, context is crucial; the thermal principle is not static but dynamic, and this flexibility has no doubt confounded analysts. Ambiguity appears to be built into the system (Kunow 2003:63), and contradictory assignments of hot or cold are common (Tedlock 1987). More on this later.

The healthy body as a whole is understood to be in a position of balance with respect to its thermal condition, neither too hot nor too cold, a common feature in seemingly all Maya medical systems. Hence the internal state of the body is crucial for maintaining health and warding off sickness. However, thermal equilibrium is easily disrupted, and cold is an especially dangerous threat. Drinking or eating something very cold can result in a drastic drop in body temperature, while a normal and healthy person can drink or eat hot (both in terms of temperature and spiciness) consumables without risking being sick. The cool mists in the early morning are risky if one goes out too soon before the body can adjust. Typically, a person's body temperature is lower early in the morning and heats up during the day, mimicking the air temperature but also reflecting the impact of physical exertion.

There are both hot and cold spirits, according to Francisco. Qaawa' is neither hot nor cold, but the Tzuultaq'a are cold "because that is where the coolness of the forest and the wind comes from." Evil spirits may "leave" their "heat" in places where they rest, to be encountered by an unsuspecting passerby. The heat can be intense in such cases, possibly even burning the individual, creating a sore. Being excessively hot from something like hard work is problematic. Manuel Choc says, "When the blood gets too hot, it's like a machine that gets too hot and burns up or gets damaged. If you put in cold water to cool it down, nothing [bad] will happen. It is the same with our body; you need to cool it down with cold boiled water." The suggestion here is that a change in body temperature can be beneficial in some instances if it returns the overall body temperature to normal. But this change must be gradual and properly managed. The use of "cold" plants for "hot" sicknesses achieves this, for instance, without risk to the patient. Plants are frequently mixed with water (for example, a "cold" plant with cool water), and therefore compatible water temperature facilitates the return to thermal balance. It is rapid changes in temperature away from the norm that creates problems. A hot individual caught in a rain, or jumping in a cool stream on a hot day, risks this sort of sudden change in body temperature.

Many mental states involving thought, worry, or "craziness" are usually classed as hot disorders (see Tables 12 and13). Emotional states also come into play. According to Francisco, an angry person is "hot" while a sad person is "cold." The logical connection to the state of the complexion is clear. He says, for instance, "Looking at a crazy person, his eyes and facial features are red, due to the heat, and that tells you he has a hot body temperature." A person who is happy would have a normal body temperature and normal complexion. As a fundamental Q'eqchi' social principle, a person should always control their emotional state, thereby avoiding any dangerous fluctuation in blood or body temperature.

Q'eqchi' preventive medicine in part revolves around thermal regulation, keeping one's body and blood temperature within the normal range by avoiding situations and actions that can alter it. Sickness does not always follow a disruption in the thermal state of the body, and we have seen already that several other factors come into play in the Q'eqchi' diathesis model. Further, sickness may take several days to emerge after a thermal breach. But sickness always entails a body or blood temperature that has deviated from normal; the nature of that deviation is key to diagnosis, which I consider in greater detail in a subsequent chapter.

The hot/cold distinction is not trivial. It provides one of the several dimensions by which the material and the meta/material—and their relationship—are relevant to human health. It provides a framework for diagnosis, treatment, and assessments of effectiveness, and more broadly a code for living a proper Q'eqchi' life. But it is only one part and may not be as essential as is suggested in some literature, or even as suggested by the iloneleb' themselves.

Mind and Body

As discussed previously, it is typically assumed within both the scholarly and popular literature that Indigenous peoples such as the Q'eqchi' have a "holistic" understanding of the human body—that they understand the mind, body, and spirit to work as an integrated whole. Characterizing whole systems as "holistic" is often a tool of convenience, in my view, as much rhetorical as anything else, when it is assumed that people lack empirical knowledge about sickness and the body. The more these are understood within local epistemologies, the less holistic a medical system appears to be (which is not the same thing as saying it is not holistic). The idea of holism in a contemporary sense is empowering as a means to coexist in a world of scientific medicine, as it carves out turf in an area, it is often argued, biomedicine cares less about. Unfortunately, this idea has often blinded researchers to the fact that these peoples also often have detailed knowledge about the workings of the various parts of the body and what they contribute to the whole. In many ways, labeling such systems "holistic" implies an epistemological simplicity that should be challenged.

Not surprisingly, the iloneleb' do not have the level of understanding of the parts of the human body (*cha'al*) that biomedical science has. They do not have a technology to view into the body (*jun xaaqalil*), and they do not undertake human autopsies. Knowledge of the body is developed analogically and empirically through animal hunting and sacrifice (Moriarty 1970), through observations of the visible aspects of the body and its functioning, through assessing the consequences of treatment that targets a suspected affected body part or system, through logical deduction, and through avenues broadly understood within the realm of popular culture, education, government policy, and biomedicine (for instance, public health campaigns). Here I want to focus on several key elements of iloneleb' knowledge that are prominent in their overall medical paradigm: the brain, mind, heart, and blood.

Some iloneleb' use the same term for both the brain and the mind, *ulul*, while others distinguish the brain as organ (ulul) from the mind (*k'a'uxl*) as the locus of the thinking activity of the brain. The brain as an organ can become disordered or dysfunctional and is implicated, for instance, in epilepsy. The brain can get "hot," causing mood and behavior problems. Headache is a symptom common to many sicknesses. But the thinking function of the brain, located in the mind, is far more problematic and is implicated in a variety of disorders.

The heart, *aam*, is also firstly understood in terms of its bodily function. Manuel Choc explains that "the heart is like a machine which pumps blood throughout the entire body." It can malfunction, creating the pain associated with angina or heart attack (*tib'l aam*), and of course it can stop altogether. A poor diet is known to create such hazardous disorders for the heart. The heart can also be frightened or be affected by the mental state of the individual, such as anxiety, with arrhythmia and tachycardia the consequence. But the heart is also the site of emotions (ch'oolej; also *eek'ank*, or feelings), where thoughts are actioned. "The brain is basically used to think of something you would want to do, and the heart is where you would take initiative to do that action," says Manuel Choc. The arteries and veins provide the connection between the mind/brain and heart; as a result, the blood can be negatively affected by poor mental states (for instance, "thinking too much"; see next chapter). While there is an alliance between the heart and mind, called the heart/mind in much medical anthropology literature (e.g., Desjarlais 1992), according to Francisco they are distinct and exist somewhat separate from the body. "The motor of the body is from the heart and the mind," he explains. "They are not a part of the body, but you can say they are connected [to it]." He will undertake ceremonies specifically to promote or repair connections among the heart, mind, and body, suggesting that they are not automatically simpatico. Emilio will also undertake ceremonies to "balance" the mind, body, and spirit together in circumstances where they have diverged as separate entities.

While the mind itself cannot make the body sick in organic terms, Francisco agrees that the heart is also the site of emotions, and these can be problematic. Some iloneleb' note that emotions originate as thoughts in the mind and then travel to the heart, where they are actioned. Others add that the heart is really the evaluative site, where thoughts are considered and judged, whereupon a signal is returned to the brain to make the body act or feel. "Yeah, there is a part of our body which does the thinking which is the brain," explains Manuel Choc. "Then it goes from the brain to the heart. Depending on the type of thought that we have, then the brain laughs." The thought/emotion/response cycle can create disorders conducive to sickness. Emilio, articulating his notion of psychosomatic processes, notes how "the mind affects the whole body because when a person thinks, the whole body is involved in [reacts to] this thinking process." To which I add Manuel Choc's explanation, "Once you have a sickness in the brain, the entire body is affected by that sickness." Emotional states originating in the heart can travel back to the brain, causing sickness. As we will see later, thinking-related and emotional disorders are common among the Q'eqchi'. Important here is to appreciate that the heart and brain are understood to be separate organs with separate functions—the brain "thinks" and the heart "feels"—but that they necessarily work together. Emilio likens the connection between them to "electricity, whereby one needs the other, so that [a person] properly, on their own, can speak and move around."

The blood (*kik'*) is understood to be the essence of human life, constantly circulating throughout the body. Its loss, through wounds or hemorrhaging, for instance, is life threatening, and the iloneleb' have clotting techniques to stem bleeding and rebuild the blood, including the use of plant medicines. Blood can get "dirty" or "corrupted," and sickness can sometimes get into the blood. Albino states that "when a person thinks negative things, the blood would become corrupted and crazy." Manuel Choc adds, "If we have good thoughts, for example, maybe with work, our heart doesn't do anything unusual. However, when we have negative thoughts, that is when our hearts get corrupted, meaning the blood, when the blood gets corrupted . . . the person will become sick."

Taqenaq kik'el, or high blood pressure, typically noticeable by observable heat in the face and head, is recognized as treatable. Blood "clots" can cause *muchkej*, or muscle cramps, and can be treated by a small amount of bloodletting at the site. Blood is the transmission vehicle in utero for the development of future medical problems as the infant develops (iloneleb' understand genetic transmission from parent to child in this manner); taqenaq kik'el is an example. The blood also carries throughout the body allergens from foods, the parasite from malaria, and venom from snakebites.[3] On a positive note, the blood also carries throughout the body plant medicine administered to cure the patient.

Different sicknesses affect the blood in different ways. Ease and speed of flow of the blood in the arteries and veins, the smoothness or jaggedness of the flow, texture (thick, thin, "lumpy"), "strength," weight ("heavy" or "light"), pulse rate (some iloneleb' count pulse beats. Francisco says seventy beats per minute is normal; above eighty means the blood is being circulated too fast, a sign of several types of sickness, including taqenaq kik'el), and temperature (hot or cold) are some of the main criteria that iloneleb' are trained to detect.

Like other aspects of Q'eqchi' cosmovision, the blood is agentive. It has characteristic healthy and sickness states, can even become frightened, and responds to sickness in a variety of ways that the ilonel must interpret. The ilonel often engages in a dialogue of sorts with the blood through xjilb'al xkik'el ("assessing the pulse") or pulsing, which is central to virtually all diagnostics and treatments and is covered in detail in the next chapter. The blood "speaks" to the ilonel separate and independent from the patient. The ilonel will "ask" the blood—typically during prayer—what is wrong with it or with the patient, anticipating that the blood will respond by offering recognizable signs that the ilonel can interpret. The ilonel may also call out likely sicknesses or situations (such as falling by a river) while pulsing for signs, such as jumpiness, that the correct one has been identified. The patient may not know what is wrong, but the blood will, and for this reason the iloneleb' put less stock in patient interviews than in pulsing as a means of diagnosis.

The gastrointestinal system is the site of many of the complaints patients bring to the iloneleb'. The digestive system is therefore well understood in its function to digest and process food and nutrients, and eliminate waste. *Q'an yaj* (ulcer or stomach "sores"), diarrhea and dysentery, indigestion and "heartburn," and general stomach upset and vomiting are some of the main problems iloneleb' treat. The gastrointestinal system is sensitive, and problems can arise by missing meals, eating foods that are too hot and especially too cold for one's current body state, or eating contaminated or rotting foods. *Lukum*, or worms (ascaris or roundworms) are understood to live in the stomach and intestines, performing an important digestive function, but they can become unruly, rustling about or biting, rising up into the mouth or out the anus. (Treatment involves settling them down, not eliminating them, as they are essential.) Stomach problems can occur when one falls down, "disturbing" the worms.

Other bodily organs are known to a lesser extent but are still a component of the medical knowledge system. For instance, Francisco understands that yellow fever can affect the kidneys and liver. Kidney stones are a well-known problem. The pancreas is implicated in several problems.

Infection and Contagion

Xmay xul, or infection, is understood to involve the entry into the body of an agent or poison of some sort that creates the sickness. Wounds, and animal or insect bites, can lead to infection. Not all iloneleb' have the same degree of knowledge on how this works. In general, there is a sense that "little animals" that cannot be seen are involved, an obvious reference to viruses and bacteria. Pain, fever, headache, redness and swelling at the site, and pus are the signs they look for. Skin disorders are a common problem, and one general disorder known as *katzkatz xox*, or itchy sores, can be caused by contact with ticks or sandflies, among others. Infections can also be caused by bad food or water, and they can be passed from other people and even animals. Wounds are routinely dressed with medicinal plants to prevent or eliminate infection, and if available, alcohol may be applied as well. Malaria is understood to come from mosquitos that have previously bitten an infected human or animal, but a few iloneleb' think it can also pass between humans through breathing. The infectious agent in malaria is in the blood; it may or may not be a "small animal," depending on the ilonel, and one suggests that the mosquito is injecting cold air into the human. The "common cold," *jolomb'ej*, is known to be contagious and to pass in the air. The sick individual, who has inhaled dust or some other noxious agent, develops the sickness and then coughs or simply breathes out the dust containing the microscopic animals that cause the sickness. Tuberculosis passes the same way, as well as through sputum, via shared drinking cups for example. Francisco, in his practice, takes care not to have such potentially contagious patients breathe on him. Sexually transmitted infections, including HIV, are known to pass from one infected human to another through sexual contact.

While iloneleb' lack detailed knowledge of the microbes involved in infectious and contagious diseases, Q'eqchi' medicine has theorized their presence, conceptualizing them in ways that make empirical sense, as little animals that one cannot see. Human-to-human transmission explains the spread of colds and flu, whereas insect vectors (including mosquitoes) are identified as agents of diseases such as dengue fever and yellow fever.

Witchcraft

It is with witchcraft and obeah that matters of sickness enter into the realm of the personalistic, as George Foster (1976) would suggest, where sickness causation is deemed to be linked to interpersonal relations. Most of the iloneleb' in this study do not distinguish among various types of witchcraft; the exceptions are Francisco and Emilio, whose advanced knowledge shows in this domain. Francisco, for instance, views obeah as a more sophisticated kind of witchcraft involving powerful spirits or the devil; the whole topic proved so unnerving to him when we talked about it that he requested that I turn off the recorder. It was not that he was afraid that talking about it would invite it but rather that if it got out that he was talking about it at all, as if he were an expert, it would be assumed that he engaged in it. "My job is not to celebrate it," he explains. "It is to stop it."

The local terms for a witch include *tuul* and "obeah man." *K'ehol yajel* means "witchcraft sickness." The term "obeah" is an import to the Q'eqchi' from Caribbean neighbors (and is originally from Africa), but its local referent is indigenous of long-standing. The ability to give someone a sickness or to otherwise cause them to fall sick through meta/material means is common the world over and takes many forms. Among the Q'eqchi', it typically involves appeals to evil spirits to create havoc and the use of various fetishes and talismans.

Witchcraft exists in the social realm, and being social in the appropriate manner is incredibly important to the Q'eqchi'. The social or interpersonal aspects of witchcraft are central to understanding its power within Q'eqchi' society. Interpersonal stresses and transgressions play out in this field largely because direct confrontation is proscribed and represents a violation of Q'eqchi' notions of morality and personhood. Envy, jealousy, and resentment are key reasons why one might be targeted. Manuel Baki explains:

> Those who practice witchcraft are persons who do not work. For instance, an individual has good fortune and the other envies that person. He would want to cause problems with the good-fortuned person. For example me, I have a farm and few head of cattle; that caused another person to do witchcraft [on me]. People would call bad luck to you.

Hence the reasons for witchcraft tend to revolve around the material and social aspects of life; a person who is wealthy, has many cattle or large plots of land, many farming implements, employment, a nice house, a vehicle, and so on is often resented, all the more so if they brag about it. Rejecting a request to lend money or a tool may also cause anger and resentment. One's spouse or partner may attract the attention of others who jealously wish they could have him or her. Indeed, with witchcraft we can see how the material and meta/material aspects of Q'eqchi' life blend together; witchcraft involves the invocation of the meta/material to reconcile tensions in the material world in contexts in which direct interpersonal engagement is considered inappropriate.

Generally, it is not necessary to connect with a specialist to employ witchcraft. In some cases, simply praying to Qaawa' that harm befall another can at least make the antagonist feel better. (According to the iloneleb', Qaawa' does not respond to such requests.) Some people have enough knowledge to undertake witchcraft in a more sophisticated form. Manuel Choc provides an example of how this is done:

> [Let's say you want to] have a person to vomit blood or grass. What they do is that they shape the image of the person from the copal incense and collect grass to put inside the image. Then they start to pray, burning candles; the candles are also shaped in the human image as well. If you want a person to vomit blood you would pray for that, burning candles. In their prayer they would ask that some part in your body breaks open, having the blood bleeding from your body. It's the same if they want to give you a cramp [pain]. They would shape the incense and put a needle in the incense. These are different ways how sicknesses can be caused by a witch.

However, it is also common to seek out a witch to do the work of harming another. Witches typically charge large sums of money and can take the assault to the maximum level, causing accidents and even death.

One can protect oneself from witchcraft in a variety of ways. Praying to Qaawa' is important in general as a means of protection. Keeping one's blood (kik') and body (jun xaaqalil) strong (kaw) helps deflect any evil directed your way. Living a proper Q'eqchi' life of humility is also essential to avoid making yourself a target of witchcraft. Francisco provides a more pragmatic example. "If you don't do anything bad to a person," he says, "and if this person prays that something happens to you, nothing will happen to you because you're free from trouble." Federico, my interpreter in this interview, elaborates: "All you got to do is keep your hands to yourself, don't touch anybody else's stuff, because if you want somebody's stuff, you will be affected with this kind of thing." This "mind-your-own-business" attitude is the other side of the witchcraft coin: do not give people a reason to dislike you. It is not foolproof, though, because you never know when someone has taken offense, at least until you fall sick from witchcraft.

The iloneleb' are often called upon to treat patients who have been witched. These patients may appear with sicknesses or report other issues, such as a string of bad luck, poor crops, or problems in their marriage. The iloneleb' usually have little trouble identifying witchcraft as the cause of the patient's troubles but are reluctant to disclose this to the patient. They are even careful not to ask too many witchcraft-related questions, lest the patient gets suspicious. The iloneleb' understand the potential for a feud should they discuss witchcraft, for the patient is sure to speculate on the source and might attempt to return the curse or otherwise get revenge. "They will kill each other," warns Francisco bluntly. The MHAB charter calls on iloneleb' to handle such cases with utmost delicacy. However, villagers understand that the ability of iloneleb' to treat witchcraft-related problems also empowers them to engage in witchcraft, and iloneleb' are frequent targets of accusations that they are in fact witches, causing sickness and then extorting money from the suffering targets to treat it. Many credible anecdotes tell of individuals, whether iloneleb' or not, doing this in Toledo. And the MHAB did remove one individual from the association for telling people they had obeah and then offering to help them for a large fee. The iloneleb' of the MHAB see all this as the price of doing business, in a sense. They understand that some are suspicious of them and their work as medical practitioners and that their association is sometimes viewed as a cabal of evildoers simply because such an organization is suspiciously untraditional. They can be targets of witchcraft if an individual thinks they have assisted another villager against him or her, and also for the same material reasons noted above. Manuel Baki, recall, experienced this because of his relative wealth in cattle. He says, "It happened three years ago. When it started I vomited foam-like stuff. I stopped eating. They fed me with a spoon; the food wouldn't go down." Suspecting witchcraft, he self-medicated with plants known to treat this problem and was subsequently able to eat again. This is a kind of empiricism common to the Q'eqchi' medical system: the outcome of treatment confirms the diagnosis. Francisco employs the same approach when dealing with cases of witchcraft. Typically, after diagnosis he assumes that the patient has been witched in the less serious form. He undertakes a procedure using a variety of plants, in sequential fashion, that are known to reverse the disorder. If this does not work, he revises his diagnosis to obeah, the more serious form of witchcraft, and changes his approach, combining all the plants into one medicine, in effect increasing the concentration of the overall dose and accentuating the synergistic properties of the individual plants.

Health and Well-being

The Q'eqchi' iloneleb' use two terms for health: *kawilal* and *sahilal*. The former speaks to health in the sense of an absence of sickness, which is also a way of saying a person is strong (kaw). Sahilal means happiness or contentment. In effect, then, the Q'eqchi' employ both aspects of the classic World Health Organization definition of health—that is, the absence of disease or infirmity, plus the broader aspects of "a state of complete physical, mental, and social well-being" (WHO 2002). I would suggest that these are conceptually two distinct states in the case of Q'eqchi' medicine. While iloneleb' work within a broader paradigm of well-being, their work as medical practitioners is largely focused on removing "disease or infirmity." For instance, when I ask Manuel Baki, "If we are to say that a person has good health, what does that mean?," he replies simply, "That is when one is not yet sick." Manuel Choc concurs: "To me, a healthy and strong man is one that has no sickness. He has his strength; he has his blood. His spirit is strong. He is healthy."

Well-being, of course, is much broader. Three Q'eqchi' terms are used to explain this concept: *chaab'il wank* (to be good or content), *chaab'il yu'am* (good life), and *sahilal yu'am* (happy or nice life). But being happy is clearly the key component of the good life, and an integral aspect of health. *Sahil*—happiness—is explained by Francisco: "The healthy person is happy all the time, happy when holding conversations, happy when traveling or walking, works contentedly and eats happily. That is how you would know that a person is healthy. No problems. He is happy."

Well-being, then, is about both public demeanor and the ability to meet one's obligations, two aspects common to the broader definition of the concept in global ethnography (Weisner 2009:229) and an idea that has been identified among other Maya groups (e.g., Watanabe 1992). The iloneleb' and their patients often equate well-being with the ability to work; not working is a sign of sickness. Manuel Choc explains that sickness is often evident by the inactivity of the victim, who becomes saddened that he cannot contribute:

> The sick person is not happy. There are days he is happy and sometimes

> he is not. He is like a sick chicken: it would walk for a while and then you would see the chicken resting or not moving anymore. That is how sickness is. It is not all the time you are happy. You have a lot of worries. . . . When a person gets cured, he is happy again.

Emilio adds the idea of sociality in his explanation:

> If a person is healthy, he is contented in his heart. He moves freely; everything is okay. He is okay in his mind and thinking. When someone does not socialize freely, does not walk normal, does not move around freely, the individual moves with discontentment. You can tell that something is wrong with him. The person would just gaze around, demonstrating that there is discontentment in his life.

When I ask Emilio what it would mean to say someone has bad health, he mirrors his previous response:

> If the person is really sick, the person does not move or walk anymore, does not do anything. He does not do anything else. You would no longer see the person around. He would be in his place [home] and would not be socializing anymore. That is when the person is really sick. When a person is really healthy, the person moves around freely and does not stay indoors so much.

So being part of the community—being seen and being socially active and communicative—is a key element of Q'eqchi' well-being. This speaks to the importance of performing social roles in an open manner. Emilio adds that health is promoted by "coming together in unity so that we are happy. Planning together as a community. Togetherness." Manuel Baki concurs: "When a person is good with the community, the community is happy with the person and the person is happy."

To dig further into the issue of well-being, I fashioned a matched set of questions based in part on the criteria of the Canadian government for the "key determinants of health."[4] The general question I asked each ilonel was, "Who will be healthier?"

Lots of family/few family
Lots of friends/few friends
Lots of money/little money
Lots of power and influence/little power and influence
Lots of education (as in schooling)/little education
Can read/cannot read
A good house/a bad house
A Q'eqchi'-style house/a town house
Water from the tap, pump, or well/water from a river
Eats a lot/eats little
Bathes frequently/bathes rarely
Woman/man
Adult/child
Knows Q'eqchi culture or ways/does not know Q'eqchi' culture or ways
Goes to the town doctor/goes to iloneleb'

The iloneleb' struggled with these questions. It is evident that they understand health, well-being, and sickness as intertwined, complex, contextual, and nuanced. They did not want to be forced into the simplistic dichotomous response categories represented in my questions. Frequently, they responded with a Q'eqchi' version of the English expression "it depends," followed by a detailed explanation. For instance, to get a sense of the broad concept of happiness in the community, I asked, "Generally speaking, are people mostly sad all the time or mostly happy all the time?" Manuel Choc responded, "There are people that are happy and some that are sad. Not all the time one would be happy. One day you would get sad. Life is not all happiness. Sickness of all kinds comes all the time. Some days people are happy while at other times they might be sad. . . . That is the way how we are."

The insistence on complexity and nuance is evident in answers to questions framed around key determinants of health. For the vast majority of factors, iloneleb' respond in a manner that makes it impossible to say with confidence that there are important distinctions in these indicators. Issues such as family composition, social networks, educational levels, quality of housing, literacy, water quality, and physical activity all are understood as having little impact on health and well-being per se. In fact, the iloneleb' often suggest that it is one's health that impacts these factors! Having a good job and having financial resources are the most predictive; three of the five iloneleb' I interviewed on this topic suggest that individuals who are wealthier through certain kinds of employment are more likely to be healthier. Financial resources are important to provide for your family and to do the things you want. And some kinds of employment—being a teacher, for instance—reduce risk of sickness in comparison to working outdoors in the fields and experiencing possible fluctuations in body temperature or run-ins with evil spirits. But, again, it is never this simple. Francisco explains:

> Money does not give health. It does not give sadness either. Health is for anyone. It is for the one that has money and for the one without. Health cuts across the board. There are some with money that have sickness and some without money that have sickness. Health does not come with money or a price. When a person is healthy, a person is happy. Someone who has lots of money, once there is no sickness, he is happy. When there is sickness, it does not matter if there is lots of money, the person would be suffering [*rahilal*] . . . when sickness gets in, it does not choose the one with or without money.

Even personal hygiene, such as regular bathing, is complex. While bathing is seen as important to wash dirt off the body, especially after a hard day of work, the water can alter the body's temperature, creating a vulnerability to sickness. In most cases, the iloneleb' feel that these factors are not by definition protective. Rather the key issue is one's maatan, or destiny. This is the confounding factor in all cases. "One's destiny is his destiny," explains Emilio. "It could be a happy destiny or a sad destiny. . . . Like us living in a thatch house; we are healthy. It is our destiny. The one in a concrete house, if that person is to get sick, it is his destiny." Adds Francisco, "The happy person is gifted that way. He is kind, he is happy, he is contented. No problem in his life. It is in his birth that he is so. He doesn't think of problems or conflicts. He is happy with his family and his relatives. It does not matter whether the home is really poor or things are lacking in the home. He is born that way, happy." So the rich person in the big house is just as vulnerable to sickness as the poor person in the thatched hut, if it is the person's destiny to be sick. Of course, the iloneleb' understand that employment and wealth are important, because they help meet the material needs of the family. But social comportment is also crucial, for those who have can be resented by the have-nots, who may engage in witchcraft against them. Humility, a key Q'eqchi' value, is essential to avoiding witchcraft-related sickness. "Good life to me is when you are humble to others," explains Manuel Choc, "not to just say anything you want to another. Live your life in the best way. Live carefully. God is watching you. Our life is long when you are happy. No fighting."

While gender does not appear to be an issue in understanding vulnerability to sickness, except for reproductive issues affecting women (De Gezelle 2014), children are considered more vulnerable than adults. This is partly a developmental issue, as their nawal (gifted energy) has not yet achieved adultlike status and their ongoing growth creates a propensity to be warmer than normal. It is partly a pragmatic issue in that children are simply not as capable of taking care of themselves and avoiding risky situations. Children are more easily frightened as well.

Health, then, is seen by these iloneleb' as an absence of disease or infirmity. Health and happiness, the Q'eqchi' idiom of well-being, are somewhat synonymous. Being sick is incompatible with being happy; these are mutually exclusive states. And health is seen more as a determinant of success in life than success is seen as a determinant of health, contrary to standard Western models of determinants of health. It is, in part, one's destiny to be sick or suffer, but humans have the capacity to talk back to this destiny, to comport themselves in a manner that, combined with key actions, has the potential to at least mitigate many life problems associated with maatan. The system is dynamic in this way, providing both an explanation for one's situation and an opportunity to take control, to some extent at least, of one's life to improve the situation. There is hope for health and happiness.

A Model of Q'eqchi' Diathesis

The idea of diathesis is borrowed here from medicine and psychology (Salomon and Jin 2013) and can be defined as "a constitutional predisposition toward a particular state or disorder and especially one that is abnormal or diseased."[5] The diathesis stress model expands on this definition and speaks to the way in which one's constitution and experiences—in particular, exposure to stress—work to create vulnerability to sickness. The iloneleb' frequently speak of this vulnerability in terms of the need for the body to be "strong," suggesting that there is a kind of protective shell—an "aura" is how Victor translated it; others refer to it as an "energy" and use the term *nawal*—that acts in a manner like the immune system. A strong nawal is essential, as is following the relational rules of propitiation. Francisco explains, in the context of planting, how one can ensure a strong spirit:

> They have to go and find the piece of land where they will plant, okay. Before they go to do the activity, they have to go and make a ceremony there. They have to ask permission so to have no accident, to have a good crop, and to have good harmony with everything, with everybody. And that is how to keep a strong relationship with all the spirits—spirit of the mountains, and spirit of the humans—and make sure no animals damage your crop. Everything is connected. This means if you do it properly, you are safe from everything.

This energy aura can be weakened, cracked, or otherwise "not prepared" to defend the body against external insults. A person with a strong nawal can still get sick, but if they do, they are much easier to cure than a more vulnerable person with a weak spirit.

"Strong" blood is essential to keeping a person healthy. This strength is in part a product of one's nawal and maatan but also a product of intentional human activity and efforts to maintain a neutral body temperature, neither too hot nor too cold. Prayer is a key element in strength maintenance—living a good and proper life that calls upon Qaawa' to be supportive. Emilio says that if any of the seven spirits of the body leaves, the blood is weakened. Nutrition is also important. Certain traditional foods are known to make the body stronger; Manuel Baki cites such foods as cabbage, callaloo, potatoes, tomatoes, and *caldo* soup. Sexual activity, which requires physical exertion followed by a decline in blood temperature, and hard physical labor, which results in a temperature rise, are both understood to weaken the blood. Loss of bodily fluids through perspiration, particularly in conjunction with hard labor, creates weakness that can be remedied, in part, by consuming water. Blood loss, caused by wounds, hemorrhage, or "worms" in the gastrointestinal tract that consume blood, is also a problem, weakening the body. Anxiety, especially thinking too much about an obsession, can "corrupt" the blood or make it "dirty" (*po'ol kik'*), which leads to various forms of "craziness."

A model of Q'eqchi' diathesis, one that helps explain the idea of vulnerability and, by extension, highlights those actions within human control that help determine health, is clearly evident. The first factor is maatan, one's destiny, which is imprinted at birth according to the day of the Maya calendar, linking "the self to the confluence of cosmic forces associated with that day" (Fischer 1999:481). Some people are inherently stronger than others, less vulnerable to sickness and early death. Further, in some cases, propensity for certain sicknesses can be inherited from parents or caused by disorders of the mother while pregnant. *Awas*, a disorder that affects infants and small children, results from an unsettling experience of the pregnant mother and leads to mental or physical malfunction or deformity. Wilson (1995:124), who provides a very detailed discussion of the types of awas among the Q'eqchi', describes it as an "inherent malformation of the victim's constitution" that will affect the child. Emilio indicates that such a child will live a short life—up to three years—if not treated. The treatment for this is not complicated and does not require a medical specialist in many instances: the parents must recall the unsettling incident, acquire some element or aspect of that experience (such as part of a pig if the mother was frightened by a pig), and burn it under the child—"smoking" (or bathing) the child in the smoke.

Maatan contributes to one's aura or energy (nawal), that external and internal bodily shield that works like the immune system, providing protection from external threats. Individual actions are the second factor in the Q'eqchi' diathesis model; while one's destiny is important, it can be mitigated to some extent by deliberate actions, and having a good maatan does not preclude sickness, especially if the individual is complacent. A healthy state is achievable if the individual works to maintain or strengthen the nawal; is spiritually responsible, praying to Qaawa' and the Tzuultaq'a for their support and gaining permission as need be; avoids sudden changes in body/blood/brain temperature; is wary in avoiding spiritually dangerous places/times; eats proper foods, particularly those identified as traditional Q'eqchi' foods; and comports in a socially acceptable manner. Conventional material aspects of life as determinants of health are less important than meta/material aspects. In effect, if one lives the "good life" from a Q'eqchi' perspective, one has a better chance of being happy, which means being healthy. The Q'eqchi' model at once encompasses factors that one has little control over and those that one can control, at least to some extent. A dialectic is an inherent part of this moral model, for the individual is agentive, required to make the correct decisions to be happy or avoid sickness, but within the context of factors that exempt them from moral retribution, because some failures, deficiencies, and sicknesses are not the individual's fault. This represents an interesting synthesis of ideas that can also be found, on the one hand, in contemporary Western public health discourse that seeks to destigmatize sickness and rejects "blame the victim" ideology and, on the other hand, in contemporary Western religious and moral discourse that presumes the "lifestyle" choices regarding so-called immoral behavior are justifiably punishable by an other-than-human power.

Conclusion

The core principles that guide the Q'eqchi' iloneleb' understanding of sickness and health relate to the need to maintain—or achieve—balance and symmetry, as so many studies of Indigenous medicine around the world have shown. More specifically, though, for the Q'eqchi', health and sickness revolve around a tension among the maatan, over which one has limited control; the nawal, which is responsive to human intervention; and one's comportment in life and in the world, over which one has considerably more control. These, to varying degrees, signal an agency on the part of the individual that is guided by a moral code of respect and reciprocity—among humans and between humans and other meta/material beings and forces—and that helps explain both sickness and health. This represents, in part, a relational epistemology (Bird-David 1999), but it is only partly animistic. The recognition of the material aspects of life—of the body, of sickness, of plant medicines, and so on—also rings clear here.

Health for these Q'eqchi' is understood largely in terms of well-being—happiness—marked by the absence of sickness and therefore the ability to be a proper Q'eqchi' person socially and economically. A balance in the material and meta/material realms that affect the individual is essential to well-being. The role of the iloneleb' is primarily restorative, focused on removing sickness from the patient. This, in turn, promotes the balance that allows for the reemergence of the patient's sense of well-being. Cure, and not the restoration of well-being, is the immediate goal of the iloneleb' when they treat the sick. How and why people get sick is the topic of the next chapter.

CHAPTER 4

Sickness and Nosology

THE GREAT CHALLENGE of this research is to identify the order and organization in a medical knowledge system that does not require either to be coherently communicated to anyone. Like any system of practice, there is a cognitive basis, sets of schemas that are constantly being constructed and amended. But in the absence of a formalized or codified set of knowledges, any epistemological model must be built inductively rather than deductively. This is a classic cognitive exercise, and one with which anthropology has some familiarity, centered on the notions that knowledge is shared yet contextual, and differentially known, distributed, and invoked. Consonance in knowledge is the core of any such model, yet it is crucial to make space for deviations, ideas that are not necessarily compatible with any emerging consensus and that often become sources of innovation. To do this, one must dive into the cognitive essence of the medical system in question, and the answers are never complete because the target—knowledge—is never static. There is no bottom to the knowledge pool, so we must be content with a "good enough" understanding that meets our purposes.

I am aware that I have not been able to identify all sicknesses known to the Q'eqchi' iloneleb' I have worked with, or the Q'eqchi' medical system more broadly. The various methods I employed produced a set of sicknesses that seemed most common and known to varying extents. A complicating factor is that, as in most medical systems, the iloneleb' identify and label disorders that can be at times causes, signs, symptoms, and physical or mental states. What is a sickness in one instance can also be a symptom of a different sickness in another. There are often several different terms or expressions used to label the same sickness. Some of these may refer descriptively to specific singular or sets of key signs, symptoms, or causes, just as with biomedicine (for example, malaria or "bad air"; jaundice or yellow fever). Further, as I noted earlier, the Q'eqchi' iloneleb' do not subscribe to the notion of strictly "natural" or material disease causation. Rather they understand sickness to be a product of agents, forces, and experiences; that is, most sicknesses have both a material and a meta/material dimension, and agency in both dimensions is in some way usually implicated. Understanding the complexity of sickness, then, is a challenge, as the iloneleb' float easily between the material and meta/material when they describe sicknesses and their causes, because they do not make the same analytical distinction I am making here for heuristic reasons.

Finally, for the iloneleb', context is everything. While they willingly engaged in the interviews, pile sorts, and other analytical exercises, these were difficult challenges because thinking abstractly about hypothetical cases is unfamiliar, and the individual nuances of a case are crucial details. Diagnosis is almost always dependent on pulsing, and verbal descriptions of pulse types are wholly inadequate to the task; pulses must be felt, and the blood communicated with directly. Subtle differences, such as mild versus strong fever, are essential to determining the sickness, its cause, and its treatment. Several sicknesses to be discussed shortly appear, on the surface, to be nothing more than different names for the same disorder, but deeper analysis highlights these subtle distinctions. Temporality is important, as sicknesses can evolve in seriousness if not treated early, and they can emerge into new sicknesses in such cases. Diagnosis and treatment are usually simultaneous and interrelated processes, which means that the interpretation of signs and symptoms shifts during the therapeutic event. Nawal (gifted energy) and maatan (destiny) are essential to understanding any sickness, and these are unique to individuals. The day someone was born is crucial information; two people with the same set of signs and symptoms but different birth dates may have different sicknesses. Further, in some cases where patient input is important (more on this in the next chapter), the patient's narrative, typically spartan but nonetheless informative, is essential to identifying the sickness. Did the person fall, and if so, was it by the river or on a path? Did they venture out in the early morning mist? Did they remember to ask for permission of the Tzuultaq'a before they hunted or planted crops? These issues are crucial to the reading of signs and symptoms and the determination of the sickness.

With these issues in mind, in this chapter I set out to provide a sense of the organizational structure of Q'eqchi' medical knowledge as exhibited by this group of practitioners, and to establish a working nosology of medical disorders. I do not suggest here that I have identified and articulated *the* singular, unified structure of *the* Q'eqchi' medical system. I do suggest, however, that the system delineated in the remains of this book will resonate with other Q'eqchi' iloneleb', who might nonetheless provide their own idiosyncratic interpretations and nomenclature. My goal here is to provide a sense of what the Q'eqchi' medical system appears to look like and to demonstrate more fundamentally that there is indeed a system.

Nosological Structure

Richard Wilson (1995:123) suggests that among the Q'eqchi' there are "two main types of human sickness," awas and spirit loss (more on these shortly). My research demonstrates considerably greater complexity, perhaps because Wilson was working with nonspecialists rather than medical practitioners. During my interviews, dozens of different sicknesses (yajel) were mentioned. Working with the interpreters and after carefully reviewing the emerging data set, I decided to select a set of sixteen disorders (the term I use here instead of "diseases" or "sicknesses") that spanned the range of material and meta/material dimensions and that were most commonly referenced. Since the pile sort task is not one with which the iloneleb' are intrinsically familiar, it proved to be time-consuming and somewhat mentally onerous. The fact that none of them could read made it more difficult. The small number of participants also meant that momentary inattentiveness or fatigue could result in a disorder being curiously placed, with spurious results, and careful confirmation was needed at all times. Despite these issues, this set of disorders, then, seems to provide the best balance to ensure productive and meaningful results.

The sixteen disorders and their English glosses are as follows. Some iloneleb' are familiar with and apply biomedical terms, but please note that these glosses should not be taken as necessarily equivalent to biomedical terminology.

choql (sickness caused by exposure to clouds or mist; sometimes glossed as pneumonia or persistent cough)
eet aj yajel (epilepsy; the "foolish sickness")
jwal naxik xk'a'uxl (thinking too much)
kaanil (spirit loss; sometimes glossed as a form of susto)
k'a'uxlak (excessive worry or anguish)
maa'usat (evil spirit intrusion)
q'an yaj (ulcer or stomach "sores")
q'an yajel (yellow fever)
rax kehob'l (malaria; chills)
rilom tzuul (sickness caused by the mountain spirit; sometimes glossed as a form of epilepsy)
taqenaq kik'el (high blood pressure)
taqenaq tiqwal jolomb'ej (headache or high head pressure)
waxk'ay (mild craziness)
wax ru (severe craziness; schizophrenia)
xiwajenaq (frightened spirit; sometimes glossed as a form of susto)
xyajel maa'us (sickness of the devil or evil spirit; sometimes glossed as a form of epilepsy)

Three analytical techniques were used, involving two programs, Visual Anthropac 1.0.2.60 (Borgatti 1996) and UCINET for Windows 6 (Borgatti, Everett, and Freeman 2002). First, multidimensional scaling (MDS) (Borgatti 1997) provides a visual representation of the pattern of proximities among the sixteen sickness disorders. The Kruskal stress function in Anthropac calculates the degree of correspondence between the distances among points implied by the MDS map and the matrix input by the user. A stress function under 0.1 is considered very good; more than 0.15 is unacceptable and invalidates the analysis.

Second, I employed a hierarchical cluster procedure in UCINET, using the average link method to reduce the impact of outliers on the analysis (Borgatti 1997; Yim and Ramdeen 2015). Cluster analysis assists in comprehending the similarities across the sickness disorders and provides an assessment of the extent to which certain items "group" together with other items according to some criteria. It is a standard technique used in the analysis of pile sort data.

Third, consensus analysis was used to measure the degree of agreement among the iloneleb'. Consensus analysis has its theoretical underpinning in cultural consensus theory, developed by Romney, Weller, and Batchelder (1986). The consensus procedure in UCINET allows me to determine the extent to which the iloneleb' agree with each other, through the calculation of Pearson correlation coefficients between the iloneleb'. Consensus analysis can provide the means for determining if observed variability in respondents' knowledge is "cultural"—literally asking if the participants' agreement is sufficient for them to be thought of as members of the "same culture" or, in this case, the same medical system. This is done through the calculation of the eigenratio. In addition, the analysis also measures each individual's "cultural competence" by comparing individual responses to those of others after first predicting the "culturally correct answer" (Borgatti and Halgin 2011). Competence scores describe how well individual responses correspond with those of the group as a whole. They are not interpreted as the proportion of answers that an individual knows or gets "correct."

While these ideas about culture and competence are somewhat dated, consensus analysis is still useful in understanding the degree of agreement among participants. Yet disagreement does not necessarily mean a lack of knowledge, as the analysis runs the risk of identifying the most knowledgeable participant as an outlier or "nonculture member" if their knowledge greatly exceeds that of the others. In other words, consensus analysis prioritizes agreement, not content. In the case of the iloneleb', this means that the variation in knowledge and experience they demonstrate as a normal phenomenon of any medical system may lead to the identification of some of them as different in their knowledge. What the analysis shows, in effect, is a distinction between general medical practitioners and specialists.

The initial pile sort undertaken by the iloneleb' was in response to my directive to sort according to "similarity," without defining this in any way. The analysis suggests that there was no single dimension invoked in creating the groupings; they were not grouped solely according to cause, for instance. Figure 7 shows the MDS plot for the sixteen sickness disorders.

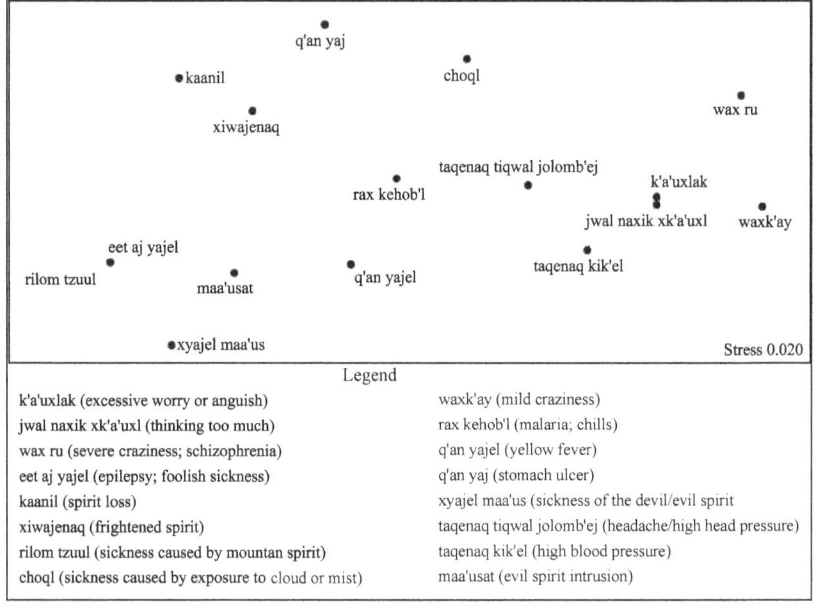

FIGURE 7. Multidimensional scale plot for sickness similarities.

There is a discernable pattern to the plot, with what could be thought of as disorders of mental, psychological, and emotional states on the right side, and disorders of spiritual states on the left. Occupying the center are four disorders: q'an yaj, choql, rax kehob'l, and q'an yajel. These patterns continue to emerge with the cluster analysis, as shown in Figure 8.

In three instances, two disorders were always grouped together, although in some cases they were grouped with other disorders as well, and in the cluster analysis, these emerged at the first level. These three clusters are:

eet aj yajel (epilepsy; the "foolish sickness")–rilom tzuul (sickness caused by the mountain spirit; sometimes glossed as a form of epilepsy)
k'a'uxlak (excessive worry or anguish)–jwal naxik xk'a'uxl (thinking too much)
wax ru (severe craziness; schizophrenia)–waxk'ay (mild craziness)

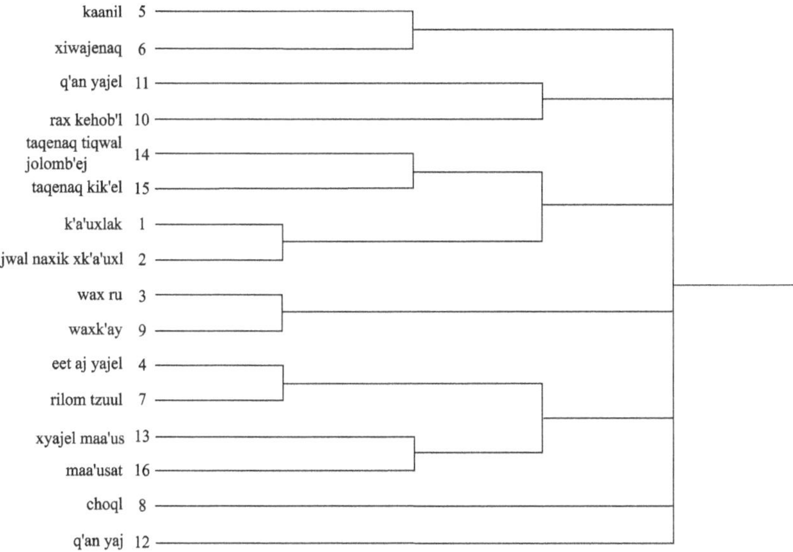

FIGURE 8. Hierarchical cluster analysis for sickness similarities.

At the next level, another three sets of paired disorders emerged. Placed in the same pile by four of the five iloneleb’, these were:

kaanil (spirit loss)–xiwajenaq (frightened spirit)
xyajel maa’us (sickness of the devil or evil spirit)–maa’usat (evil spirit intrusion)
taqenaq tiqwal jolomb’ej (headache; high head pressure)–taqenaq kik’cl (high blood pressure)

Two outliers, which were not placed in any group by four of the five iloneleb’, were choql (sickness caused by exposure to a cloud or mist) and q’an yaj (ulcer or stomach “sores”).

Overall, the cluster analysis at four partition levels reveals the following categories (the labels, of course, are mine):

Category 1: Disordered Psychological and Emotional States
k'a'uxlak (excessive worry or anguish)
jwal naxik xk'a'uxl (thinking too much)
taqenaq tiqwal jolomb'ej (headache or high head pressure)
taqenaq kik'el (high blood pressure)

Category 2: Disordered Mental States
wax ru (severe craziness; schizophrenia)
waxk'ay (mild craziness)

Category 3: Disordered Interpersonal Spiritual States
eet aj yajel (epilepsy; the "foolish sickness")
rilom tzuul (sickness caused by the mountain spirit)
xyajel maa'us (sickness of the devil or evil spirit)
maa'usat (evil spirit intrusion)

Category 4: Disordered Personal Spiritual States
kaanil (spirit loss)
xiwajenaq (frightened spirit)

Category 5: Disordered Physiological States—Vector-Related
q'an yajel (yellow fever)
rax kehob'l (malaria; chills)

Category 6: Disordered Physiological States—Internal
q'an yaj (ulcer or stomach "sores")

Category 7: Disordered Environmental States
choql (sickness caused by exposure to a cloud or mist)

Both q'an yaj and choql failed to cluster with any other disorder.

To understand the organizational or nosological structure at work here, it is necessary to dig into each category.

Category 1: Disordered Psychological and Emotional States

The general commonality in this group is that these disorders affect mental and emotional states with the locus of the problem largely in the brain or mind (with the blood that circulates to the brain having a role). The iloneleb' tend to view taqenaq tiqwal jolomb'ej (headache; high head pressure) and taqenaq kik'el (high blood pressure) as symptoms of these disorders as well as disorders in their own right.

Let me look first at the "thinking" disorders: k'a'uxlak, which literally means "to think" but is used by the iloneleb' in the therapeutic context to mean excessive worry or anguish, and jwal naxik xk'a'uxl (thinking too much). The global literature is replete with references to similar disorders (e.g., Yarris 2011; Kaiser et al. 2015), demonstrating a profound concern of peoples everywhere with what might be depressive or anxiety states. In the Q'eqchi' case, all five iloneleb' placed them together in a pile (sometimes with other disorders), a consensus that highlights the importance of these in the everyday lives of the people. The source of the anxiety or worry with these two disorders tends to be found in external factors, particularly the social and material realms, and in this manner they are distinguishable from the mental disorders in Category 2. Francisco explains that "the brain can be disturbed, can be affected from various things like too much thinking or too much worries. Sometimes they start to worry about different things like the present, the future, or other problems that bring some weakness. Sometimes they can't sleep due to thinking one idea or a lot of ideas, until it starts to disturb the whole body." Witchcraft can be the ultimate cause, but not in every case, and the hallmark here is that people literally drive themselves to distraction. In this sense, these represent internal states that lack the outrageous and problematic outward behavior associated with waxk'ay and wax ru. As Francisco explains, "They are similar in the cause of wanting. But in the case of waxk'ay and wax ru, a person gets crazy, but on the other hand with jwal naxik xk'a'uxl, it's just your imagination of wanting [something or someone], but it is never achieved. The person never gets crazy but keeps on wanting." K'a'uxlak and jwal naxik xk'a'uxl are fundamentally emotional disorders, Francisco says, "but it can get worse and lead to waxk'ay and wax ru." "Craziness," he adds, "starts with extreme thinking."

Francisco describes the typical course of k'a'uxlak:

> They start to show on the face, on her face, on his face, the motive of plight. This means they come to look sad and angry, and they have no more willingness to do their activities. They forget the balance of life, and they start to not talk, lose the sense of life. What I mean is just everything is boring, they can't have a conversation, can't say nothing. They change totally their behavior.

The similarity of what Francisco describes to what is known within biomedicine as depression is striking. There are other Q'eqchi' terms for depression, such as *po'b'il k'a'uxl* (disturbed mind) and *po'ol xch'ool* (disturbed soul), demonstrating various facets of the disorder. The root *ch'ool* (soul or spirit), Francisco adds, "is like the center of his life, like the balance of everything."

The "wanting" is key to these two disorders, which are so close to each other as to be almost indistinguishable. Yet, as Manuel Choc explains, "they are caused due to too much worries about material things, or about a man or a woman." Interpreter Rehinalio Maquin clarifies after further discussion. "With the jwal naxik xk'a'uxl, it is like a young man wanting a young lady," he says. "With the k'a'uxlak, it is caused by worrying too much about material things, such as money." Francisco explains, "Thinking too much happens when a person wishes good things in his life but does not achieve them. It causes some problem with the way of thinking." Excessive worry, on the other hand, "is a mental problem caused by worrying too much about certain problems with family or things that happened to him/her." Jwal naxik xk'a'uxl is considered to be the more severe of the two disorders, and can be fatal. Memory loss is a possible consequence of both if left untreated.

Both jwal naxik xk'a'uxl and k'a'uxlak have physiological manifestations, including the pressure disorders taqenaq tiqwal jolomb'ej (headache; high head pressure) and taqenaq kik'el (high blood pressure), and these are common symptoms in some extreme cases of other sicknesses. This led to Lorenzo placing all four of these disorders together in one group. Emilio recognized taqenaq kik'el also as a key early symptom of the thinking disorders and placed it together with k'a'uxlak and jwal naxik xk'a'uxl. Manual Choc indicates that both pressure disorders could be caused by extreme worry. But they can also result from a sudden change in temperature of the body and especially the head. Explains Francisco, "Yes, whenever cold hits the head, it causes the blood to cool very rapidly, thus clotting in the vein, allowing it to hurt. This can happen too if you get wet by heavy rain, or with heavy wind too."

Francisco indicates that there is a strong similarity between taqenaq kik'el and taqenaq tiqwal jolomb'ej. "In this case of taqenaq kik'el," he explains, "the sickness causes extreme high pressure on the head. The person would not feel good. In the case of taqenaq tiqwal jolomb'ej, the person easily gets vexed, and tired due to the heat. These are almost the same problems." Rehinalio adds, "When a person has these sicknesses, the person tends to get tired and gets miserable very quickly or short-tempered quickly." While physical fatigue is characteristic of taqenaq kik'el, with taqenaq tiqwal jolomb'ej, the individual has trouble concentrating and focusing attention. The connection between these two is clear in that taqenaq tiqwal jolomb'ej is a common symptom of taqenaq kik'el. Further, both, and especially taqenaq tiqwal jolomb'ej, are known symptoms of other sicknesses. And, as Emilio explains, "sometimes taqenaq kik'el is caused by you [in the sense that] it just develops in you," positing an internal biological explanation, in particular a buildup of blood unrelated to anything else.

The iloneleb' appear to place these four in close proximity to each other by gauging similarity in both etiology and symptomology. The essential features of these four common disorders are:

- Patterns of thinking create disorders of anxiety, worry, or depression, as the individual finds himself or herself unable to concentrate on anything but the material target or issue of their infatuation or concern.
- A more generic "thinking too much," or excessive consternation or distraction, is also a symptom and cause of other problems as well.
- Physiological features include headaches and high blood pressure.
- These are problems of the mind or brain—"the thinking place"—and the emotions, and to a lesser extent they are physiological problems.

Category 2: Disordered Mental States

The two disorders in this group, waxk'ay (mild craziness) and wax ru (severe craziness; schizophrenia), represent forms of "insanity." These are sicknesses understood to affect the mind or brain. A person can literally "think too much" or obsess (often about another person) in a way that damages how the mind functions, or they can be driven this way by witchcraft. Manual Baki explains the relation between waxk'ay and wax ru:

> You will not suffer from both sicknesses at the same time. But both of them are similar, and one of them is mild and the other is a worse case. Waxk'ay is the mild form of wax ru. Both of these sicknesses can be caused by witchcraft. . . . Some people would cause sickness to another because they're jealous or dislike someone that is acquiring wealth, or just because of some family dispute. . . . Waxk'ay will cause you trouble, not having your mind at one state. You will not have any more peace of mind; wax ru, however, is the worse form of it. The patient would rip off his or her clothing, run around naked, or even run into the bush.

Francisco distinguishes the two in similar behavioral terms: "A person who has waxk'ay would only laugh, talk to himself. His mind is not correct. He doesn't concentrate fully on his work." With wax ru, on the other hand, "the crazy person sees something that nobody can see, which causes his problem. . . . The person is crazy. He sees people coming after him, trying to hold him, and he tries to get them off him." With respect to wax ru, Lorenzo adds, "these people are violent especially to the ilonel. When the ilonel tries to give him treatment, he is very violent, and he might want to bite him. With the family members, they are afraid of him, and he might be violent to them also." "The mind is not functioning well," Emilio says of wax ru. "He may behave like a drunkard." Physiologically, in both cases the patient likely experiences a headache, flushing, and "high blood pressure." These are the products of a mind that is literally speeding up in a disorganized fashion, the way an automobile engine would overheat when revved.

So "craziness," or insanity, is a sickness that affects the mind. Its genesis can be found in both the realm of the interpersonal and the realm of the intrapersonal, reflective subject. The multidimensional scaling demonstrates a connection to the "Disorders of Psychological and Emotional States," occupying the same general area in the plot that establishes these two groups as distinct and apart from the others. This suggests that what we might call psychiatric disorders are understood as nosologically different from other disorders involving physiological and spiritual manifestations, an important observation, as it brings into question the degree of mind-body-spirit holism frequently ascribed to Indigenous peoples, including the Maya.

There is wide consensus, then, about the nature of waxk'ay and wax ru and the relationship between them. They appear to be grouped according to similarity in cause and symptomology. To sum:

- Both can be caused by witchcraft—that is, "somebody altering your mind," according to Emilio.
- They can also be caused by thinking too much.
- Waxk'ay is the milder form.
- If untreated, waxk'ay can turn into wax ru.
- Symptoms include talking to yourself or to invisible people (waxk'ay), hearing voices (both), hallucinations (both), and violent, dissociative "running" behavior (wax ru).
- There are few physiological symptoms, primarily headache and "high blood pressure" in the head.

Category 3: Disordered Interpersonal Spiritual States

These four disorders—eet aj yajel (epilepsy; the "foolish sickness"), rilom tzuul (sickness caused by the mountain spirit), xyajel maa'us (sickness of the devil or evil spirit), and maa'usat (evil spirit intrusion)—can be characterized by the involvement of an external agentive entity that encounters, confronts, or attacks the individual. While only Emilio grouped all four together, Manual Choc grouped three of them—xyajel maa'us, eet aj yajel, and rilom tzuul—and the other three iloneleb' generated consistent pairings of xyajel maa'us–maa'usat and eet aj yajel–rilom tzuul. Let me break this down by starting with the pairings.

According to Francisco, the root *eet* in *eet aj yajel* refers to being foolish, referencing a person's behavior, giving some sense of the nature of this sickness. Its English-language gloss, used locally, is "epilepsy," and the symptoms would be familiar to a biomedical practitioner. The individual loses consciousness and falls, clenching the teeth and often foaming at the mouth, with eyes rolling back, limbs twisting and convulsing, and the face turning blue. The collapse, according to Francisco, is precipitated by the stoppage of blood circulation in the body, whereupon the person faints and falls. In addition, headache, fever, vomiting, and diarrhea often follow after the seizure, and several seizures in succession are common. Death is a real possibility.

The iloneleb' see eet aj yajel as very close to rilom tzuul, which literally means to be "looked upon by the mountain spirit," but it is also glossed as epilepsy. The symptoms of rilom tzuul are essentially the same as for eet aj yajel, and several iloneleb' see these two as variations of the same disorder. One connection between them is the involvement of evil spirits. Further, violation of the moral responsibility to ask permission is implicated. Manuel Choc explains, "Sometimes they are caused by the mountain's spirit or by going into the forest and resting in an abandoned place; it's due to not asking permission for going to that place. The mountains are alive, and they have spirits. If you don't ask permission, you will be an easy target for the sickness."

Lorenzo Choc adds that one can contract these disorders simply by resting in a place where the spirit has recently vacated. The evil spirit may "hit you," or you may simply walk into it, but in both cases the first sign is falling down. "Weak blood" renders one especially susceptible to these affronts. The general sense is that rilom tzuul is the more serious of the two, likely due to the more direct involvement of the demanding and easily angered Tzuultaq'a, which are more powerful than the evil spirits that roam the forest and can cause sickness simply through encounter.

This pairing, then, brings together one sickness labeled according to signs and another according to cause. Yet the actual signs and symptoms of the two are largely indistinguishable, with the only clear distinction being etiological. Within the Q'eqchi' medical system, however, the distinction between the Tzuultaq'a and the *maa'us*—evil spirits—is crucial.

Another pairing in this cluster is xyajel maa'us (sickness of the devil or evil spirit) with maa'usat (evil spirit intrusion). The obvious connection here is the etiological significance of evil spirits. With xyajel maa'us, the sickness is caused by an encounter with an evil spirit, but that spirit does not enter the body, as in the case of maa'usat. Interpreter Romulo Caal elaborates that with maa'usat, "this evil spirit is able to penetrate into the heart and mind, and it is this powerful spirit which can normally enter people."

The symptoms of xyajel maa'us are detailed by Francisco: "You can see on the person's body that some type of infection develops on the skin. Or that the person's feet or hands are disabled or crippled. The person suffers with fever, headache, and chills." Other iloneleb' describe the development of sores, rash, or swelling on the body as a distinguishable sign, something not found with eet aj yajel, rilom tzuul, or maa'usat.

The crippling nature of xyajel maa'us explains the frequent local use of the gloss "epilepsy" by the practitioners and others, and some include as a sign that the patient falls to the ground. But maa'usat also presents as a form of epilepsy as understood by the iloneleb', even though the gloss was less frequently used by them. Emilio explains that, with spirit intrusion, "the spirit plays with the patient, making him twist all kinds of ways, but while unconscious. And the mouth and lips twist as well." In general, then, the Q'eqchi' medical system recognizes a variety of forms of "epilepsy," although any equation with biomedicine must be done with extreme caution, as it is likely that the general term "epilepsy" has been adopted by Q'eqchi' practitioners from English-language biomedical practice and applied to a variety of disorders that are similar. These four disorders are categorized together because of the connection to external spiritual factors, but the commonality of the gloss "epilepsy" cannot be denied.

All four disorders in this cluster are curable. The iloneleb' do not see them as chronic, remitting/relapsing disorders, but rather each attack is a separate occurrence that can be successfully treated to achieve complete cure. In some cases, however, where this proves difficult, the iloneleb' work to both control the symptoms and achieve a cure over a longer term. Upon cure, any subsequent episode is understood as a new incident, although susceptibility to the new attack may rest in preexisting disorders and circumstances, such as body and blood strength, maatan, and so on.

There is a strong consensus among the iloneleb' regarding the similarity in nature of these four disorders. The following features emerge:

- All have a spiritual etiology involving encounters, confrontations, or attacks.
- All have a mechanical and physiological manifestation, specifically seizures.
- All are thought locally to be variants of epilepsy.
- The strong similarities among the disorders make them somewhat indistinguishable for some iloneleb'. Hence they are approached as essentially the same in treatment.

Category 4: Disordered Personal Spiritual States

Kaanil (spirit loss) and xiwajenaq (frightened spirit) were grouped together by four of the five iloneleb'. Kaanil and xiwajenaq are another pair in Q'eqchi' nosology that can appear indistinguishable at first blush, and both are locally glossed as susto when translated. Yet they represent distinct disorders, related by the idea of some affront to the spirit, causing sickness. Kaanil results when a person is surprised or frightened by another human or animal, causing the spirit to jump out of the body. This surprise typically takes the form of an unexpected encounter, ranging from an animal suddenly crossing one's path to a person being discovered in a compromising situation (such as in marital infidelity). The more serious xiwajenaq is the product of a fright, caused when a person falls on a roadway or trail, falls by or in a river, or more generally falls down unexpectedly, similarly causing the spirit to jump out. The river is an especially dangerous place for the Q'eqchi'. Manual Choc explains:

> It is dangerous because the river has a living spirit just like the mountains. They have spirits that we cannot see. Some streams are angry just as some people are and may not want you to pass by or interfere with it. These are the streams that can affect you bad when you fall at its bank or in it. Even if the riverbed doesn't have any water over it, your spirit can still be affected because of the spirit of the river that holds onto your spirit.

In both kaanil and xiwajenaq, the alienated spirit does not typically travel

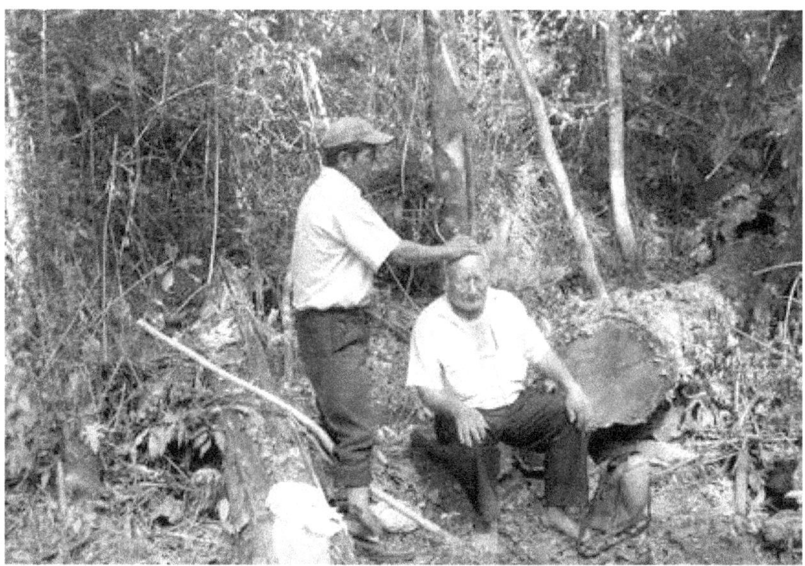

FIGURE 9. Francisco Caal (left) treating Manuel Baki for *xiwajenaq* (frightened spirit), Toledo District, 2006. Photo by author.

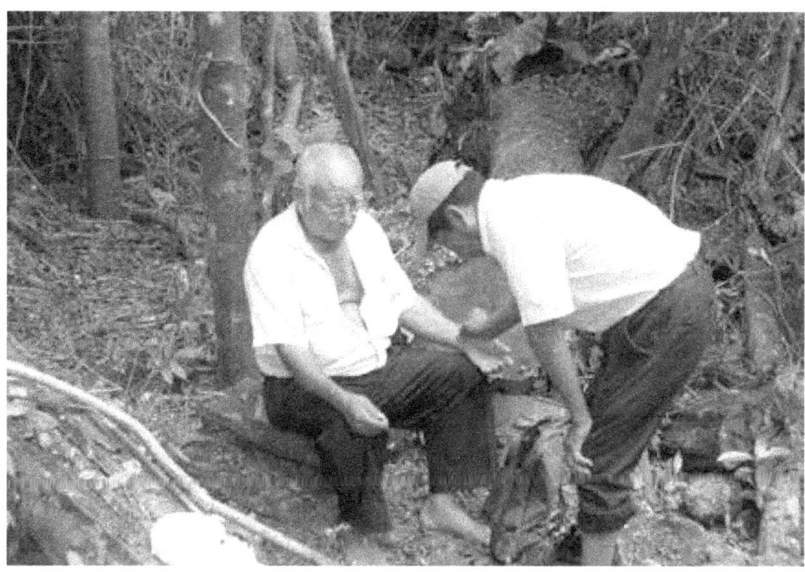

FIGURE 10. Francisco Caal (right) checking Manuel Baki's pulse during treatment for *xiwajenaq* (frightened spirit). Toledo District, 2006. Photo by author.

far, tending to stay in the vicinity where the surprise or fright occurred. The treatment of the ilonel, then, usually involves returning to that location. For this reason, the patient may be required to reflect on recent events to help pinpoint the exact cause. In both disorders, the physical manifestation of spirit loss, such as chills, fever, headache, or vomiting, may not become apparent for several days.

As these are discrete disorders that do not evolve into one another when left untreated, diagnosis must be specific. In the research exercise, the iloneleb' used a combination of signs (absence of one of the body's spirits, for instance), symptoms, and cause to determine that the two disorders belonged in the same category.

There is significant consensus on the nature of kaanil and xiwajenaq. In many ways they resemble susto, as understood in the literature. The term "susto" may refer to either kaanil or xiwajenaq. Like "epilepsy," it has been adopted from elsewhere but made relevant to the specifics of Q'eqchi' medicine. The two disorders would seem to be categorized together on the basis of similar symptoms and causes in general, but with a focus on a causal outcome: the loss of spirit. The main features are:

- They are caused by surprise or fright, resulting in the spirit exiting the body.
- They are discrete sicknesses with different kinds of fright as causes but with a similar outcome, spirit loss.
- They are identifiable by certain physiological signs and symptoms.

Category 5: Disordered Physiological States—Vector-Related

Q'an yajel (yellow fever) and rax kehob'l (malaria; chills) cluster at the third partition. Two of the iloneleb' grouped q'an yajel and rax kehob'l together, while two kept q'an yajel and three kept rax kehob'l as separate and distinct from all other disorders. Signs and symptoms were the main factors in categorization, although Emilio put choql and taqenaq tiqwal jolomb'ej together with rax kehob'l on the basis of similar treatment. The main similarity between the two disorders in this group relates to the role of vectors (insects) and how they are understood to affect physiological states. These disorders demonstrate that the iloneleb' are aware of microorganisms as disease agents.

The term *q'an yajel* is translated as "yellow fever" and sometimes "hepatitis." *Q'an* means "yellow," so the term literally means "yellow sickness." Within biomedicine, yellow fever and hepatitis are understood as separate diseases, and references to hepatitis were relatively rare in this research. As for the term *rax kehob'l*, *rax* translates as "green" but can be taken as a reference to a swamp or a marsh, the home of malaria-bearing mosquitos. The term *kehob'l* refers to cold or chills, so *rax kehob'l* literally means "swamp chills." The result of viral or parasitic infections, yellow fever, hepatitis, and malaria are known biomedically to affect the liver and can cause a yellowish tinting of the skin. The iloneleb' focus on the physiological aspects of skin discoloration and fever in diagnosing, plus excessive thirst and weight loss. The fever is considered milder in q'an yajel than in rax kehob'l. But the distinction between them is often subtle. Francisco explains the differential diagnosis:

> It's the symptoms that are related or almost the same and can be confused if it is not diagnosed properly. In the case of q'an yajel, a person experiences chills, fever. It's almost like malaria [rax kehob'l]; the difference is that the person's eyes and fingernails are yellow [with q'an yajel]. If you don't see the difference in skin, you can say it's malaria. These are two different sicknesses.

Q'an yajel is less understood than some other disorders, and in multiple ways. For instance, Manuel Choc believes that q'an yajel comes from eating too much of certain foods, such as sugar or mangoes. (In the latter case, the yellow color of the fruit causes the skin discoloration.) Lorenzo suggests that it can be contracted "through the air," referencing mists and spirits. Emilio is uncertain what causes it but suggests a mosquito link. The main symptom is the yellowing of the skin and fingernails, although fatigue, loss of appetite, and weight loss were also mentioned. Rax kehob'l is understood by all to come from mosquito bites. Francisco refers to the "insect poison" that is injected as the cause. Fever, chills, and body aches are the key symptoms. While both q'an yajel and rax kehob'l are seen as serious disorders, there was greater agreement (80 percent) that q'an yajel was a serious sickness than that rax kehob'l (60 percent) was a serious sickness. If left untreated, both can lead to death.

While meta/material forces are always at play in Q'eqchi' cosmovision, these sicknesses are characterized by their predominantly material causes and manifestations.[1] Other literature on Indigenous therapeutics would likely refer to these as "natural" sicknesses.

The main features are:

- There is external causation; the sicknesses are vector-borne.
- Skin discoloration is unique and indicative.
- Fever and chills are positive signs and symptoms.

Category 6: Disordered Physiological States—Internal

Four of the five iloneleb' felt that q'an yaj (ulcer or stomach "sores") was distinct from all other disorders. Q'an yaj is one of the most common ailments the iloneleb' treat. Locally, the Spanish term *ulcera* is also often used. The main symptom is stomach pain, with other bodily pains sometimes occurring, although changes in complexion were noted by two iloneleb'. Q'an yaj can take two forms: the first is caused by a disruption in eating patterns, such as missing a meal; the second is caused by disruption to the stomach itself, caused by a fall, which in some cases also results in kaanil (spirit loss). In the latter case, the spirits are more directly involved. Explains Francisco: "Yes, these disorders [q'an yaj and kaanil] are different. For a person who falls, it is necessary to bring back his spirit to its human form from where the person fell, and there it is treated. For a person who misses a meal, I give some medication and that is enough."

In the first variation, the problem arises over a period in which meals are missed or consumed at unusual times. In the second, the sickness can come on quite suddenly. In both variations, however, the root of the problem lies with the "worms" (lukum) that live in the digestive track and that normally assist in digestion. When they are disturbed, q'an yaj can result. With missed meals, the worms begin to eat the stomach itself because there is nothing to feed on, and this will result in bleeding. Falling agitates them. The main features of this category are:

- They are characterized by internal physiological signs and symptoms.
- The stomach is the primary locus of the distress.
- Normal bodily functions are disrupted.
- Etiology is related to an external event, the act of eating (or not), or an incident.

Category 7: Disordered Environmental States

There is only one sickness included here, an isolate called choql, or sickness caused by exposure to clouds or mist. Some iloneleb' see it as a form of pneumonia with a persistent cough. *Choql* translates simply as "cloud." There are several other disorders that could reasonably be included here had they been part of the pile sort (a few are contained in Table 12), all characterized by an environmental etiology, defined here as an encounter with a material or meta/material aspect of the physical environment, such as air, wind, water, rain, mist, or darkness. One can quite literally bump into a sickness the same as bumping into a tree, an idea that confounds any clean material–meta/material dichotomy. Francisco suggests that "trees, mountains, rocks, and all living things have a spirit." These are "spirits of the environment," adds Emilio, things that "have life and give life." Evil spirits also lurk in the environment. Manual Choc says that "the evil spirit is everywhere. . . . A person can find evil spirit on trees, ground, rock." Snakes and other animals can leave an evil spirit or a "bad vibe," as Emilio says, on trails. Wind is seen as potentially dangerous, as it can carry sickness as well as evil spirits, even as it is understood to be the breath of the Tzuul and necessary for humans to breathe. Explains Manuel Choc, "The sicknesses are encountered because we don't respect our environment. This is how we get sick. The environment has a spirit like a human. When we don't ask for permission of these spirits, it causes sicknesses to us, because we have no respect for the environment through damaging it."

Considerable consensus was demonstrated in the case of choql, as four of the five iloneleb' set it aside as not similar to any other sickness in the pile sort exercise. Emilio grouped it with taqenaq tiqwal jolomb'ej (headache; high head pressure) and rax kehob'l (malaria; chills), based on similar symptoms. Its etiology is found in human contact with air, wind, and mist, as Francisco explains: "This sickness is caused by clouds that run in the wind . . . infected with sicknesses. Also, a person can be affected by early morning dew, which causes extreme headaches, coughing, eye pain, and blurred vision. It is the coldness of the cloud that would affect you. It can affect you in three ways: your sight, coughing, and headache."

More specifically, it is the reaction engendered in the contact between human and environment that creates the conditions for the sickness. "It is like fire and water that makes smoke," explains Francisco. "Your body is hot, and the cloud is cold; that causes the problem." The sudden drop in body temperature is the key mechanism, and it is essential that humans avoid emerging too quickly into the cool morning air, which is a particular risk factor. There is potential for evil spirits to be involved as well as the infectious agent. "A spirit can also be in the wind," he says. Manual Choc adds importantly, "Everything has spirits, and the choql may have spirits as well." Lorenzo is more certain: "The spirits are in the mist."

The essential features of choql and any other disorders that might fit into this category are:

- Etiology relates to a human–environment interaction.
- As spirits exist in the elements of the environment, they can be encountered, causing sickness.
- Clouds and mist are considered to be cold, so a disruption in the body's thermal state is a trigger.
- Sickness is caused by a kind of atmospheric infection.

Additional Nosological Dimensions

To delve further into the underlying nosological structure of Q'eqchi' medicine, I invited the iloneleb' to undertake several different pile sorting exercises with the same set of disorders. There proved to be considerable overlap in the sorts for "cause" and "treatment," reinforcing the nosological structure

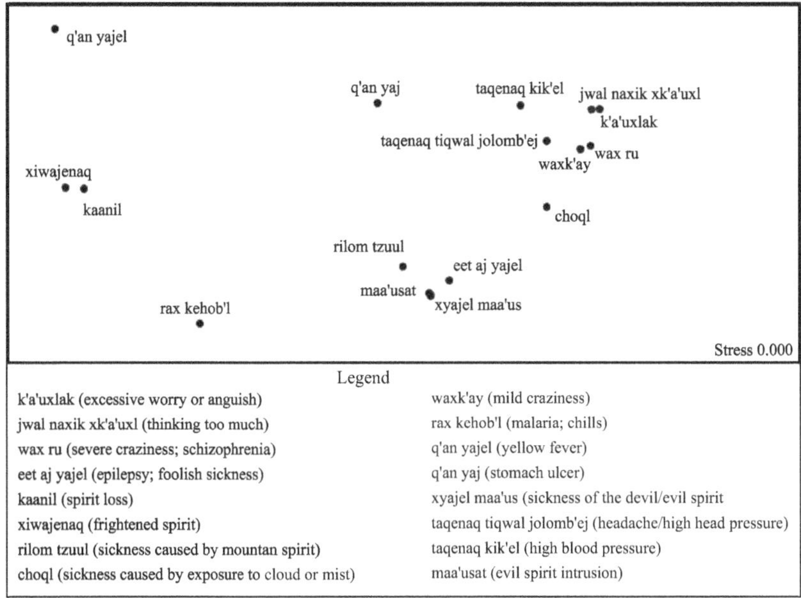

FIGURE 11. Multidimensional scale plot for sickness causation.

that emerged from the similarities exercise, demonstrating coherence and synergy in the medical knowledge system. However, the mapping of the results one upon the other also demonstrates that the categorizations were not rote and that the iloneleb' do indeed distinguish among general similarity, cause, and treatment in the structure and application of their knowledge.

Since so much of the literature on Indigenous medicine suggests that etiology is the main means of categorization, let me present those results first. The results of the multidimensional scaling for causation are shown in Figure 11.

In the upper right we find the psychological, emotional, and mental states disorders largely together (my Categories 1 and 2), as we saw in the multidimensional scaling for similarities. We also see the same clustering of the "Disordered Interpersonal Spiritual States" (Category 3) in the bottom center and "Disordered Personal Spiritual States" (Category 4) on the far left, with the remaining disorders from Categories 5, 6, and 7 somewhat orphaned.

Figure 12 contains the results of the cluster analysis. As causation is multifaceted, it is not surprising that the data here are a little less coherent. In comparison to the similarities sort, we see that two of the three pairs of disorders that emerged in the first level of clustering were the same: k'a'uxlak (excessive worry or anguish)–jwal naxik xk'a'uxl (thinking too much) and wax ru (severe craziness; schizophrenia)–waxk'ay (mild craziness). Joining them as a distinct pair of causation at this first level was kaanil (spirit loss) with xiwajenaq (frightened spirit). Xyajel maa'us (sickness of the devil or evil spirit) joins with maa'usat (evil spirit intrusion) at the second level. Also at the second partition, taqenaq tiqwal jolomb'ej joins with wax ru and waxk'ay, demonstrating the link between headache and mental illness (with the former understood as both a sickness and a cause). Eet aj yajel (epilepsy; the "foolish sickness") and rilom tzuul (sickness caused by the mountain spirit) are paired at the third partition, along with xyajel maa'us and maa'usat, thus defining nicely the "Disordered Interpersonal Spiritual States" nosological category. Also coming together at this third partition are "Disordered Psychological and Emotional States" and "Disordered Mental States" categories.

Rax kehob'l (malaria; chills) and q'an yajel (yellow fever) remain isolated throughout, suggesting the possibility that the role of a vector in causation is understood more latently than overtly; in other words, cause is understood in more subtle ways than I was able to tease out. Q'an yaj (ulcer) and choql (sickness caused by exposure to a cloud or mist) also remain essentially isolated until well into the clustering. These data suggest that disorders in the categories "Disordered Physiological States—Vector," "Disordered Physiological States—Internal," and "Disordered Environmental States" are, in etiological terms, less coherent than disorders in the other groups, and this may reflect that my categories here are less salient.

What is evident is that while there is considerable overlap between the similarities and causation pile sorts, the iloneleb' are not using causation as the sole factor in structuring their nosology. Rather, their knowledge appears to be organized in much more complex, multifaceted ways.

Figure 13 presents the MDS plot from the pile sort for treatment similarity. The figure demonstrates a clustering of disorders according to treatment that is very similar to the previous figure for causation. The "Disordered Psychological and Emotional States" are situated in close proximity to the

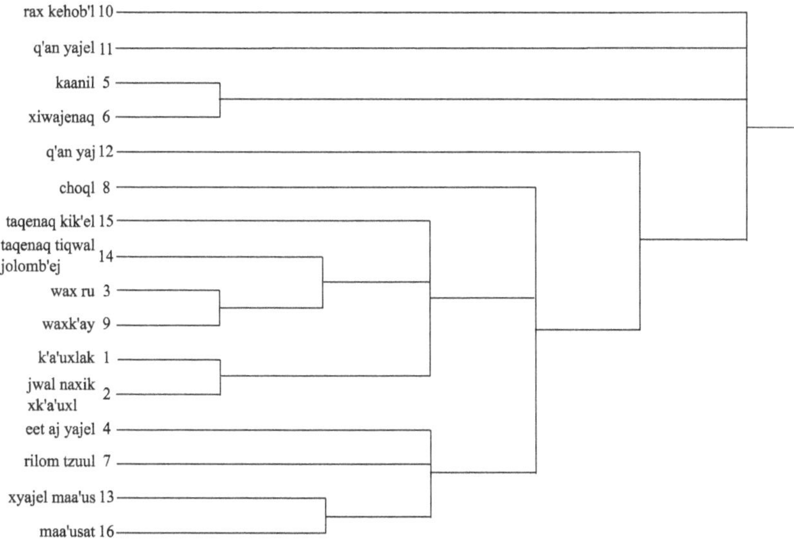

FIGURE 12. Hierarchical cluster analysis for sickness causation.

"Disordered Mental States" on the lower right. The "Disordered Interpersonal Spiritual States" (center) and the "Disordered Personal Spiritual States" (far left) cluster again but remain isolated from each other. And the remaining disorders appear free-floating. These observations are confirmed in the cluster analysis for treatment, as seen in Figure 14.

Figure 14 shows that the "Disordered Personal Spiritual States" (kaanil and xiwajenaq) cluster immediately, along with two of the "thinking" disorders (k'a'uxlak and jwal naxik xk'a'uxl) in the "Disordered Psychological and Emotional States" category and two in the "Disordered Interpersonal Spiritual States" category (xyajel maa'us and maa'usat). By the third partition, all four disorders in the "Disordered Interpersonal Spiritual States" category have come together, as have most of the disorders in the "Disordered Psychological and Emotional States" and "Disordered Mental States" categories. Yet again we see that disorders of personal and interpersonal spiritual states remain apart from each other, suggesting that despite the apparent "spiritual" connection, treatment is unique for each set.

The pile sort data for prayer yielded similar results. Figure 15 confirms that

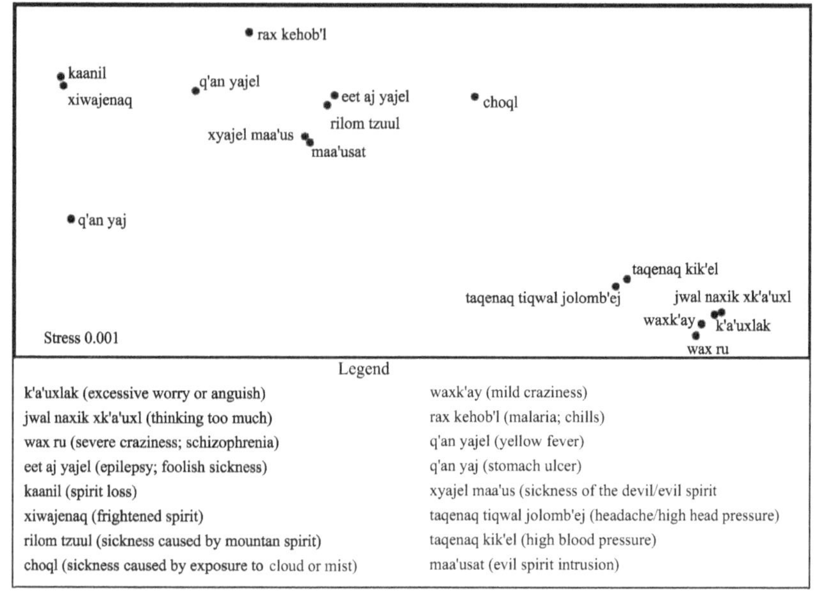

FIGURE 13. Multidimensional scale plot for sickness treatment.

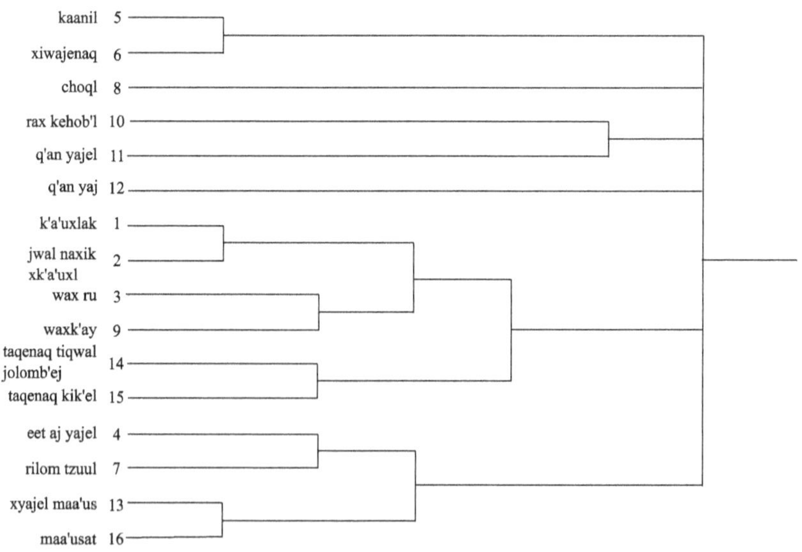

FIGURE 14. Hierarchical cluster analysis for sickness treatment.

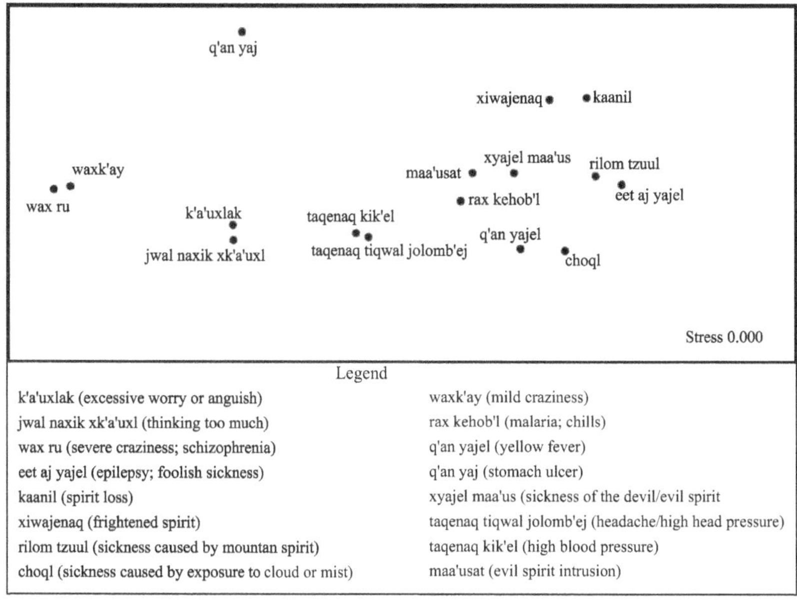

FIGURE 15. Multidimensional scale plot for sickness prayer similarity.

disorders of psychological and emotional states, and those of mental states, occupy the left side, demonstrating the clear break between these and the other disorders. Similarly, disorders of spiritual states are gathered on the right side of the scale. The latter suggests that the prayers employed in their treatment bear some similarity, underscoring their meta/material connection even though they are typically distinct in the other ways shown above.

The hierarchical cluster analysis echoes this finding. What is striking here is that by the second partition, all four of the most analytically robust nosological categories (1 to 4) have formed. Figure 16 also shows how the "Disordered Mental States" category does not this time join with the "Disordered Psychological and Emotional States" category in a meaningful way, reflecting their distance in the multidimensional scale and suggesting that combining these two into a single category (that is, mental health) would be premature. Also notable is that the disorders in the "Disordered Interpersonal Spiritual States" and "Disordered Psychological and Emotional States" categories cluster quite quickly into distinct groups, in both cases in the second partition.

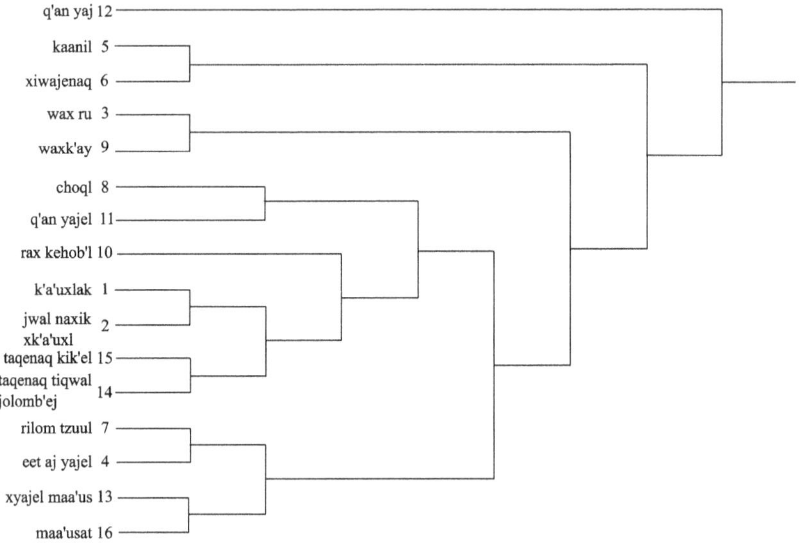

FIGURE 16. Hierarchical cluster analysis for sickness prayer similarity.

This is in contrast to the treatment analysis, where it was not until later, in the third partition, that they come together, suggesting that treatment is not synonymous with prayer but rather that these are both more nuanced.

Combining data from three pile sorts of similarity, causation, and treatment confirms the broad analysis generated from each individual pile sort. The multidimensional scale plot is in Figure 17. The distinction between the psychological, emotional, and mental disorders, on the lower left, and the interpersonal and personal spiritual disorders, on the upper and far right, respectively, is palpable. However, also significant is that interpersonal spiritual and personal spiritual disorders still remain distinct from each other and that the remaining four disorders are less connected to the other categories or to each other.

A different kind of sorting exercise was done on the matter of seriousness, presented as a simple dichotomous exercise in which "more serious" disorders were separated from "less serious" disorders to understand the structure of prognosis. The mechanism operative here, as it became apparent in the

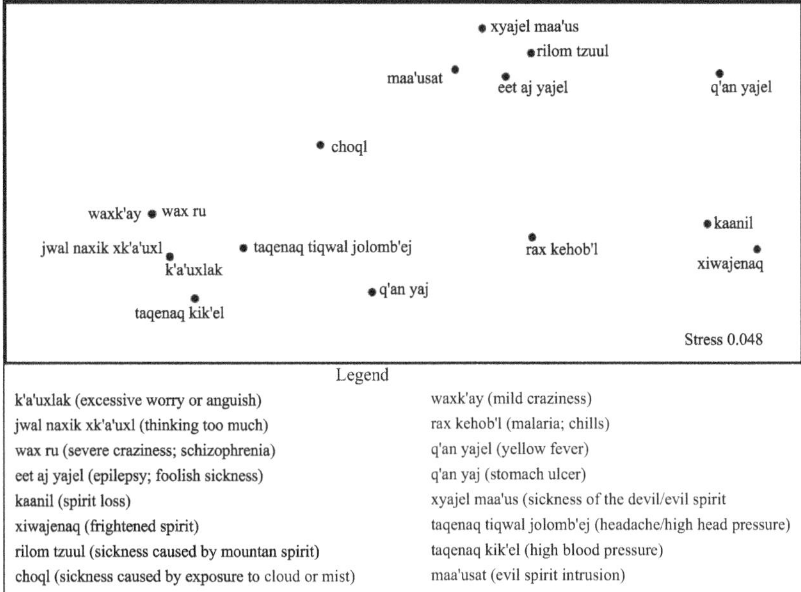

FIGURE 17. Multidimensional scale plot for sickness similarity, causation, and treatment combined.

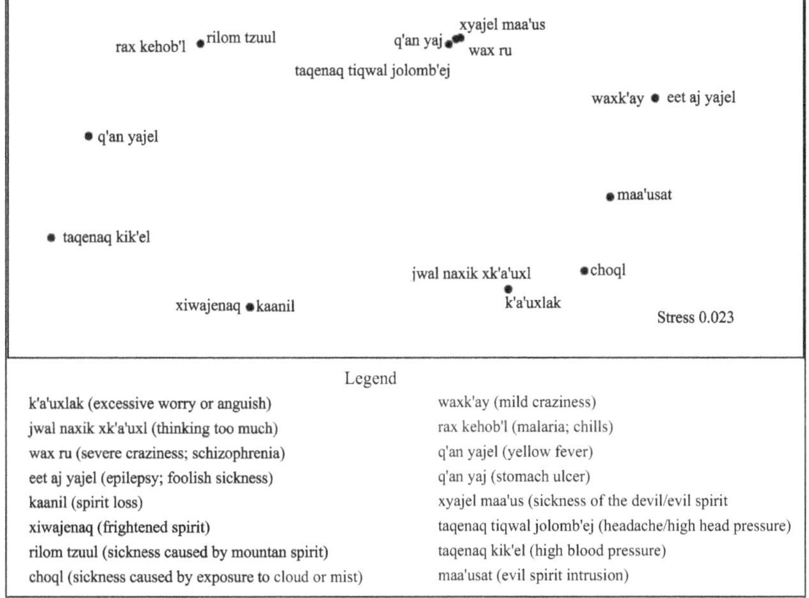

FIGURE 18. Multidimensional scale plot for sickness seriousness.

follow-up interviews, related to either the distinct possibility of death or the possibility that a less serious disorder could develop into a fatal one if left untreated. The analysis reveals very different results than other analyses, as disorders that were clustered together in the previous sorts are recombined with disorders that are often very different. Figure 18 provides the multidimensional scale analysis of these data.

Seriousness in this figure is on the vertical axis, with the less serious disorders near the lower end of the scale and more serious disorders nearer the top. It is evident that the iloneleb' make nuanced prognostic judgments according to a variety of criteria and are not just applying in a rote manner their understanding of other nosological factors, such as cause. Very similar disorders, such as wax ru and waxk'ay, are in part distinguished by prognosis. Further, not all spiritual disorders are equally serious; nor are all psychological and emotional disorders. Some simply have better likely outcomes than others, and treatment is often appropriately applied according to prognosis, in part to prevent a turn toward a more serious disorder. Disorders that so far have never been positioned near each other, such as rax kehob'l and rilom tzuul, come together only because of their perceived seriousness. In general, however, these data suggest that less serious disorders are more likely to be found in the "Disordered Psychological and Emotional States" and "Disordered Personal Spiritual States" categories, and the more serious disorders in the "Disordered Mental States," "Disordered Interpersonal Spiritual States," and "Disordered Physiological States—Vector-Related" categories. In other words, iloneleb' distinguish between psychological/emotional states and mental states, and between personal and interpersonal spiritual states, in determining seriousness, suggesting an invocation of deeply informed nuance rather than simplistic, categorical, or "recipe" thought.

Assessing *Ilonel* (Practitioner) Agreement

Obviously, agreement is an important consideration in any effort to elucidate a cognitive system. Agreement is especially pertinent here because the iloneleb' have had different training and clinical experiences, and only in recent years, with the formation of their association, have they taken the opportunity to meet as a group to discuss sickness and its treatment and to begin to learn directly from each other. Emilio and Francisco, as both medical practitioners and Guia Espiritual Maya, simply have greater knowledge and experience, and this is recognized by the other iloneleb' and the broader Q'eqchi' community in Belize and Guatemala. This plays out in important ways in understanding consensus.

Table 1 presents the agreement matrix for similarities. The high eigenratio indicates a good fit to the consensus model: there is significant agreement among the iloneleb'. We can see here that agreement varies, expectedly, with the highest levels of agreement being among Manuel Baki, Manuel Choc, and Lorenzo Choc. The lowest level of agreement is, perhaps surprisingly, between Francisco and Emilio, the two most experienced iloneleb'. Overall, we see in Table 2 that these two have the lowest competence scores. Keep in mind that these scores describe how well individual responses correspond with those of the group as a whole. They are not interpreted as the proportion of answers that an individual gets "correct."

TABLE 1. Practitioner Consensus Agreement Matrix for Similarities

	FRANCISCO CAAL	MANUEL CHOC	LORENZO CHOC	MANUEL BAKI	EMILIO KAL
FRANCISCO CAAL	1.00	0.78	0.77	0.83	0.67
MANUEL CHOC	0.78	1.00	0.85	0.92	0.82
LORENZO CHOC	0.77	0.85	1.00	0.93	0.83
MANUEL BAKI	0.83	0.92	0.93	1.00	0.83
EMILIO KAL	0.67	0.82	0.83	0.83	1.00

Eigenratio: 6.15

TABLE 2. Competence Scores for Similarities

PRACTITIONER	COMPETENCE SCORE
Francisco Caal	0.821
Manuel Choc	0.932
Lorenzo Choc	0.939
Manuel Baki	0.990
Emilio Kal	0.856

The pattern for causation agreement is a little different, as Table 3 demonstrates. Here we see that Manuel Choc has the lowest paired levels of agreement, with Francisco and Manuel Baki, and that the agreement between Francisco and Emilio remains relatively low. Manuel Choc's competence score in Table 4 is also the lowest.

TABLE 3. Practitioner Consensus Agreement Matrix for Causation

	FRANCISCO CAAL	MANUEL CHOC	LORENZO CHOC	MANUEL BAKI	EMILIO KAL
FRANCISCO CAAL	1.00	0.48	0.70	0.82	0.67
MANUEL CHOC	0.48	1.00	0.78	0.53	0.78
LORENZO CHOC	0.70	0.78	1.00	0.75	0.83
MANUEL BAKI	0.82	0.53	0.75	1.00	0.68
EMILIO KAL	0.67	0.78	0.83	0.68	1.00

Eigenratio: 8.28

TABLE 4. Competence Scores for Causation

PRACTITIONER	COMPETENCE SCORE
Francisco Caal	0.781
Manuel Choc	0.758
Lorenzo Choc	0.940
Manuel Baki	0.822
Emilio Kal	0.896

The greatest degree of agreement among the iloneleb' can be found in their pile sorts according to treatment similarity. Table 5 presents the consensus agreement data. This extensive agreement among the iloneleb' is highlighted by complete agreement between Francisco and Manuel Choc. The competence scores are correspondingly high, as Table 6 shows.

Overall, in terms of the three main pile sorting exercises—similarities, causation, and treatment—there is strong evidence of significant agreement among the iloneleb'. Although they trained independently of one another,

TABLE 5. Practitioner Consensus Agreement Matrix for Treatment

	FRANCISCO CAAL	MANUEL CHOC	LORENZO CHOC	MANUEL BAKI	EMILIO KAL
FRANCISCO CAAL	1.00	1.00	0.88	0.73	0.87
MANUEL CHOC	1.00	1.00	0.88	0.73	0.87
LORENZO CHOC	0.88	0.88	1.00	0.72	0.75
MANUEL BAKI	0.73	0.73	0.72	1.00	0.87
EMILIO KAL	0.87	0.87	0.75	0.87	1.00

Eigenratio: 14.51

TABLE 6. Competence Scores for Treatment

PRACTITIONER	COMPETENCE SCORE
Francisco Caal	0.975
Manuel Choc	0.975
Lorenzo Choc	0.880
Manuel Baki	0.812
Emilio Kal	0.916

with different masters and often in different regions of Guatemala and Belize, what emerges here is indicative of a coherent medical system shared throughout the Q'eqchi' region. However, we also see that the two most experienced iloneleb', Francisco and Emilio, often demonstrate lower competency scores than the others, suggesting that their knowledge is significantly different from the other three. Yet the degree of agreement between Francisco and Emilio is often (relatively) quite low in comparison to the others, in particular in the similarities and causation data. So not only are they distinct from the others, but they are somewhat distinct from each other, and this may explain how they determine who is best able to help a patient when they are working together. Figure 19, the multidimensional scale plot for similarities by practitioner, shows in stark fashion this pattern.

There is also evidence of the "art" of Q'eqchi' medicine when we look at the consensus data for prayer similarity in Table 7, where we see relatively low

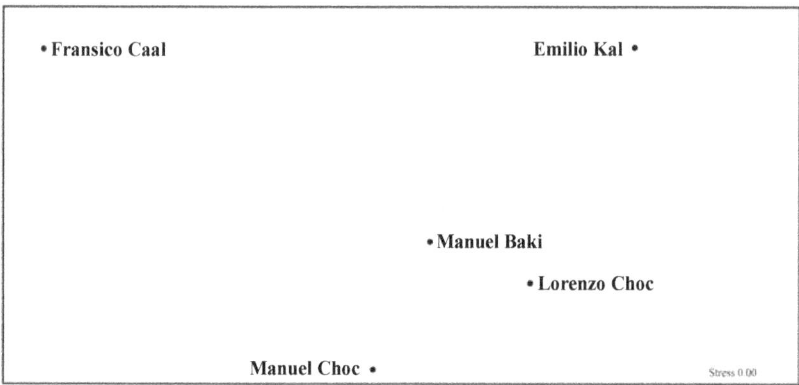

FIGURE 19. Multidimensional scale plot for similarities by *ilonel.*

degrees of agreement. The difference between the treatment data and the prayer data suggests that while prayer is an essential element of treatment, each ilonel has their own approach to prayer use, and further that the iloneleb' understand treatment to be multifaceted. Clearly, some other factors are at work in the distinctions made throughout the pile sort exercise.

TABLE 7. Practitioner Consensus Agreement Matrix for Prayers

	FRANCISCO CAAL	LORENZO CHOC	MANUEL BAKI	EMILIO KAL
FRANCISCO CAAL	1.00	0.32	0.53	0.43
LORENZO CHOC	0.32	1.00	0.38	0.28
MANUEL BAKI	0.53	0.38	1.00	0.43
EMILIO KAL	0.43	0.28	0.43	1.00

Eigenratio: 31.89

The relatively low degree of agreement on prayers results in somewhat lower competence scores, especially for Lorenzo and Emilio. See Table 8.

Finally, let us look at the consensus data for thermal properties, shown in Table 9, where four iloneleb' were asked to sort the sixteen disorders into four possible categories: hot, cold, neither, or both (depending on context).

TABLE 8. Competence Scores for Prayers

PRACTITIONER	COMPETENCE SCORE
Francisco Caal	0.704
Lorenzo Choc	0.480
Manuel Baki	0.758
Emilio Kal	0.592

TABLE 9. Practitioner Consensus Agreement Matrix for Thermal Properties

	FRANCISCO CAAL	MANUEL CHOC	LORENZO CHOC	EMILIO KAL
FRANCISCO CAAL	1.00	0.03	0.03	0.12
MANUEL CHOC	0.03	1.00	0.30	0.08
LORENZO CHOC	0.03	0.30	1.00	-0.02
EMILIO KAL	0.12	0.08	-0.02	1.00

Eigenratio: 0.601

Several important observations can me made here. There is no strong agreement among the iloneleb' regarding thermal properties; the weak eigenratio indicates a lack of fit to the consensus model. This observation is compatible with research that indicates that thermal qualities often play a minor role in classification (e.g., Tedlock 1987), suggesting both that other factors may be more important in how sickness is conceptualized and that knowledge, experience, and context are significant in the interpretation of these disorders. Emilio, recognized as the most knowledgeable of the iloneleb', identified almost half of the disorders as being potentially both hot and cold, and in the interviews he expounded on the contextual basis for making such determination. For instance, in the case of choql, he considered specific symptoms rather than offering a rote, categorical determination, stating, "It's cold, but at times headache can affect him as well, so we say it's both." Several disorders were considered to have no thermal properties whatsoever by at least one ilonel.

Conclusion

The structure and nosology of the Q'eqchi' medical system detailed here is not necessarily the structure of *the* Q'eqchi' medical system; there is no reason to believe that such a singular structure would exist in such a dynamic system. It is a structure that emerges from the analysis and is clearly a product of a host of factors: the particular iloneleb' involved, the methods used and ability of iloneleb' to understand and execute the tasks, the sixteen disorders selected, and so on. As I noted in the introduction, my assumption is that Indigenous knowledge systems such as that of the Q'eqchi' are fluid and contextual rather than fixed or rigid, and therefore even the addition of one more ilonel could potentially impact this particular structure. We need to appreciate that a dynamic system, which is inherently cognitive and contextually, historically, and experientially based, informs Q'eqchi' medical practice, including diagnosis and treatment. Both the "art" and the empiricism in Q'eqchi' medicine are apparent.

That said, what we see here are several important patterns. There is a clear distinction between disorders of psychological, emotional, and mental states, and those of spiritual states. With respect to the former, mental states ("craziness") seem distinct from the "thinking" and depression/anxiety disorders. With respect to the spiritual disorders, those involving interpersonal states, where something happens *to* the individual from the application of an external force, are clearly understood differently than personal spiritual states, where the problem lies with an internal element of the individual being affected or lost. Several disorders were understood to be primarily physiological, and I draw the distinction between those caused by specific external vectors and those caused by internal disruptions.

There is strong evidence of agreement among the iloneleb' in evidence here, suggesting that the medical system of which they are a part experiences a kind of ongoing centripetal or involutionary force on knowledge, despite their isolated training and practice. It is also evident that iloneleb' practice is much less based on the application of formulaic, "recipe" notions of thermal principles than is often thought, although as we shall see in the latter parts of this book, these thermal disorders remain central to their understanding and treatment. I would propose that the idea of thermal properties—of sicknesses and of medicines—provides an organizational framework through which sickness can be approached and ordered in a complex world full of challenges to health and means to restore it but that effectiveness of treatment ultimately lies elsewhere. So too is the case with prayer. The Q'eqchi' medical system is not arbitrary in the sense that each distinct sickness must have a distinct prayer associated with it, one that is part of the medical canon. It is the *idea* of the prayer, and the basic notions contained therein, that seems to be therapeutically engaged—not the specific content of prayers.

Finally, the data suggest that the iloneleb' in this research represent different kinds of practitioners. Manuel Choc, Manuel Baki, and Lorenzo Choc seem to share similar knowledge and are what we might call "general practitioners." Their practice tends to be local. Francisco Caal and Emilio Kal, however, are clearly specialists, although not necessarily of the same kind. Their greater knowledge and experience are reflected in their separateness from the others, characterized by greater attention to context and nuance, precisely what one would expect of specialists. The fact that they are called upon to attend patients throughout Belize and Guatemala attests to their status.

CHAPTER 5

The Diagnostic Process

CLINICAL DIAGNOSIS WITHIN Q'eqchi' medicine involves three interrelated assessments that engage both the material and meta/material aspects of sickness. These are narrative, signs and symptoms, and the blood/prayer/pulse triad. Unlike some other Maya groups (e.g., Fabrega 1970), diagnosis for the Q'eqchi' iloneleb' is not usually separate or distinct from treatment, involving different practitioners or locales. Rather, there is a somewhat seamless flow, back and forth, between diagnosis and treatment, depending on the sickness. Indeed, the distinction between diagnosis, treatment, and the assessment of effectiveness is quite fluid. The ilonel constantly assesses a diagnosis in reference to certain signs that the treatment is working, and contrary signs are taken as indications of an incorrect diagnosis. In this chapter, I focus on the diagnostic process, and in the next I describe Q'eqchi' medical treatment and assessment of outcomes.

Narrative Diagnostics

Since some sicknesses are clearly related to specific contexts or experiences of the patient's life, iloneleb' will typically explore these if they have indications that a diathetic or an event-related sickness is the issue. As discussed previously, Q'eqchi' diathesis is centered on notions of nawal and maatan, the strength of one's energy or spirit, and one's destiny according to the Maya calendar. These are essential data for those iloneleb' trained specifically in these complex diagnostic areas. For these specialists, any diagnosis must be filtered through the lens of nawal and maatan to properly understand the signs and symptoms of any patient's sickness. For iloneleb' lacking this training, emphasis is placed more on situational or experiential aspects of the sickness.

In my observations of treatment sessions, as well as in the reports of iloneleb', Q'eqchi' patients are not elaborate storytellers. Nonetheless, understanding if there has been an incident of some kind is important to the process of differential diagnosis. Francisco, after treating a patient with stomach pain that could be q'an yaj (ulcer or stomach "sores"), admits that, "Yes, I have to know by asking him if he has fallen in a creek, river, or on land. If no, that means hunger caused it." While stomach pain is a strong indicator of q'an yaj, as discussed earlier, Francisco understands that a fall can cause a similar symptom but indicate a very different, potentially more serious disorder. Missing a meal and losing one's spirit have similar stomach symptoms but cause very different sicknesses.

Many sicknesses can result from an experience, be it a fall, an encounter with a snake or other animal, or something less dramatic, like walking out into the morning mist or taking a cold drink or bath on a hot day. Even experiences of a pregnant woman can imprint on the developing fetus and create a disorder for the newborn, as in the case of awas. Typically, with falls or encounters by (nonpregnant) adults, there is a delay of several days before symptoms begin, and patient memories fade. So while patient reports are an important aspect of the diagnostic procedure, they are often incomplete or inaccurate. One of the characteristics of Q'eqchi' diagnostics is iloneleb' skepticism about the ability of patients to relay accurate information. Manuel Choc describes the problem thusly:

> Most of the time when the questions are asked, in terms of if the person has fallen down, if the person has fever or something, or where the person has been for a certain number of days. . . . Most of time these questions are not really reliable in terms of what the sickness is. They are not really, because most of the time the sickness would be related to other events. Oftentimes, the patients would not really remember if they fell down or had a fever or something. So it is the responsibility of the ilonel to feel the blood pulse, do the massage, to detect what sickness this person has.

The hallmark of this aspect of diagnosis is the relating of the story of an experience that identifies to the ilonel an etiological incident. This is not a narrative in the sense that this concept is typically used in medical anthropology (e.g., Mattingly 1994, 1998a, 1998b; Waldram 2012b). Emplotment is slim if extant at all, and the narrative tends to take the form of a relating of precise, factual events.[1] The practitioner may call upon the patient to reflect about past experiences, searching for the one that is the cause of the sickness. Simply put, Q'eqchi' patients do not typically tell stories about their sicknesses. This would contrast significantly with Harvey's (2013:96) description of the clinical "polyphonic" nature of K'iche' Maya treatment in Guatemala, where narrative is essential to diagnosis. What the disclosures by these Q'eqchi' patients do is identify to the ilonel, as much as possible and in specific instances, a likely occurrence and locale that are involved in the sickness in some manner; this is important because the treatment may necessitate a return to that locale, one of the few ways in which the diagnostic and treatment processes are temporally distinct.

Diagnosis by Signs and Symptoms

The first information that the ilonel obtains regarding a patient is typically associated with the initial request to consult. The patient may visit the ilonel or send a communication via a family member, requesting medical services. Typically, some information about the nature of the problem is provided, usually a brief detailing of symptoms. This gives the ilonel some sense of the kind of preparation that may be needed, including which medicinal plants should be acquired and whether the ilonel's abstinence is necessary (in which case the treatment will not occur for several days).[2]

As detailed above with respect to narrative, Q'eqchi' patients are not known to offer elaborate details on their symptoms, and quite typically one hears from them that a "real" practitioner should be able to determine the sickness without such reports. Further, the ilonel may not inquire in any meaningful way, accepting, as the patient does, that he has the ability to discern the sickness without patient input (Waldram 2015b). In particular, the blood pulse diagnostic is especially effective for many disorders. "It is not necessary to ask," explains Manuel Choc, referring to a suspected case of sickness caused by a tuul, or witch. "You can detect what is wrong with the person by just checking the blood pulse."

But typically, some report is offered at the time of treatment, and it assists in the process, even if it is fractured, generalized, or incomplete. Pain, headache, dizziness, fever, chills, gastrointestinal complaints, and emotional problems such as anxiety tend to be the chief complaints raised with the iloneleb'.

As an augment to the pile sort exercise, iloneleb' were asked to detail the signs and symptoms of the sixteen disorders used. The results are shown in Table 10. Together, the data demonstrate the typical signs and symptoms of each disorder and which have the most elaborate presentation and possibly are better known. Visual inspection of the table demonstrates that some disorders are particularly well developed, with high degrees of ilonel agreement, but idiosyncrasies are also evident, reflective of unique clinical understandings. Disorders of the psychological and emotional states, and the mental states, present signs and symptoms that are primarily psychological or behavioral. However, there is also recognition of somatic components. For instance, headache, fever, chest pains, and high blood pressure may also be noticed. Somatic signs and symptoms are clearly prominent in the other disorders. The physiological disorders have signs and symptoms that are almost entirely somatic. Disorders of interpersonal spiritual states, disorders of personal spiritual states, and the lone disorder of environmental states have signs and symptoms that are entirely somatic.

What these data clearly suggest is that the iloneleb' are very much in tune with the somatic, physiological aspects of most of these disorders, including those that are understood to be fundamentally psychological or mental. Understanding these psychological issues to have physiological components suggests some support for the mind-body holism thesis. But across all the disorders there is no clear union of the mind and body, as the holism thesis would suggest there should be, at least at the level of the material engagement of these disorders.

The idiosyncrasies evident in Table 10 demonstrate variability in sign and symptom assignment. Some iloneleb' identify significantly more signs and symptoms than others. Francisco, for instance, lists seventy-six signs and symptoms across the sixteen disorders, more than double that listed by Manuel Choc. Clinical experience is important of course, and the more experience an ilonel has with a particular problem, the easier it is to recognize. Francisco, treating a case of taqenaq tiqwal jolomb'ej (headache or high head pressure), notes, "I have many patients who suffer from this

TABLE 10. Free Listing of Signs and Symptoms by Disorder and *Ilonel*

SIGNS/SYMPTOMS	DISORDERS															
	1	2	3	4	5	6	7	8	9	10	11	12	13	14	15	16
fever/ feels hot (subjective)		LC	MB	FC EK LC MB MC	FC EK LC MB MC	FC EK LC MB MC	FC MB	FC LC	MB	FC EK MB MC	FC LC MB	FC MC	FC LC MB	FC MB	FC MC	FC EK LC MB
chills		LC	LC	FC LC	EK LC MB	FC EK LC MB	LC	LC	MB	FC EK MB MC	FC EK LC	FC	FC LC	MB	FC	FC EK LC
stomach pain			FC LC	LC	LC	LC	LC	LC	LC	LC	FC LC	FC EK LC MB MC	LC	LC		LC
body pain/ cramps				MB						FC MC	FC	FC			FC	
eye pain								LC MB								FC
diarrhea			FC	FC EK	FC EK MC	FC MC				FC		MB				
vomiting	EK LC MB	FC LC MB MC	EKL CM B	FC LC MB MC	FC EK LC MB MC	FC EK LC MB MC	FC EK LC	FC EK LC MB MC	EK LC MB	EK LC MB	FC EK LC	FC MC	FC LC	FC EK LC MB MC	FC EK LC MB	FC LC
seizure/ body contortions				FC LC MB FC	LC	LC	FC EK MC MB						LC	LC	FC	EK MC
fatigue/ weakness				EK		FC EK					EK MC					
weight loss				EK						FC	FC LC	FC				
vision problems		LC		LC	LC	LC		FC EK MB MC			LC		LC	LC	FC	
yellow complexion		LC	LC	LC	LC	LC	LC	LC	LC	FC LC	FC EK LC MB			LC		LC
											MC					
other complexion										MB		FC LC	LC MC		FC MB	
speech problems				LC				MB					LC			LC

TABLE 10. Free Listing of Signs and Symptoms by Disorder and *Ilonel (continued)*

SIGNS/SYMPTOMS	DISORDERS															
	1	2	3	4	5	6	7	8	9	10	11	12	13	14	15	16
infection/ swelling/ inflammation									FC				FC LC			
rash/sores													FC LC			
cough				FC				FC LC MC		FC	FC					
insomnia														FC		
loss of appetite	FC			FC		FC				MB	FC MB					
photophobia								FC			EK					
chest pains		LC MB														
high blood pressure			FC LC MC													
worry	FC EK LC MB	LC MB														
"thinking too much"	MB	FC MB MC												MC	MC	
paranoia/ hysteria/ running away			FC EK LC MB MC													
talking to self	MB								FC EK LC							
concentration problems		EK							FC							
hallucinations			FC						EK LC							
"acting crazy"									FC LC							
flat affect	FC	MC														
agitated		LC												EK	EK	
sadness	FC			EK							FC					

Legend: Disorders

1. k'a'uxlak (excessive worry or anguish)
2. jwal naxik xk'a'uxl (thinking too much)
3. wax ru (severe craziness; schizophrenia)
4. eet aj yajel (epilepsy; the foolish sickness)
5. kaanil (spirit loss)
6. xiwajenaq (frightened spirit)
7. rilom tzuul (sickness caused by mountain spirit)
8. choql (sickness caused by exposure to cloud or mist)
9. waxk'ay (mild craziness)
10. rax kehob'l (malaria; chills)
11. q'an yajel (yellow fever)
12. q'an yaj (stomach ulcer)
13. xyajel maa'us (sickness of the devil)
14. taqenaq tiqwal jolomb'ej (headache; high head pressure)
15. taqenaq kik'el (high blood pressure)
16. maa'usat (evil spirit intrusion)

Legend: Practitioners

FC: Francisco Caal
MC: Manuel Choc
LC: Lorenzo Choc
MB: Manuel Baki
EK: Emilio Kal

problem. I only need to hear of the symptoms, and I already know what is the problem."

The actual physical state of the patient often gives clues, to varying degrees of certainty, as to the appropriate diagnosis. Simply put, as in biomedicine, some disorders are easily apparent through superficial examination, such as by looking at the patient. A good example of this is q'an yajel, or yellow fever, a disorder that biomedical practitioners also recognize readily by appearance (Costandi 2011). Certain sicknesses can be diagnosed reliably simply through observational examination of the patient: how they look or their behavior. Others require more detailed diagnostics. Emilio Kal and Manuel Choc identify such sicknesses from the list of sixteen disorders in Table 11, agreeing on eleven of them.

TABLE 11. Diagnosable Disorders through Observational Criteria

NOSOLOGICAL CATEGORY	DISORDER	EMILIO KAL	MANUEL CHOC
Psychological and Emotional States	k'a'uxlak (excessive worry or anguish)		
	jwal naxik xk'a'uxl (thinking too much)		X
	taqenaq tiqwal jolomb'ej (headache/high head pressure)		
	taqenaq kik'el (high blood pressure)	X	X
Mental States	wax ru (severe craziness)	X	X
	waxk'ay (mild craziness)	X	X
Interpersonal Spiritual States	eet aj yajel (epilepsy; the "foolish sickness")	X	X
	rilom tzuul (sickness caused by the mountain spirit)	X	
	xyajel maa'us (sickness of the devil or evil spirit; sometimes glossed as a form of epilepsy)	X	
	maa'usat (evil spirit intrusion)	X	
Personal Spiritual States	kaanil (spirit loss; sometimes glossed as a form of susto)		
	xiwajenaq (frightened spirit)		
Physiological States	q'an yajel (yellow fever)	X	X
	rax kehob'l (malaria; chills)	X	X
	q'an yaj (stomach ulcer)	X	X
Environmental States	choql (sickness caused by exposure to clouds or mist)		

Although only two iloneleb' were involved in this exercise, the other iloneleb' at different times also identified certain sicknesses that were readily observable, and overall these data still resonate with the broader understanding of the nosological system, in particular with respect to disorders that have obvious physical manifestations. For instance, both iloneleb' agreed that all three disorders of physiological states, as well as "high blood pressure," can often be diagnosed through observation alone. They also agreed that both forms of "craziness," as well as classical epilepsy, where the physical manifestations of a relapse are dramatic, also require no further investigation. For instance, Francisco explains that with wax ru, "you don't have to diagnose the sickness but rather just do the treatment. Some crazy people don't allow diagnosis because they would fight back." Only after the treatment has been initiated and the patient is calmer can any more treatment ensue. The initial goal is to calm the patient. This would suggest that even though there is a spiritual component, iloneleb' are well in tune with the material aspects of these disorders, which they recognize as central to their respective diagnoses. Emilio's unique ability to diagnose all four of the disorders of interpersonal spiritual states through observation alone reflects his deeper knowledge and training as a Guia Espiritual Maya.

To dig deeper into the diagnostic process, I arranged certain signs and symptoms into variable sets that could be suggestive of a variety of different sicknesses and requested the iloneleb' to offer a diagnosis. I chose sets that I believed would reflect known physical and psychological issues; those readers who are biomedically inclined will no doubt recognize some possible sicknesses. In doing this I was acutely aware that this is *not* how iloneleb' actually diagnose, and this chapter in totality seeks to explain the dynamic process in which they engage. Nonetheless, this represents an effort to understand the role that material and meta/material signs and symptoms play in the diagnosis of sickness and to further uncover the extent to which there is agreement among the iloneleb'. While as part of this exercise I requested information on sickness names, etiology, treatment, prayers used, pulse characteristics, and thermal properties, in Table 12 I present only the data for names and thermal properties. In addition, however, I assign each sickness to a nosological category as determined in the previous chapter. In some cases this was self-evident; when the sickness identified was one actually used in the pile sort tests from which the nosology was derived, I accessed the other information to affirm. In other cases though, the other information offered, especially etiology, was used more directly to help identify the appropriate category, especially since the sickness name could be somewhat misleading if taken literally (and some sicknesses have several local names), and some names were sign or symptom descriptions rather than sickness labels per se. Table 12 presents nine of the total of fifteen such cases to demonstrate a variety of features of the diagnostic process.

TABLE 12. Hypothetical Sickness Diagnosis

DISORDER 1: SADNESS, INSOMNIA, CRYING, FATIGUE, LOSS OF APPETITE					
	Francisco Caal	**Manuel Choc**	**Manuel Baki**	**Lorenzo Choc**	**Emilio Kal**
NAME	maak'a' xmaatan (no luck, worry)	k'a'uxlak (worry)	ra xch'ool'ej (hurt heart, sadness)	No specific name (very emotional)	po'ol xk'a'uxl (disturbed mind, worry)
THERMAL PROPERTY	cold	hot	hot	hot	hot
NOSOLOGICAL CATEGORY	1	1	1	1	1
DISORDER 2: HEARING VOICES, TALKS TO SELF, LAUGHS BY SELF, SEES PEOPLE WHO ARE NOT THERE					
	Francisco Caal	**Manuel Choc**	**Manuel Baki**	**Lorenzo Choc**	**Emilio Kal**
NAME	wax ru (severe craziness)	tont aj yajel ("foolish sickness")	roksimbil xjolom (affected head/mind)	wax ru (severe craziness)	waxk'ay (mild craziness)
THERMAL PROPERTY	hot	hot	hot	hot	hot
NOSOLOGICAL CATEGORY	2	1	3	2	2
DISORDER 3: CRYING A LOT, SADNESS, FEELING LONELY					
	Francisco Caal	**Manuel Choc**	**Manuel Baki**	**Lorenzo Choc**	**Emilio Kal**
NAME	q'un xch'ool (weak soul, weak mind from birth)	awas yajel (spirit sickness, mentally disabled from birth)	k'a'uxlak (worry)	does not know sickness	po'bil k'a'uxl (disturbed mind, mind not settled, worry)
THERMAL PROPERTY	cold	hot	hot		hot
NOSOLOGICAL CATEGORY	2	2	1		1

DISORDER 4: PAIN IN CHEST, DIFFICULTY BREATHING					
	Francisco Caal	**Manuel Choc**	**Manuel Baki**	**Lorenzo Choc**	**Emilio Kal**
NAME	tib'l aam (pain in heart, heart attack)	ke aj muchkej (cold body cramps)	muchkej (body cramps)	muchkej kik' ("cramps in blood," "blood ache")	may (pain, body aches)
THERMAL PROPERTY	hot	cold	cold	cold	hot
NOSOLOGICAL CATEGORY	5	5	5	5	6

DISORDER 5: FEVER, SORE THROAT, COUGH, BODY ACHES					
	Francisco Caal	**Manuel Choc**	**Manuel Baki**	**Lorenzo Choc**	**Emilio Kal**
NAME	muchkej (body cramps, aches)	ojb' (cough)	jolomb'ej (head cold)	kaq jolomb'ej (fever, head cold)	choql (sickness caused by exposure to clouds or mist)
THERMAL PROPERTY	Cold	cold	cold	cold	hot
NOSOLOGICAL CATEGORY	5/6	5	6	6	6

DISORDER 6: DIARRHEA, VOMITING, STOMACH PAIN					
	Francisco Caal	**Manuel Choc**	**Manuel Baki**	**Lorenzo Choc**	**Emilio Kal**
NAME	kaanil (spirit loss, susto)	ha'sa'il ("devilish water," bad water consumed); or tib'l sa' (stomach pain)	k'otakil (diarrhea)	ha'sa'il ("devilish water," bad water consumed)	kaanil (spirit loss, susto) or xiwajenaq (frightened spirit)
THERMAL PROPERTY	cold	cold	cold	cold	hot
NOSOLOGICAL CATEGORY	4	5	5	5	4

TABLE 12 (*CONTINUED*)

DISORDER 7: WEIGHT LOSS, FATIGUE, LOSS OF APPETITE, PALE COMPLEXION					
	Francisco Caal	**Manuel Choc**	**Manuel Baki**	**Lorenzo Choc**	**Emilio Kal**
NAME	empacho (indigestion)	nume' sa' (weight loss, diarrhea)	t'anenaq se' ha' (fall in water, with fright)	ya xchiké ix sa' ("shaken insides," fall)	xiwajenaq se'ha' (frightened spirit from fall in water) or t'anenaq se' ha'
THERMAL PROPERTY	cold	hot	cold	cold	cold
NOSOLOGICAL CATEGORY	5	5	4	5	4

DISORDER 8: COUGHING UP BLOOD					
	Francisco Caal	**Manuel Choc**	**Manuel Baki**	**Lorenzo Choc**	**Emilio Kal**
NAME	choql (sickness caused by exposure to clouds or mist)	choql (sickness caused by exposure to clouds or mist)	xa'ank kik' (vomiting blood)	xyajel maa' us (sickness of the devil, evil spirit, epilepsy) or choql	xyajel maa'us (sickness of the devil, evil spirit, epilepsy)
THERMAL PROPERTY	hot	hot	cold	hot	hot
NOSOLOGICAL CATEGORY	6	6	3	3/6	3

DISORDER 9: PERSON ALTERNATES BETWEEN VERY SAD AND TIRED, AND VERY HAPPY AND VERY ACTIVE					
	Francisco Caal	**Manuel Choc**	**Manuel Baki**	**Lorenzo Choc**	**Emilio Kal**
NAME	not a sickness	ra ch'oolej (hurt heart, sad soul)	look aj k'a'uxl (crazy thinking)	not a sickness	not a sickness
THERMAL PROPERTY		hot	hot		
NOSOLOGICAL CATEGORY		3	1		

Disorder 1: Sadness; insomnia; crying; fatigue; loss of appetite. All five iloneleb' refer to this disorder in psychological or emotional terms. Francisco's *maak'a' xmaatan*, or bad luck related to one's maatan or destiny, is understood to create worry in the suffering individual. Emilio's *po'ol xk'a'uxl*, or disturbed mind, likewise is manifest as excessive worry. Manual Choc uses the term *xk'a'uxl*—technically "his mind"—simply to mean "he has worry" as a psychological state. (Manuel Baki also does this for Disorder 3.) Identifying these in the nosological category Disordered Psychological and Emotional States was straightforward.

Disorder 2: Hearing voices; talks to self; laughs by self; sees people who are not there. Three iloneleb' identify this disorder as wax ru or waxk'ay, severe or mild "craziness" or insanity. Although Manuel Choc refers to it as *tont aj yajel*, or "foolish sickness," in the interview he suggests that this is a disorder of excessive worry. Manuel Baki simply indicates that the person's mind has been affected, the likely result of witchcraft; I have categorized it with the Disordered Interpersonal Spiritual States as a result.

Disorder 3: Crying a lot; sadness; feeling lonely. Manuel Baki and Emilio see this as a psychological or emotional disorder, referencing worry or an unsettled mind. Emilio refers to this as *po'b'il k'a'uxl*, another term for "disturbed mind" but with a connection to the soul or spirit. He distinguishes this from the similar po'ol xk'a'uxl in Disorder 1 by the greater presence of crying in the former. Both Francisco and Manuel Choc indicate that the problem links ultimately to birth and especially awas, the disorder of infants and small children caused when a pregnant woman has an unsettling experience and that in some cases presents as an intellectual disability. For this reason, I have categorized *q'un xch'ool* (weak soul or spirit) and *awas yajel* (the awas sickness) identified by Francisco and Manuel Choc, respectively, as disordered mental states.

Disorder 4: Pain in chest; difficulty breathing. Francisco understands this as tib'l aam, or "pain in the heart," which can be glossed as a heart attack. His explanation is entirely physiological and connects a bad diet to too much fat around the heart. Manuel Choc, Manuel Baki, and Lorenzo all refer to muchkej, or cramps, a broadly glossed term that typically denotes pain; they relate it to a sudden drop in body temperature. Emilio has a somewhat different diagnosis and suggests that the disorder could be pain resulting from a chance encounter with the spirit or "vibe" of a snake or other animal that has recently been in the vicinity or crossed a path ahead of the person. He did note, however, that a person who has allowed his or her blood to "cool down," for instance after sexual activity, would be especially vulnerable to this sickness.

Disorder 5: Fever; sore throat; cough; body aches. Four of the five iloneleb' identify a sickness related to the key symptoms resembling jolomb'ej, the common cold. The causes identified varied, however. Manuel Baki indicates that it is a "normal" sickness that you get from the cold weather. Lorenzo focuses on the communicability of the sickness, suggesting that the *ojb'* (cough) could pass through the air from person to person, although initially it can come from the wind or air. Emilio referred to it as choql, a sickness also related to exposure to air and wind. Since these three all anchored their diagnosis in the temperature, air, wind, or mist, it makes sense to consider these sicknesses as disordered environmental states (keeping in mind that the Q'eqchi' concept of the environment, sutam, includes both material and meta/material elements). Francisco relates it to a rapid drop in body temperature (which is typically caused by changes in environmental states), while Manual Choc relates it to bad food. Hence for both Francisco and Manuel, their diagnoses are best thought of as disorders of physiological states (and in Francisco's case, a cause of a disorder of environmental states).

Disorder 6: Diarrhea; vomiting; stomach pain. Both Francisco and Emilio diagnose kaanil (spirit loss), although Emilio also adds the possibility of xiwajenaq (frightened spirit), both disorders of personal spiritual states. The others see this as a problem related to the consumption of bad food or water, which would identify this set of signs and symptoms as a disorder of physiological states.

Disorder 7: Weight loss; fatigue; loss of appetite; pale complexion. Manual Baki and Emilio diagnose fright-related sicknesses—in the category Disordered Personal Spiritual States—caused by falling in water. Lorenzo also relates it to a fall, but he suggests that the impact literally shakes the digestive track (which can irritate the lukum, or worms, that live there). Manuel Choc sees the problem as weight loss due to the lukum not properly digesting food. Francisco focuses on irregular food consumption causing indigestion. These last three fall within the category of Disordered Physiological States.

Disorder 8: Coughing up blood. Francisco and Manuel Choc identify this disorder as choql, "sickness caused by exposure to a cloud or mist" (a disorder of an environmental state in the nosology), and Lorenzo lists choql as an alternate diagnosis to xyajel maa'us (sickness of the devil or evil spirit). Emilio also diagnoses this disorder as xyajel maa'us. Manual Baki uses a sign descriptor to identify the sickness as *xa'ank kik'* (vomiting blood), not making a distinction between coughing and vomiting. As he relates it to witchcraft, I have categorized it as a disorder of an interpersonal spiritual state, along with xyajel maa'us.

Disorder 9: Person alternates between very sad and tired, and very happy and very active. Francisco, Lorenzo, and Emilio all note that these signs and symptoms were not characteristic of any specific sickness. As Fabrega, Metzger, and Williams (1970) found in their study of the Tenejapa medical system, many "strange and atypical" disorders are recognized as such but not as a sickness per se, and this is precisely how Francisco and Emilio understand it. They did think it could be linked to maatan, one's destiny based on the day of birth, or else passed to a child from a parent in utero. In contrast, Manuel Choc felt it could be *ra ch'oolej* (variant of *rahil ch'oolej*), sadness or "sad soul," caused by an evil spirit. Manuel Baki suggested *look aj k'a'uxl*, or "crazy thinking" caused by excessive worry. These two sicknesses fit best in the categories Disordered Interpersonal Spiritual States and Disordered Psychological and Emotional States, respectively.

The artificial nature of this exercise cannot be underestimated. Signs and symptoms—or "indicators" for simplicity's sake—are sometimes understood in the context of possible experiences, such as falling. In other words, any particular constellation of indicators may also signal the likelihood of an experience, and that experience is crucial to diagnosis (and treatment). Nonetheless, that on occasion an ilonel would report that a sign and symptom pattern did not constitute a recognizable sickness indicates that the diagnostic process does indeed involve discernment. It also suggests that iloneleb' understood the intent of the exercise despite its contrived nature and took care to consider the information presented to them rather than simply uttering the first thing that came to mind.

Overall, this exercise demonstrates both consensus and variability based on signs and symptoms. The ambiguous nature of both characterizes biomedicine as well as Q'eqchi' medicine, and in the case of the latter, the exercise as a whole decontextualizes the diagnostic process. Nonetheless, what we see here is strong evidence of an ability to engage with the material markers of sickness and apply learned diagnostic criteria.

Diagnosis by Thermal Principle

As noted in the introduction to this book, it is unreasonable to expect a complete consensus on medical matters when consulting with practitioners of any medical system, as their knowledge is a combination of training and experience. For the iloneleb', context is crucial, and this is evident when we look at what some might assume would be a fairly straightforward classification system of sicknesses based on thermal principles. Table 13 provides results of a pile sort in which each was asked to sort the sixteen disorders according to their hot (*tiq*) and cold (*ke*) characterization (with the options of "both" or "neither" as well). Of the sixteen disorders, only four (25 percent) were unanimously and clearly identified as either hot or cold; three more disorders were identified as hot or cold by three of four practitioners. However, thinking back to the knowledge hierarchy among the practitioners, we see that Emilio—the practitioner with the most advanced knowledge of the material and meta/material aspects of sickness, in the estimation of the others—frequently (seven times) placed disorders in the "both" category, noting in our interviews in each instance that the actual designation would depend on the specific circumstances of the patient and etiology. If we add those "both" designations to the categories selected unanimously by the others, we see that seven of the sixteen categories (44 percent) could be thought of as unanimous. The responses are dispersed to a much greater extent for the other sicknesses, with less or no evidence of consensus. And four sicknesses were identified by at least one ilonel as having no hot/cold properties at all.

Similarly, the data in Table 12 demonstrate significant, but rarely unanimous, agreement on the thermal properties of the nine sign and symptom sets. This is, of course, a way of thinking about sicknesses that is totally unfamiliar to the iloneleb', an issue identified by others, such as Tedlock (1987), as leading to largely useless, contradictory "etic" classifications. Rather than dismiss the approach entirely, I think the data here show evidence of a system of thought regarding thermal principles. It is not surprising to see a lack of unanimity on the thermal properties of each disorder. This is in part due to

TABLE 13. Hot/Cold Determination for Selected Disorders

DISORDER	HOT	COLD	NEITHER	BOTH
wax ru (severe craziness; schizophrenia)	FMLE			
taqenaq tiqwal jolomb'ej (headache; high head pressure)	FMLE			
xiwajenaq (frightened spirit)	FMLE			
taqenaq kik'el (high blood pressure)	FMLE			
eet aj yajel (epilepsy; the "foolish sickness")	FML			E
waxk'ay (mild craziness)	FML			E
k'a'uxlak (excessive worry)	MLE			F
jwal nak'a'uxlak (thinking too much)	ME		LF	
rilom tzuul (sickness caused by the mountain spirit; epilepsy)	FM	L		E
xyajel maa'us (sickness of the devil or evil spirit)	ML	F		E
maa'usat (evil spirit intrusion)	ML	F		E
kaanil (spirit loss)	ML	FE		
choql (sickness caused by exposure to cloud or mist)	L	F	M	E
rax kehob'l (malaria; chills)	F	L		ME
q'an yaj (ulcer)	LE	F	M	
q'an yajel (yellow fever/hepatitis)	L	F	M	

Legend
F: Francisco Caal
L: Lorenzo Choc
M: Manuel Choc
E: Emilio Kal

the abstract and unfamiliar nature of the exercise and to a different reading of the sign and symptom constellation, as these general symptoms can point to several different sicknesses. It is also likely due to less salience being given to thermal properties than previously assumed, as noted earlier.

In general, psychological and emotional disorders, and disorders of the mind, tend to be understood as hot, whereas disorders involving spiritual forces are more complex. Problems exemplified by an apparently simple material manifestation, such as coughing up blood or the symptoms associated with a viral infection or cold, often also have a meta/material dimension. But thermal properties are just one source of information for the iloneleb', of course.

Diagnosis by Prayer and Blood

Prayer (*tij*) is an essential ingredient in diagnosis, treatment, and judgments of effectiveness, and it is not easy to distinguish its use in these aspects as the process is quite iterative and dialogical. While I pick up the topic of prayer again in the next chapter, here I want to foreground that discussion somewhat by detailing how prayer is used as part of the diagnostic process. Prayer, of course, is in the first instance a vehicle of communication between the material and meta/material aspects of life. Thompson (1970:172) notes that "Maya prayer is directed to material ends," rather than for spiritual insight per se. But for the iloneleb' prayer is also intertwined with the body, the blood, and the pulse of the patient, and of course the meta/material world. Prayer has the capacity to allow the ilonel access to the interiority of the body simultaneously with access to the broader meta/material forces that affect that body. It is this interrelationship, its connectedness, that gives Q'eqchi' medicine its holistic dimension.

Qaawa' (God) is immediately called upon in all prayers to assist in diagnosis; the Catholic influence is obvious in this opening prayer segment from Manuel Baki:

> In the name of the Father, the Son, and the Holy Spirit. You're the Father in heaven. You have seen and know what this particular individual encountered among the people, among the mountains on earth. Now I will

> stand up to the four corners of his body to find out what's affecting her. And only you heavenly Father will help me as I hold on to her hands and feet to diagnose the problem.

While many scholars have assumed that Catholicism and Maya religion simply blended into a hybrid, Astor-Aguilera (2010) documents the use of key symbols, such as the cross, in precontact times, and Gonzales (2012) suggests that Indigenous knowledge and spirituality was "veiled" within Catholicism, allowing the traditional ideas to continue while somewhat superficially mimicking the religion of the dominant society. This intriguing idea is in evidence in what Manuel says above. The reference here to the "four corners" is also the four "cardinal points" on the body: the head, the two hands, and the two feet together. These points are central to pulsing, as I discuss below, but are also part of the diagnostic process and are reflections of the broader four cardinal points of the earth discussed in the previous chapter. Different prayers are often required, depending on which points of the body are relevant to the sickness; Emilio will pray to the planetary points in an effort to learn which part of the body is indeed involved, thus bringing the broader Q'eqchi' cosmovision into play.

Prayer, then, is used initially in treatment to request that the sickness identify itself, or that Qaawa' reveal it to the ilonel. It is the vehicle by which communication is established and elements of the sickness story are revealed. "What have you found?" asks Manuel Baki in his diagnostic prayer. It is not a rhetorical question. He is not talking to the patient directly, however, and does not anticipate a verbal response. "What have you got? Where did you get it? Is it in the air? Is it in a creek? On a tree? Or on a rock that you found your sickness?" The answers he receives through the blood pulse will guide his diagnosis.

The experience of the sufferer, then, is something addressed in the prayer, offering a sign that the ilonel would interpret in the context of the relationship between certain kinds of experiences and certain sicknesses. The ilonel seeks a diagnosis partly through ascertaining if there is an etiological narrative involved, especially one that the patient does not recall or recognize. Francisco details his approach. "First I ask to Qaawa' that in his name I will tend to this sickness. And then I start to feel the blood pulse and in the name of Qaawa', I ask what she has encountered or what is happening to her. Then I start to feel how the blood is reacting to my question." This reaction is crucial to the diagnosis. Lorenzo elaborates:

> I have no other ways to find out [what is wrong], but only when I say the prayer do I find out the sickness of the patient. When I hold his hand, the blood will respond to what is causing the problem when I'm saying the prayer. I would ask what is wrong, what is affecting the blood, and the blood will respond to those questions. It will be found in the blood. If it's a fright [that caused the problem, for instance], the blood will be frightened. After that you'll tell the patient that she has fallen in water and ask if that is not the case. The patient would agree.

As Lorenzo suggests, iloneleb' may also utter a series of possible sicknesses in their prayer, feeling the pulse and waiting for a reaction indicative of a positive diagnosis. "It is with the prayer that I'm saying that allows me to know what sickness the person has," Manuel Baki elaborates. The blood is capable of many different responses, but generally it will "jump" when the correct sickness is called out. Manuel Baki continues:

> As you're saying the prayers and you mention the sicknesses, the pulse would jump to it. That is how you would know what's the cause of the sickness. When we are treating that person we're asking all those sicknesses that we think are affecting that person. If we reach to that certain verse in the prayer, the blood would respond to the prayer. It is the same as how the doctor's do using the stethoscope.

A sickness can be belligerent, too, when it comes to identifying itself. Lorenzo refers to the need to occasionally "scold" the sickness to reveal its identity.

The prayer known generically as remeer is the basic one used in most cases during the diagnostic phase, although other prayers may be added to it throughout diagnosis and treatment. As part of the diagnostic exercise shown in Table 12, the iloneleb' were also asked to identify the prayers they would use for each disorder. A total of thirty-six prayers were mentioned, and of these, twenty-six (72 percent) were remeer, either alone or in conjunction with others. This is a prayer that is used to directly communicate with the blood, via the pulse, in an effort to learn the sickness. Remeer is not a standardized prayer, in the sense that all iloneleb' recite the same words, but the label refers more generally to a prayer type used to diagnose. Yet while each ilonel appears to have learned a somewhat different text, all texts share the same characteristics: an appeal to Qaawa' to enable the ilonel to diagnose and treat, and a request that the sickness identify itself through the blood in the pulse or in some other manner.

Diagnosis by Pulsing

Several Q'eqchi' terms are used to describe the process of pulsing, including *ch'e'ok kik'*, meaning "feeling/touching the blood," *xjilb'al xkik'el* (checking the blood), and *xjilb'al ich'mul* (checking the artery). Pulsing creates a bond among patient, ilonel, sickness, and both the material and meta/material elements. It provides the physical, tactile, and spiritual aspect of connectivity. By feeling or, more accurately, reading the blood that runs through the arteries, the ilonel gains access to and opens a dialogue with the patient's interior state. As Groark (2008:42) notes for the Tzotzil, the pulse "provides an involuntary (and unfailingly accurate) form of self-disclosure," allowing the ilonel to gain insights into the patient's disorder and the relevant broader aspects of their life, of which the patient may not be cognizant. The blood does not lie even when the patient does, or fails to disclose relevant information, is unable to provide details due to age or infirmity, or even just forgets.

Pulsing has long been a subject of interest among students of Mesoamerican medicine (e.g., Fabrega 1970), and there has not always been agreement as to its intent. Nash (1967) and Groark (2008) both argue that the blood pulse essentially reveals social information—that is, "the patient's relations with others," what Nash calls "sociopsy" (1967:133) and Groark (2008:442) calls "social gnosis." Nash argues that "physiological clues" are not what practitioners seek, an argument that is compatible with the broader focus of much medical anthropology on the symbolic rather than the material. Others, such as Metzger and Williams (1963), suggest that the blood pulse can reveal considerably more information about etiology, including specific locations implicated and specific prayers and plant medicines required. My approach here, as in the rest of the book, is to explore both the material and meta/material aspects of pulsing.

Pulse diagnosis is common to many medical systems throughout the world, including biomedicine, and listening to the pulse more than the patient is rather ubiquitous (e.g., Craig 2012:52). Researchers have shown a particular interest in the similarities between Maya and traditional Chinese medicine (TCM) (García, Sierra, and Balám 1999). Balick, De Gezelle, and Arvigo (2008) utilize a set of twenty-eight "pulse types" derived from a TCM manual in an interesting experiment with a Mopan Maya practitioner in Belize. As with the Q'eqchi' iloneleb', this practitioner did not have names for the different pulse types but did appear to recognize them from the descriptions provided by the researchers, typically offering a diagnosis. As in the diagnostic exercise I undertook with the iloneleb', the experiment by these researchers does not reflect how the practitioner actually diagnoses; by definition, pulsing is tactile and intercorporeal, not textual. So perhaps it is best to focus not on the specific disorders apparently diagnosed from pulse descriptions but rather on the extensive variability in pulse types that seem to resonate in some way. As these researchers had worked with the practitioner for several years prior, they were able to generate a list of forty-one disorders that he had diagnosed in the past through pulsing; these include sixteen physiological disorders, seven "insanity" disorders, and three spiritual disorders. While their nosology is different from what I have presented here, their exercise demonstrates the comprehensive and nuanced skills needed to pulse diagnose, and it further establishes the preeminence of physiological signs, symptoms, and disorders in the broader medical system.

Working with the iloneleb', I did not ask them to detail all the disorders that were diagnosable though the pulse. As noted above, several disorders do not require it; they are determinable by observation alone or in conjunction with a report from the patient. Further, in the diagnostic exercise, Francisco and Emilio report to a much greater degree that they do not always use pulsing, with Emilio indicating that in only one case would he do so, employing other diagnostic procedures instead. This pattern is no doubt a reflection of Emilio and Francisco's greater knowledge and experience.

The pulse is typically read in three areas, reflecting the four cardinal points of the body. The pulse can be read at the wrist by palpating the radial artery (Figure 20). Either wrist will work, and in some cases both are read simultaneously. Depending on the suspected sickness, the pulse is also read on the forehead, by palpating the supratrochlear artery with either the thumb (Figure 21) or the hand (Figure 22), and on the feet, by palpating the dorsalis pedis (Figure 23). Generally, the carotid artery is not a site of pulse reading, but on occasion an ilonel might place his hand on the chest over the heart. In some cases, the pulse is read at more than one place throughout treatment. The normal sequence of pulsing in such cases is head–wrists–feet, but the sequence may vary depending on the suspected disorder. "What we do to a patient is that we place our hand on the forehead to feel the pulse," explains Lorenzo. "It is from that you will find out what is causing the problem as you were saying the prayer. You will always start on the head, then to the hands or wrist, and to finish on the foot." Later explaining his diagnostic approach for what turned out to be a fright-related sickness, he adds, "When you reach to the feet and one of the feet does not seem to have blood, [I know] that person has fallen somewhere, because the blood is no longer rising up or getting higher in the body." So different pulsing sites can provide different information, and sometimes it is necessary to survey all of them. Lorenzo adds, "For example, for a xiwajenaq (frightened spirit) case, if a person falls in a river and only his feet slipped, the feet will have low blood signals. The head and the hand will have good blood pulse." Different prayers are usually used, depending on the part of the body being palpated, and diagnostic pulsing prayers transition seamlessly together and then into treatment pulsing prayers in a way that the patient is unaware of. Francisco likens this to "chapters" linked to each area being pulsed, all connected in one long prayer.

The manner in which a given pulse is described is variable, and again I note that having to describe in words what a pulse "feels" like is not something they are trained to do, nor is it how they learn. The translation of their descriptions into English adds yet another layer of distortion. But a process of differential diagnosis is apparent in how the pulses are understood. Describing a case of eet aj yajel (epilepsy; the "foolish sickness"), Francisco describes the pulse this way: "Her blood flows rapidly and seems as if it is scared and moves rapidly again." With wax ru (severe craziness or schizophrenia), "a crazy person's pulse jumps very hard, calms down, then jumps again very crazily, slow then fast, slow then fast." He distinguishes wax ru from waxk'ay (mild

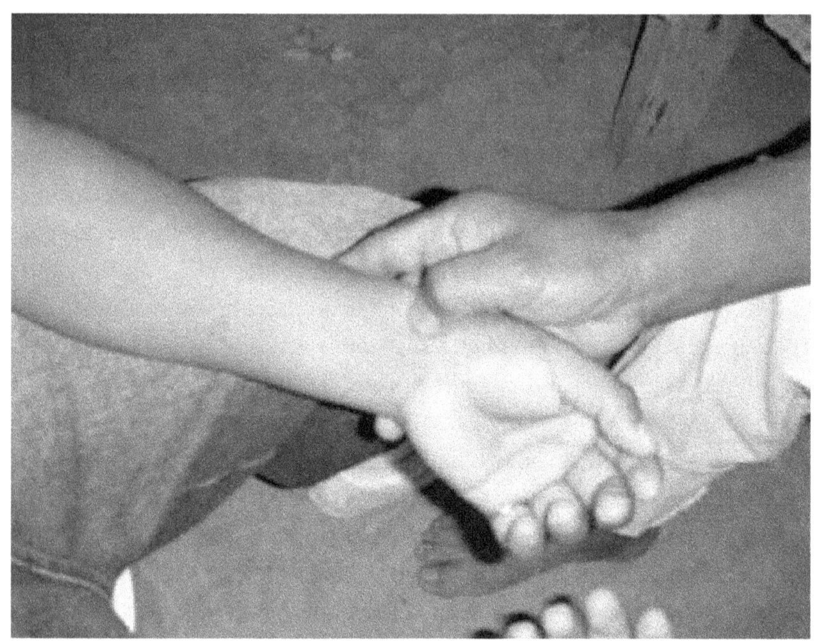

FIGURE 20. Checking the pulse at the wrist (radial artery). Itzamma (Indian Creek), 2013. Photo by author.

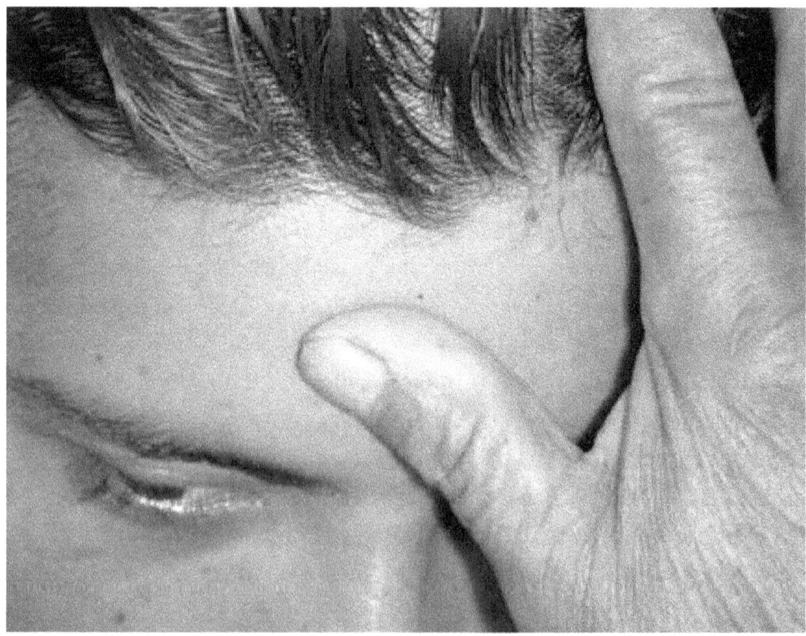

FIGURE 21. Checking the pulse at the forehead (supratrochlear artery) with thumb. Itzamma (Indian Creek), 2013. Photo by author.

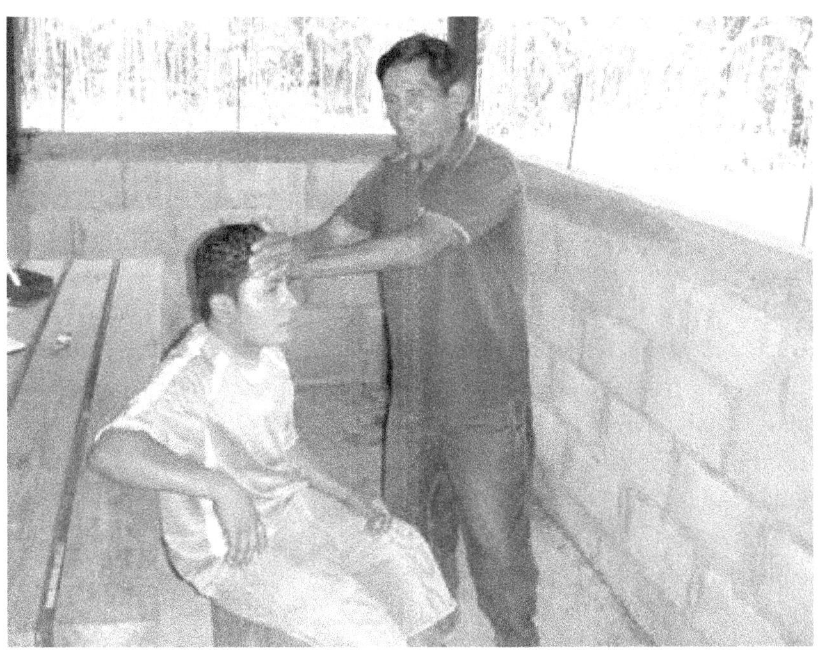

FIGURE 22. Checking the pulse at the forehead (supratrochlear artery) with hand. Itzamma (Indian Creek), 2013. Photo by author.

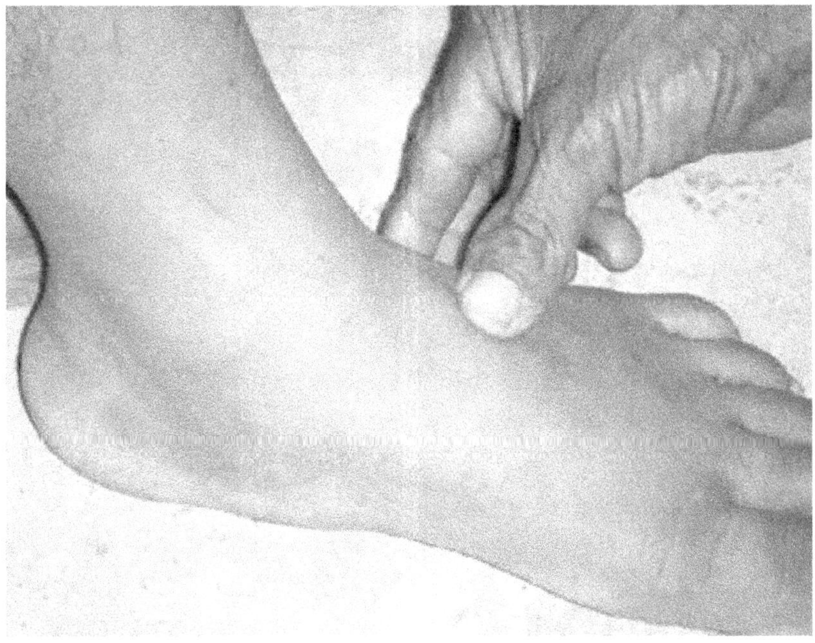

FIGURE 23. Checking the pulse at the foot (dorsalis pedis). Itzamma (Indian Creek), 2013. Photo by author.

craziness): "Yes, it's a little different; you can feel that the pulse with waxk'ay is just like the kaanil (spirit loss), which is fast, due to being frightened, because the person is not extremely crazy." So he uses other clues, such as the person's behavior, to distinguish between waxk'ay and kaanil. Lorenzo describes the pulse of a patient with rax kehob'l (malaria): "The blood would be moving slow because of the chills." In contrast, he describes a patient with rilom tzuul (sickness caused by the mountain spirit): "Moving fast. Like frightening a snake, it would go fast. The blood is like that too." He describes eet aj yajel: "The epileptic pulse would feel the blood moving fast, but unlike rilom tzuul it moves in sections, but pumping fast." Emilio explains how he tells the difference between eet aj yajel and kaanil: "If it's eet aj yajel, then you hold the wrist and touch the [arteries], and it's pumping hard or heavy. If it's kaanil, the [artery] is pumping slowly. When it's eet aj yajel, the pumping can stop for a second." And not every sickness is diagnosable by pulse. Francisco discusses jwal naxik xk'a'uxl (thinking too much):

> What I find with this problem is there is not much change in the pulse flow [from normal]. Only his mind and thoughts go astray, or he worries a lot. The only thing that can happen to the person is hurt, causing injuries to himself, be it a fall, cut, or anything due to not concentrating on what he is doing by worrying too much. But the pulse, nothing is wrong with it.

Here are some of the most common descriptors of the blood pulse that emerged throughout the research:

- Faster than normal; light
- Slower than normal; tired
- In "sections"—that is, there is a pulse, then nothing, then a pulse, as if "sections" flow through every few seconds.
- Back and forth. It changes directions.
- Jumpy
- Heavy or thick
- Thin
- In clumps

This is not an extensive list by any means, and several recognizable sicknesses have a pulse that could be described in similar terms. The list itself is not discerning. The problem here is in the exercise of describing verbally something that is tactile. When a disorder is such that pulsing is considered necessary, the information it provides is often partial and is added to other diagnostic information to determine a global diagnosis. For instance, in describing eet aj yajel (epilepsy; the "foolish sickness") Francisco explains, "The pulse is very fast and light in its movement. Other symptoms might be present, such as fever, diarrhea, vomiting. Only by feeling the pulse and its flow can you be certain of the problem." With maa'usat (evil spirit intrusion), he notes that "the pulse flows normally, but the only problem might be pain in certain areas on the foot or arm. The blood is not affected in any way except it is a little too heavy in its flowing, but this doesn't cause anything." And in the case of choql (sickness caused by exposure to a cloud or mist), "the person's pulse will be heavy or slow. The patient will have symptoms such as headache, coughs, painful eyes, blurred vision." Pulsing, then, is typically used in tandem with other signs, symptoms, and patient reports, to ultimately determine the diagnosis, a synergistic blending of material and meta/material sources of data.

While counting of beats is not a necessary feature of Q'eqchi' pulsing, the emphasis on the quality of blood flow certainly is. And here there are some notable similarities with biomedicine. For instance, in a popular clinical examination manual (Gidrewicz and Wen 2005:252), we find some strikingly similar pulse descriptors linked to ECG wave forms:

- "Sudden rapid pulse with a full expansion followed by a sudden collapse"
- "Double peaked pulse with a mid-systolic dip"
- "Alternating amplitude of pulses"
- "Small, slow rising pulse with a drop or notch in the ascending portion"

The "presence and quality of pulses" is a core element of the peripheral vascular exam, in fact, and both the "rate" and the "rhythm" are to be assessed. Rhythm is judged as "regular," "regularly [consistently] irregular," and "irregularly irregular." Some characteristic pulses found during palpation are described as:

- "Small, weak"
- "Small, slowly rising pulse that is delayed with respect to heart sounds"
- "Strong, bounding pulse"

So while the specific descriptors differ, there remain strong similarities between Q'eqchi' medicine and biomedicine, in which the pulse and the feel of the blood flow provide essential diagnostic information.

Therapeutic Disclosure

While within biomedicine, the principle of diagnostic disclosure seems fundamental to the idea of patient autonomy, in practice, clinicians often withhold or alter information about a patient's disorder (McCabe, Wood, and Goldberg 2010). Referred to as "therapeutic non-disclosure" or "therapeutic privilege," it is an accepted practice "if disclosure is believed to be medically contraindicated" (Snyder 2012:77). So too do the Q'eqchi' iloneleb' withhold information, and nondisclosure might be thought of as a "best practice" in some instances. In particular, where the diagnosis implicates some social etiology, the iloneleb' are inclined to be circumspect. A clear distinction is made regarding what is disclosed, according to the diagnosis. Manuel Choc explains:

> There are times when it is, well, it would not be necessary to tell a patient what the sickness is, and this is in terms of witchcraft and so forth. Because if you tell a person that a certain person has given you these sicknesses, then it would bring other problems, because the person would want revenge. So what the ilonel would do is basically say that your sickness is not really great, it's not really high, and the ilonel would just try his best to cure his sickness. . . . If a person has regular sickness, such as fear, fever, and so forth, the ilonel would tell them, "This is your sickness." However, when it comes to witchcraft, it wouldn't be acceptable to tell them that is their sickness, because the next question would be, "Who did it?" And it would cause a lot of problems.

Albino concurs: "No, you wouldn't say it's witchcraft. You would create a problem if you tell them. They might end up killing each other. I would just give them some plant medicine and tell them that would help with the problem."

Essentially, beyond the issue of witchcraft and related phenomena with a clear interpersonal dimension, the iloneleb' ultimately share some information about the diagnosis. This is partly to confirm the diagnosis, by requesting that the patient think into the past about places they might have traversed or incidents they might have experienced. But the iloneleb' also tend to provide only basic information on the assumption that sickness is too complicated for laypeople to fully appreciate. Further, since diagnosis and treatment often blend seamlessly, the patient is not afforded the opportunity to learn the diagnosis or prognosis, or to discuss treatment prior to treatment commencing. Often, the only break in the process comes later, after the ilonel has concluded his pulsing and praying and is preparing the medicinal plants that will also be used. In effect, a Q'eqchi' patient consents, at least in part, to treatment when they engage with the ilonel in the diagnostic process, even if they are unaware of the diagnosis and the subsequent treatment regimen.

Conclusion

Diagnosis within this Q'eqchi' medical tradition is complex and multifaceted. It adheres to processes of differential diagnosis to distinguish among the large number of potential sicknesses that can affect the mind and body of the individual. In most cases, diagnosis involves the use of several techniques in an integrated manner. The patient's role is relatively small in the diagnostic process, but not entirely invisible. And while meta/material forces are most certainly involved in diagnosis, it is too simplistic a rendering to suggest that diagnosis is essentially about discerning issues in the social order (broadly conceived to include humans and other entities). The iloneleb' are clearly in tune with the material indicators of sickness as well.

CHAPTER 6

The Clinical Context of Treatment

THERE ARE COMMON general approaches and techniques for many sicknesses and specialized techniques for others. More serious sicknesses require different approaches than less serious ones. Sicknesses where evil spirits are involved require more complex and dangerous (for the iloneleb') procedures than those involving disorders of physiological states. The iloneleb' have different knowledge and experiences, and this is reflected in the way they approach treatment of similar sicknesses. The art of medical practice is in evidence as the iloneleb' invoke favored approaches to treatment they have used successfully in the past, adapt approaches to specific clients and their circumstances, and change course in diagnosis and treatment when needed.

In this chapter I distinguish certain aspects of medical treatment for heuristic reasons, recognizing that to do so risks failure to see the whole—an integrated system—for the parts. Further, it is not possible to do justice to the variability in knowledge, experience, and technique of the members of the MHAB. Here, I can only try to focus our attention on some key aspects. This book is about the specialized knowledge and experience of specific Q'eqchi' medical practitioners. Understanding how they approach clinical treatment is crucial to understanding the broader manifestation of empiricism that underscores it.

The Goals of Medical Treatment

Central to my analytical framework in understanding treatment outcome is the distinction between transformative and restorative processes I made previously (Waldram 2013). To recap: Transformative therapeutic processes work from the assumption that the individual's original psychosocial or health state, whatever it was, does not represent a desirable or attainable status achievable through therapeutic intervention, and that the individual must transform to a new state of health or well-being, with associated psychosocial changes, as opposed to a return to the old. This transformation is often a long-term process, sometimes without end, and the idea of "cure" is alien to understanding the intended outcome.[1] Any hope of improving health is linked to a break from a problematic or pathological past. Successful treatment involves helping the individual deal with concurring and ever-present stresses and challenges while they transform their self-identity in a prosocial and pro-healthy direction.

Restorative therapeutic processes work from the assumption that the individual's normal state is one of health, more or less; that sickness is an undesirable if not threatening disruption to that state; and that the goal of treatment should be to eliminate whatever pathology—be it a microorganism, an envious neighbor, or an evil spirit—is causing the problem. Successful treatment means to cure the individual; the pathology that once afflicted the individual is removed, and they are returned as close to the pre-sickness state as possible, which means they can resume appropriate psychosocial functioning. While transformative healing often necessitates ongoing vigilance by the patient to avoid relapse, aided by support groups and often an ongoing relationship with the healer, with restorative treatment, the goal is to terminate the patient status and thus the relationship to the practitioner.

Q'eqchi' medicine, like all medical traditions, invokes both transformative and restorative processes, and patient and practitioner perspectives typically vary as to the goals of treatment and assessments of its effectiveness. The Q'eqchi' term *b'anok* (from *b'an*, or medicine) is often translated as both "to cure" and "to heal." However, what distinguishes Q'eqchi' medicine from that described for some other Indigenous groups is that the focus of therapeutic intervention is restorative, not transformative.[2] Q'eqchi' medical knowledge, then, revolves around the identification and treatment of specific, diagnosable pathologies. Even chronic, recurring disorders as understood by biomedicine, such as epilepsy (called xyajel maa'us, or sickness of the devil or evil spirit), are curable according to the iloneleb'. The goal here, to quote Francisco, is "to get rid of it completely from the person . . . so that it doesn't happen to the person again." Adds Manuel Choc, "With our treatment, the sickness goes away." Q'eqchi' iloneleb', then, have an imperative to cure. Detailing the treatment of a female patient with a stomach problem, Francisco declares, "She will have to get better. My job is to make sure of that." Emilio, with respect to his treatment of a child with a skin rash, states, "It is my duty as an ilonel to treat the problem. What I expect to see is the patient gets normal." Treating a case of xyajel maa'us, Lorenzo states confidently, "I expect that she will fully recover from her sickness."

Simply put, the standard by which the success of treatment is measured is the extent to which the pathology is removed and the patient returned to as near a normal state as possible, as understood by both the ilonel and the patient. Once the patient is cured, the job of the ilonel is done, a phenomenon noted by earlier researchers such as Fabrega (1970:397), who writes that "a good cure . . . is one that eliminates symptoms permanently." Manuel Choc, after treating a young woman four times for maa'us aj musiq'ej (sickness caused by evil spirits), "told her that I will not continue to treat her because her problem went away." Any subsequent sickness is understood as new unless a connection can be drawn to the previous sickness in a manner that implicates a mistaken diagnosis or the failure of the patient to complete the treatment. Patient compliance is as important an issue for Q'eqchi' iloneleb' as it is for biomedical practitioners, and patients who feel better enough to resume their proper social and economic roles and activities—that is, invoking a notion of well-being—may fail to continue to undergo treatment or take medicines. This represents a key tension in the Q'eqchi' medical system: iloneleb' treat to achieve a cure, and patients often undergo treatment to restore well-being.

The iloneleb', like most traditional practitioners throughout the world, are remunerated for their efforts. This may take the form of cash or an in-kind payment or service. Typically, the ilonel is offered a sum at the outset, when a request is made for treatment; accepting the money sends a signal that he will put his best effort into curing the patient. "If I [accept the money]," explains Albino, "I assure to do my job 100 percent; no doubt the patient will get better." However, it is also common for the bulk of the payment to be made only after treatment, and especially after a successful cure (keeping in mind that the patient and ilonel may differ on what constitutes a cure). "I am not paid," Lorenzo elaborates, "until the patient recovers fully." Since, according to custom, the form and amount of payment are entirely at the discretion of the patient or their family, the imperative to cure clearly also has a material dimension for the ilonel.

The Four Pillars of Q'eqchi' Medical Treatment

Q'eqchi' medical treatment, while dynamic, centers on four pillars: pulsing; prayer; pharmacology; and jilok, or massage. While prayer and the use of plant medicines have been recognized by other researchers (e.g., Metzger and Williams 1963:225) as central elements of Maya treatment, the roles of continued pulsing and jilok have not been as well documented. Most treatments involve these four components, and while they are typically adapted to specific cases, where a case is understood as a particular sickness in the context of a specific individual, in their general form they work in an integrated manner to diagnose, treat, and ultimately assess effectiveness.

PILAR 1: PULSING

Pulsing is extensively discussed in the previous chapter on diagnosis, so I will not delve specifically into it here other than to emphasize that pulsing continues at various points throughout many treatments to monitor progress and evaluate outcome. As treatment progresses, pulsing continues to provide valuable information on the state of the patient and the sickness to the practitioner, allowing the ilonel to determine if a change in diagnosis or treatment approach is warranted. The pulse not only reacts when a plausible sickness is mentioned, but it continues to react and inform in response to the other three pillars, to be discussed next.

PILLAR 2: *JILOK*

Jilok is a general term, typically translated as "massage," but the meaning in Q'eqchi' really does not translate well.[3] This is not the kind of massage typically associated with massage therapists; it does not involve significant amounts of pressure and is not aggressive. The iloneleb' do not attempt to manipulate the muscles or manually alleviate muscle tension.[4] Jilok "is done basically by passing the hand over the person's entire body," explains Manuel Choc. "It is a mild touch." Typically, it is done in a downward motion, the hands gliding over the body without firm pressure. The ilonel may blow on his hands several times before applying them or do so intermittently during the process. According to Manuel, the breath of the ilonel applies the good spirit of Qaawa', his power, which the ilonel channels because of his praying. In effect, blowing provides a direct physical connection between the patient and the Creator, who has the actual power to cure, as the mouth serves the dual function of uttering prayers and expelling air that symbolizes essential life force. Manuel Baki adds that the blowing also helps "cool down" the body and blood of a patient who is experiencing a hot sickness. In cases where there is discernible pain, such as with q'an yaj (ulcer or stomach "sores") or back pain, the ilonel may stop at the locus of the pain and press lightly while praying. Francisco relates the importance of massaging in the area of the kidneys and liver for patients with q'an yajel (yellow fever), for instance, as these organs are directly affected by the virus.

Jilok also forms part of the diagnostic process, as well part of the assessment of effectiveness, working in tandem with pulsing, according to Albino. Adds Emilio, "Checking the blood pulse is part of massaging. Like when a person is massaging, he would then feel the arteries, checking the blood pulse, whereby he would ask questions of the sickness [asking it to reveal itself]." Further, during the jilok, the ilonel also prays, usually with remeer. "Talking to the blood" is how Francisco explains it. Some treatments involve prepared plant medicines, which are passed lightly over the body. So, while I am treating these pillars as separate here for heuristic reasons, they are more integrated in the overall treatment process.

There are variations of jilok, specialized techniques used for specific problems, including those related to women's reproductive health (De Gezelle 2014). Francisco, treating a pregnant woman with back pains, used a common treatment known as *b'ak'ok*, which includes tying a broad cloth tightly around the abdomen along with simultaneous use of prayer and plant medicines. For uterine distress, including excessive bleeding after childbirth, a variation called *b'ak'ok kub'sa'* (*kub'sa'* means "uterus") is used. A procedure known as *b'ak'ok b'aqel* (literally "tying the skeleton") is used to treat skeletal pains experienced by women after childbirth, caused by pelvic expansion during delivery. In each case, the hands of the ilonel are positioned over the site of the pain or discomfort.

Jilok allows the ilonel to remove sickness from the body. For a case of muchkej, or cramps, Manuel Choc massages the pain from the upper body to the knee, where he applies a poultice of medicinal plants to cure the problem. Other iloneleb', working characteristically from the upper body to the lower, from the head to the toes, and from the core to the extremities, explain that they are pushing the sickness out of the body. It is common to start with the head. Francisco notes, "You cannot just start anywhere. It has to be on the head, because the person's central nervous system starts there. That is where the person suffers most. It is required that you start concentrating on the forehead." Interpreter Romulo Caal, Francisco's son, adds, "It is necessary to start at the head because the head is the most important part of the body; it has eyes, which are interconnected to other systems. When a person is sick he feels most of the pains in the head," an observation confirmed in my discussion of symptomology in the previous chapter, where headache and head "pressure" are affiliated with many sicknesses I tested. "It is important to start up and not down." Adds Manuel Choc, "When a person is sick, it is normal, when doing a massage, to bring it [sickness] down, so that it would come out. If you bring it up, it would kill an individual. The sickness normally comes out of the feet at the toes." According to Francisco, "It will be coming out as air or wind," or as a spirit in a form resembling steam or fog.

PILLAR 3: PRAYER DIALOGUE

Prayer (tij) is a central element of Q'eqchi' religious and medical practice, and it serves as a kind of technical language learned by iloneleb' for the purposes of treatment. It is a vehicle of communication, then, in a language largely understood only by other "specialists"—that is, practitioners, Qaawa', and spirits—in the Q'eqchi' medical world. The iloneleb' are among several specialist types with access to prayers for a variety of purposes, such as to ensure a successful crop, to ask permission of the Tzuultaq'a to travel, and even to settle strife within marriages. Prayer knowledge, like all specialist knowledge, is differentially known, and only some individuals are culturally authorized to know and recite certain prayers. Further, there is evidence of variability across Q'eqchi' groups in Central America in terms of the content of prayers, although the structure tends to remain fairly consistent (Kahn 2006). In medical treatment, prayers constitute proprietary knowledge, and masters are paid to teach the prayers by apprentices seeking to learn.

Virtually all treatment sessions involve prayer, and frequently multiple prayers are employed at different points and for different reasons. Some iloneleb' note that the prayers are different ones, used at specific moments, while others think of them as "verses" of a single prayer. It is not easy to discern when a prayer transitions from its diagnostic to its treatment function, and indeed these often continue interchangeably throughout the clinical encounter. While opening prayers to Qaawa' are somewhat monological in the sense that a direct response is not expected, once the practitioner enters the diagnostic and treatment modes, prayer becomes dialogical in the sense that some response, be it from the pulse, the body, the spirits, or the disorder, is expected.

During an interview with Francisco regarding his treatment of a case of xiwajenaq (frightened spirit), where he is pulsing at three points in sequence, the forehead, wrist, and feet, I ask him, "Are you using different prayers for these different places on the body, or is it the same prayer you're saying?" He responds, "Different prayers. The first prayer is to find out if the person was frightened; we speak to the blood, that it should not get frightened again. The other prayers are to use the spirit of the light, air, and the environment to clear out the problem that he has, so that his spirit calms down. Each prayer is different, step by step." Specific sicknesses have specific prayers, as do specific places on the body. But, as noted previously, the iloneleb' do not share the specific prayers in the sense that the text is identical. Rather they share the general format of the prayers; from their individual masters, each ilonel has learned unique prayers to be employed to achieve the same ends.

Despite this variability in text, iloneleb' are taught the importance of accuracy in the use of prayer. "It is not just made up" on the spot, asserts Francisco; nor is it a "prayer" in the sense of a person praying in a church. Rather it is a very specific prayer or set of prayers to be used in a specific case. Speaking of the very long prayer he uses to treat xiwajenaq, he explains,

"Everybody can say [a prayer] from the heart, like what you want to say [in church]. But this is not a prayer only from the heart; this was learned as a specific prayer for each process or step of the treatment until the end. This is different. I am not just making it up." In a sense, then, equating ilonel medical prayer with religious prayer is misleading, as is the English term "prayer" itself. "Prayer," for the ilonel, represents a means to establish a relationship with the material and meta/material forces that affect human health, just as a biomedical practitioner would establish a relationship with other specialists or pharmaceutical representatives to ensure that patients receive the best possible care. Prayer helps ensure that the necessary resources for treatment are available.

Learning the appropriate prayers is typically a starting point in the training of iloneleb', and some very long ones can take months to commit to memory, so that they can be recited to the satisfaction of the master. To provide an example, Francisco's longest prayer is for q'an yaj, or stomach ulcer. "That is a very long prayer and is very, very hard," he explains. "It took five months to learn and would take half an hour to recite if I went quickly!" One can imagine the effort needed to commit to memory such a long passage, which contains little repetition, especially with the emphasis on getting it exact. There are serious repercussions for failure to do so. "It's very important to learn as it is, no change, no cuts," warns Francisco. "It has to be exactly the same words. If you make a mistake, it can bring the sickness into your body." At the very least, an incomplete prayer will likely lead to a failed treatment.

In this research, I encountered at least fifteen to twenty distinct prayers used in treatment, plus the opening remeer. Some have names; others do not. Where some iloneleb' see a single prayer, perhaps with verses or segments, others see several distinct prayers. Prayers during treatment serve several clinical purposes. Working together with pulsing and jilok, prayers continue to aid diagnosis and invoke the powers of Qaawa' and other spirits to make the patient better, and they allow the ilonel to know if the treatment is working. Prayers provide a language with which to communicate with the blood of the patient and the afflicted internal organs. They act as a catalyst to render the medicinal plants effective; they act on the sickness to obey the dictates of the ilonel, for instance by migrating within the body, following the practitioner's hands, to an exit point in an extremity; and they propitiate the spirits, who do their bidding by departing from the sick person. While, at the start of treatment, it makes sense to think of practitioner utterances as monologue "prayers" in the conventional sense of an appeal to a deity, at some point during treatment, the practitioner adds in or shifts toward a dialogical component, talking to and interpreting responses from the patient's body, blood, pulse, and the sickness itself, as well as various relevant spiritual entities. The term "prayer" does not adequately account for this dialogical process involving so many players, one in which any "god" figure may be only superficially involved or otherwise be supplanted. This is why it makes sense to speak of "prayer dialogue" rather than simply "prayer." These are clinical conversations or consultations with meta/material forces.

While one could also argue that the prayer dialogue provides the rich symbolic context necessary for "healing," the fact is that the patient is largely ignorant of prayer content (Waldram 2015b). The prayer dialogues—always vocalized—are uttered quickly, often in a low, inaudible voice. Typically they include, at least partially, aspects of the Q'eqchi' language that are somewhat ancient and not known to lay speakers, along with what we might think of as specialist medical and religious language not understandable to nonspecialists. The iloneleb' are not talking to patients with these prayers; they are talking to Qaawa', the spirits, the blood, and the sickness. While most patients recognize these utterances as prayers, and even that they are somehow relevant to their treatment, they do not normally understand anything being said or with whom the ilonel is conversing, and of course the patients are oblivious to the meta/material forces "talking back" to the ilonel.

PILLAR 4: PHARMACOLOGY

The rich biosphere of southern Belize provides a breathtakingly large number of plant species that are known within the Q'eqchi' medical system to have medicinal properties. The vast majority of medical treatments involve these plant medicines (including bark, roots, and leaves), sometimes singly but often in combinations. More than one hundred distinct plant names or name variations were mentioned during the research in direct reference to the treatment of specific medical disorders. This is on the low side in comparison to studies focused specifically on plants. It was not my intent to delve deeply into the specifics of the plants used or to comment on their pharmacological properties—I am not trained in either botany or pharmacology—and fortunately there is significant evidence of both already in existence from research with Q'eqchi' and other Maya groups and, significantly, with the MHAB iloneleb' themselves.

Several quantitative studies documenting research with members of the MHAB resonate strongly with the argument I am making in this book: that Q'eqchi' medical knowledge represents a shared system of complex ideas about the material and meta/material aspects of the world that affect human health. Pesek et al. (2010) demonstrate that the Q'eqchi' iloneleb' have a more detailed knowledge of environmental zones in southern Belize with respect to the location of medicinal plant species than does current ecosystem science. Amiguet et al. (2005, 2006), Bourbonnais-Spear et al. (2005, 2007), Awad et al. (2009), De Gezelle (2014), and Choco (2015) all document the detailed knowledge of plant medicines and, importantly, the high degree of consensus in the identification and uses of specific plants for specific sicknesses. Amiguet et al. (2005), for instance, working with the same iloneleb' as me, collected 169 medicinal plant species from sixty-seven different families; more than 75 percent of these species were noted for their usage by at least half of the practitioners, and nineteen species were used by all nine iloneleb' from the MHAB with whom the researchers worked. Studies from other Maya regions of Central America support the idea of strong within-group consensus in the knowledge of plant medicines (e.g., Heinrich et al. 1998; Ankli, Sticher, and Heinrich 1999, Ankli 2002; Michel et al. 2007). While laboratory analysis of some of these plants is ongoing, results so far suggest that the compatibility between Q'eqchi' knowledge of the sicknesses they treat and the plants' pharmacological properties is significant. To date, much scientific research focus has been on "mental health" and the uses of key plants with anxiolytic and antiepileptic properties (Bourbonnais-Spear et al. 2007; Awad et al. 2009)—plants typically used by the iloneleb' to treat sicknesses such as kaanil (spirit loss) and eet aj yajel (epilepsy; the "foolish sickness"). This is not to suggest that scientific validation is needed to accept that the Q'eqchi' practitioners have extensive knowledge of plants in their region, but these investigations do provide an additional lens through which

FIGURE 24. Manuel Choc (left) and Manuel Baki demonstrating medicinal plants at Maya Day. Blue Creek, 2012. Photo by Andrew Hatala.

to understand and appreciate this knowledge, a kind of methodological triangulation.

The evidence is strong, then, that the iloneleb' have at their disposal a significantly large number of medicinal plant species, many of which are similar in the outcomes they produce for specific sicknesses. The iloneleb' have many options, in other words, when it comes to determining the best plants to use. To join the MHAB, candidates must undergo a test of this knowledge, identifying medicinal plants in situ and detailing their use and means of preparation. Of course, there is variability in use, and the iloneleb' have favorite go-to plants for specific sicknesses, often selecting from locally available options before considering the need to travel to remote regions. Working with biologists, they have constructed and continue to maintain a medicinal plant garden—some fifty acres of natural forest where they transplant and cultivate important species—which is fairly easy to access for most (Audet et al. 2013).

The manner in which the medicinal plants are prepared and used varies according to the case. It is essential that the ilonel requests permission through prayer to pick the plants if he is to ensure their therapeutic power

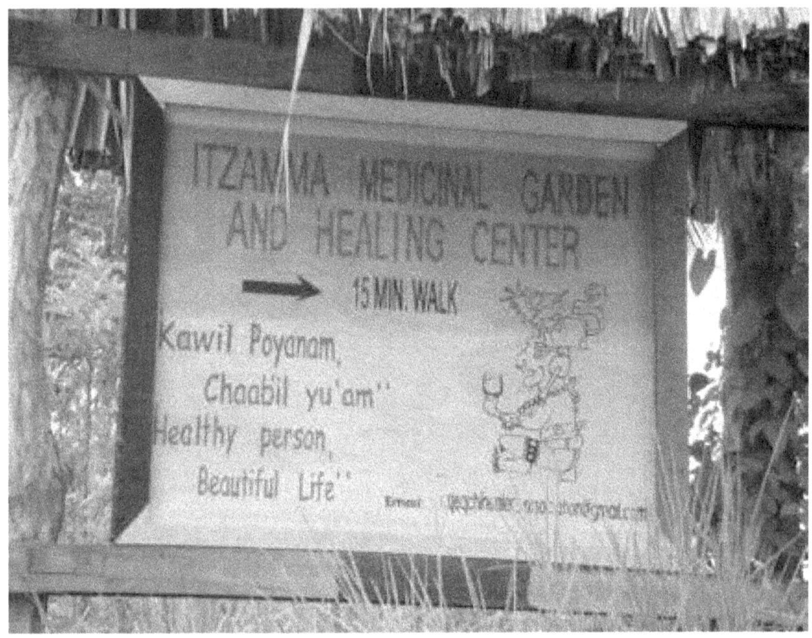

FIGURE 25. Itzamma Medicinal Garden and Healing Center entrance sign, 2013. Photo by author.

and avoid personal calamity. The plants were left on earth by Qaawa' for people to use, and they are protected by the Tzuultaq'a; the iloneleb' act as human stewards of the resource. It is preferable to use freshly picked plants, and multiple treatments often involve daily trips to harvest, but the iloneleb' also make use of plants they keep handy in case they are needed.

Two main ways of using medicinal plants are bathing and oral consumption. In both cases, the plants are crushed and mixed with water, with chlorinated tap water avoided where possible. The thermal properties of the sickness are important in this step, as the ilonel seeks to rebalance the patient. For instance, a "hot" sickness logically requires a "cold" plant, and it will typically be mixed with unheated water. In some cases, the plants are cooked in water that has been boiled and then cooled. Bathing usually involves the medicine being poured onto the patient, often starting from the head. However, localized disorders may be treated more directly, with medicine being poured on the lower back, for instance, if that is the site of pain. Manuel Baki likens it to getting an injection from the doctor. The mixture "cools down" the patient and the sickness, and it is understood to enter the body through the skin. Bathing may also be done by splashing the medicine on the patient with a flick of the hand. Bathing sometimes occurs separately from oral consumption, and the same mixture is used for both. Thus the patient receives the medicine in two ways, which work synergistically on both the exterior and the interior of the body.

Dosage—both the quantity of plants and water—is largely calibrated visually. The iloneleb' are careful to ensure that a patient uses the medication properly, especially if they need to leave some with the patient to be taken on a regular basis. They will explain how to use the medicine, how to mix it, and how much to use, but typically they will leave only a small amount, returning frequently to check on the patient and replenish the supply if needed. They are also concerned if the patient has been seeking care elsewhere or using home remedies, as these could either interfere with the medicine they are providing or lead to an overdose.

A third method for the delivery of medication is the poultice. Manuel Choc used this in the treatment of a man with a knee injury. The medicinal plants were soaked and placed on the knee, then bound with a cloth to keep them in place. He changed them twice over a half-day period. The poultice works in three ways: by introducing medication into the body through skin absorption, by drawing out the pain-causing sickness, and by reducing inflammation. "Yes, it worked," explains Manuel, when I inquire about the outcome. "Because he was able to walk when he left from here. He left his walking stick! He had it when he came to me." Poultices are considered particularly effective for inflammation, swelling, and infection; they can be used as part of the treatment for snakebite, drawing out the venom. The leaves from poultices, along with any other medicinal vegetative matter remaining from bathing or drinking, must be carefully handled because of their proximity to the sickness. They are contaminated and must be disposed of in an isolated or out-of-the-way place, where humans are unlikely to encounter them.

Different single plants may be used sequentially. Manuel Baki describes the treatment of a woman suffering from rilom tzuul (sickness caused by the mountain spirit), which caused her to fall, resulting also in xiwajenaq (frightened spirit). "First, I gave her medication to stop the fever," he explains, "because it was really high. Now I'm cooling it [sickness] down." Depending on how the patient responds, he considers the option of a third plant to use, as well as a bath. The mixing of plants is also common. Francisco, working with a patient suffering from an itchy skin disorder he believed had been caused by ant bites, describes using eight different types of leaves and bark. "This problem is in the person's body and blood, so it is necessary to use many plants to treat the itchiness and kill the problem," he explains. "All of these plants treat that problem." The leaves and the bark, shredded with his machete, are combined into one pot and cooked before the patient consumes and bathes in the mixture. It is important that these be cooked together as well and not administered singly; it is in the mix that potency is achieved. "I have tried these plants individually but couldn't treat the problem," he elaborates. "When it is combined together like this, then it's able to treat the itching problem. This itching problem is a very serious problem, and it requires strong medication."

The iloneleb' are not averse to using pharmaceuticals and other over-the-counter products in their work. Analgesics, in pill form and as rubs, and antibiotic creams are sometimes used, for instance. However, these are expensive, and even when they are thought to be more effective than available plants, the latter remain important because of their financial and physical accessibility.

Medical Technology

Q'eqchi' iloneleb', like all medical practitioners, employ technology to assist in their work. As Cassell (1997:63) defines it, medical "technology . . . refers to modalities and instrumentalities that greatly extend the power of human action, sensation, or thought, independently of their user." In other words, technology expands "therapeutic power." This includes medication. Of course, for the Q'eqchi' we are not talking about X-rays or MRIs but rather material items found in or manufactured from the local environment that facilitate curing of patients. While their materiality is obvious, the mechanism by which these work is often embedded in the meta/material. Indeed, these tools reinforce the conceptual integration of the material and meta/material worlds characteristic of Q'eqchi' medicine.[5]

Several technological items are used to assist in drawing out or otherwise removing the pathology. For the most part, the technology is secular. It involves items that are commonly found and easily accessible. Sometimes the patient is responsible for providing them. Eggs, for instance, are well-known throughout the Maya world as instruments to treat evil eye and other disorders in which spirits or other meta/material forces are implicated (e.g., Rubel 1964; Tenzel 1970; Cosminsky and Scrimshaw 1980; Foster 1985; Orellana 1987; Kunow 2003). The iloneleb' in this research describe using eggs to treat a variety of disorders, such as q'an yaj (ulcer or stomach "sores"). Francisco, in one treatment, describes carefully pressing two eggs into the stomach ulcer while doing the jilok and praying. The treatment is done once per day for three days, for about fifteen minutes each time; medicinal plants are also used. This is an ordinary egg, from a turkey, goose, or duck provided by the family, and between treatments it is placed in a jar of water to protect it. A coin is placed under the egg as it is pressed down on the site of the ulcer pain. Francisco understands that an "eye" that can "see" lives in the stomach and that this eye is also affected by the sickness; it is necessary to "close" the eye by placing the coin on it. The egg's function is to draw out the sickness causing the ulcer and pain, which is upsetting the eye and the lukum (ascaris worms) that live normally in the gut. Like other medical waste, both the coin and the egg, now contaminated, must be disposed of in a place in the forest away from human habitation. Otherwise, a person with a weak "immune system" (here Francisco means spiritually not physically weak) who happens upon them could contract the sickness. The ilonel is protected from contracting the sickness, even if the egg breaks. "There is a prayer that the iloneleb' say when treating a patient," explains Francisco, "that safeguards them from getting this sickness, whereby someone without any safeguard would be weak in spirit and would be affected."

Other items of technology are used to entice sickness out. These include tortilla and meat from animals such as chickens, provided by the family of the patient. These are usually used together. The sickness is personified and must be treated in a humanly fashion. "It is just like you're feeding humans," says Manuel Choc. "We eat tortilla with meat; we can't only eat meat alone. That is why we have to feed the evil spirit so that they leave the patient." Lorenzo explains that the spirit of the sickness "will be asked to feed on these items, and in return they would leave the sick person. You will be asking them to eat and drink, using the prayers of curing." They are typically placed against the body of the patient during the process. When it's done, just like the eggs, the tortilla and meat are considered contaminated, possibly imbued with the sickness, and they must be disposed of carefully and away from humans.

This notion of offering or sacrifice or *xk'eeb'al toj* (offering tribute or payment) represents a dynamic use of technology. Corn tortilla, tobacco, animals, and fish are medical tools that serve an integral function in treatment by being offered to the spirits or the sickness in return for the release of the patient from the infirmity. This idea that sickness, in the form of spirit, needs to be lured or compensated, or simply kept happy, looms large in the Q'eqchi' medical system and is a component of the larger perceived ethic of permission and reciprocity. Food offering—literally giving something of significant value—represents a supreme form of payment to the sickness or the evil spirit, accompanied by a request or even exhortation from the ilonel to accept the offering in return for leaving the patient alone. Meat is more difficult to acquire; hence it has greater value as a payment than corn tortilla. Atonement for the patient's sins, if such transgression is implicated in the patient's disorder, may also require a sacrifice, employing a procedure known as *isink awas* (meaning "to remove the awas") or simply *awas*. (This treatment is unrelated to the awas that affects infants and young children.) Frequently, this sacrifice takes the form of an animal butchered for the purpose in advance, but sometimes the animal is sacrificed during the treatment itself. Fowl, such as a turkey, chicken, or goose, are commonly used. Any animal owned by the family will suffice, although the ilonel may prefer to match the animal in certain characteristics with the patient. A young turkey, for instance, might best match with a sick child; a noisy animal with a patient with wax ru or waxk'ay (forms of insanity); a black bird for someone with a sickness involving the "black" devil. All of this reflects what is known as the doctrine of signatures (Kunow 2003): treating with plants or animals that resemble in some way a sickness or an afflicted body part or organ. In this case, the freshly killed animal will be passed over the patient's body to the four cardinal points while the ilonel prays and calls upon the sickness to exit the patient.

Another important item of technology is pom, incense made from the sap of the copal tree (though there are several different varieties) that gives off a thick, black, pungent smoke and a strong odor when burned. It too is part of the sacrificial complex at the core of Q'eqchi' medicine, but in its natural state it is not sacred in itself. Indeed, the iloneleb' sometimes buy it in town. Often formed into a lump or ball, the pom is used in many ways, most commonly as an offering. "The pom is normally used to ask for blessing to or from the Tzuultaq'a," according to Francisco. "Whenever activities are done, cleaning milpa [plantations] and planting, or treating sickness, the pom is used to ask permission. This is an offering to make a connection between the human and the earth or cosmos." Francisco, while praying, rubs it on the wrist of a patient suffering from xiwajenaq (frightened spirit) "to tell the sickness to leave him and that his spirit be restored." Similar to the meat and tortilla, the pom is discarded, in this case at the site where the original fright occurred. Emilio notes that pom is often burned at the site where meat and tortilla sacrifices are deposited in the bush. "It is burned along with praying to dedicate the sacrifice to the spirits," he says, "to whichever he [the patient] has done wrong, and that his sacrifice is accepted so that he gets better."

Pom may be used on a variety of body parts or rubbed on the body more generally. Pom may also be burned in a procedure referred to as *sib'te'enk*, or "smoking" the patient. Emilio explains: "It is burned along with praying to dedicate the sacrifice to the spirits, to whichever he has done wrong and so that his sacrifice is accepted so that he gets better." But it is also used to "chase off whatever is causing the sickness of that person." Contained within an incense holder, the smoking pom may be carried around the patient, filling the air with smoke as the holder sways back and forth. It may also be burned in a pot in front of the patient. In some cases, the patient may be encouraged to inhale the smoke, especially if there is an internal dimension to the sickness, but in other cases, inhaling will not help the problem. The rising smoke is understood to reach the spiritual realm and to communicate the request of the ilonel, on behalf of the patient, for the return to health.

Unfortunately for the iloneleb', like many medical technologies, pom can also be harmful. It is known to be used in witchcraft; the protagonist shapes it into the form of the victim. Lorenzo has been forced to acknowledge this problem and uses pom carefully. "I can't burn it because we're in the village," he says. "If they [other villagers] smell the scent of the copal, they would think about something bad. They would say we're doing witchcraft."

Candles are employed in a similar fashion. Typically, candles are used as offerings, to help convince Qaawa' to restore the patient to good health. During treatment they are passed, unlit, over the patient's body or are placed on particular areas of the body, while the ilonel prays to Qaawa'. They may also be lit and then deposited in a fire or a pot serving as a fire pit, sometimes with pine kindling, and are typically positioned in front of the patient. Most treatments requiring candles use four colors—red, yellow, black, and white—each symbolizing an element of the body and a cardinal direction (as we saw in chapter 3). In some cases, two other colors—blue (sky) and green (forest)—are added. Following treatment of a child with a form of epilepsy that Emilio calls *rajlal po nat'ane'k* ("falls monthly" or falls regularly), he provides an additional explanation for the candle colors and the pine:

> These candles, there are six different types that are used. The red is for our life, our blood. It asks for a blessing for this individual. This is placed where the sun rises (East). I used white. The white is for our life. The yellow is for whatever problem is affecting an individual. The blue is used to ask for good luck in a person's life or what gifts he has in his life. There are two types of candles, the blue and the green, that serve the same purpose for good luck in the future. The black signifies the sunset (West); it is in this direction that all the evil things are in the dark. It's the dark side of life. We ask from the spirit of this direction that we avoid problems. The pine is for the well-being or the strength of an individual to overcome the sickness.

During his treatment for rajlal po nat'ane'k, he uses red candles. After passing them through the smoke of the burning pom "to take the power of the flame so to cool down the problem of the child," he places them up against the child's forehead while he prays. He does this in recognition that the brain was involved in the sickness. "Because it is in the head that we think, and his mind is being affected, so I have to ask help to relieve this problem," Emilio explains. Red, symbolizing blood, is used, as interpreter Federico Caal articulates: "Along with the brain, the blood has to work, the blood has to flow, so

FIGURE 26. The altar of Emilio Kal showing candles (back left, front right), medicinal plant bundles (left and right front), medicine bag (back right), saint, and crucifix (back center). Jalacte, 2013. Photo by author.

the candle as well resembles the blood. So he is asking the blood to help, to start flowing through. It's not functioning well, so that is what causes much of this problem." The candles will draw out the sickness; they will be deposited into the pot with the burning pom and left until the fire burns out. During this treatment, Emilio also uses a lime, rubbed on the child's head, also to take out the sickness, and this too is deposited in the fire.

Alcohol in various forms is an important element in Q'eqchi' medicine. There is ample evidence for a long history of the production of alcohol among the Maya, augmented in more recent times by commercially available products, including rubbing alcohol, liquor (especially rum), and colognes with high alcohol content, such as *agua florida* (a mixture of several fragrant plants with some alcohol content, considered by some to be medicinal). Alcohol's connection with spiritual ceremonies is strong, and the contemporary use of alcohol in treatment seems ubiquitous (e.g., Nash 1967; Fabrega 1970; Foster 1985; Watanabe 1992; Chevalier and Bain 2003; Kunow 2003). Its medical uses are well known, especially as an antiseptic and analgesic. It is also known to have important thermal effects on the body, with an ability to warm a cold body and cool a hot one, depending on the sickness (Watanabe 1992; Chevalier and Bain 2003). The particular form of alcohol matters to the iloneleb', since rum is considered hot and agua florida is cold. A small amount may be offered to the patient to consume, especially if he or she is experiencing pain or cramps. Some iloneleb' in the MHAB also use it to "cleanse" the patient. One method is to shower the patient: the ilonel takes a small amount into his mouth and sprays it over the head and upper body of an afflicted individual, typically on all four sides to represent the cardinal points. Interpreter Tomas Caal elaborates on the process as articulated by Emilio:

> So, in order for the rum to actually help the person, there must be the healing prayer that goes with it. So the ilonel would have been saying the prayer [first]. Then the rum would have much more power to help the individual. So that is the reason why they would use their mouth, to symbolically take away the evil spirit. And their words are powerful so that the rum is also powerful. In this way you know that we are helping somebody. We are not abusing anybody.

Taking the rum into the mouth, the place from which the prayers emanate, imbues it with the spiritual power to achieve the treatment goals, analogous to the use of blowing during jilok.

Some iloneleb' consume drinkable alcohol for its protective and antiseptic properties, combining a material understanding with a meta/material one. "If a person is sick, we come in close contact with the person," explains Francisco. "He might also have tuberculosis, or other sickness that is contagious. We breathed and talked together. That is why I have to drink some rum to help against these problems. It kills the germs that are causing the sickness." Commercial rum is considered to be the very best for this purpose, but it is expensive. When alcohol is not available, medicinal plants can be chewed by the practitioner, but this provides less protection. Francisco also is testing a new formula as an insect repellant, since Q'eqchi' people cannot afford products from the store: "We have something that we're experimenting with, jack ass bitter [a plant] and alcohol. Not everybody knows how to make it. This helps to guard you from these insects. We prepared some for our trip into the forest reserve, and it was very effective."

But there are meta/material uses of alcohol as well, to spiritually protect and strengthen the ilonel. In this research, only Francisco and Emilio used it this way because, as Manuel Choc said, only they do the "spiritual ceremony" as part of their treatments. Any engagement with potentially malevolent spirits is a threat to iloneleb'. They must be prepared. "If the ilonel does not have a longer period of [sexual] abstinence, they are weak," according to Emilio. "So, in order for you to combat the evil spirit, you need to be strong. You need to go to the patient with a stronger blood. If your body is not prepared, it could be then that, you know, maybe you can get affected or your patient does not cure." Levels of mild intoxication may be reached when dealing with serious cases, with alcohol consumed between rounds of treatment. Alcohol may also be consumed by the iloneleb' prior to or after a treatment session, a feature noted by other researchers as well (e.g., Holland and Tharp 1964; Tenzel 1970; Fabrega and Silver 1973).

Alcohol also fits into the ethical relationship between humans and the spirits, especially the Tzuultaq'a. It is used as an offering, to ask the Tzuultaq'a for permission to use their resources. As well, it can be offered to help ensure prosperity and health. According to Emilio:

> If you want good in your life for your family, you would need to give this to Mother Earth. Mother Earth is our mother, and that's where we get our money [resources] from. That's where we get whatever our household needs. So we would need to give it to Mother Earth to drink. In spiritual ceremonies, you would find spiritual guides pouring rum on the four cardinal points. This is to give back to Mother Earth what it deserves, as you're asking for the well-being of your family.

Before a treatment begins, if the sickness warrants, Emilio and Francisco might make an offering to the cardinal points by sprinkling alcohol on the ground in the area where the treatment will occur. This demarcates a kind of therapeutic space for the next steps in the process and propitiates the spirits through payment for the services they are about to be requested to offer.

Finally, I need to touch on how iloneleb' treat snakebite. There are several very poisonous snakes in southern Belize, including the fer-de-lance (a pit viper; *Bothrops asper*), and it is common for the iloneleb' to be called upon to treat a bite victim. If the bite is very recent, the ilonel is most likely to begin treatment by sucking the poison out with his mouth, perhaps after having made a small incision at the site of the bite. This application of suction is known the world over and meets with varying degrees of success. The iloneleb' know this is dangerous for them as well, and while the mouth-suction technique represents a kind of traditional "instrument," they see no reason not to seek out an improved method. Commercial snakebite kits, with plastic suction pumps, have proven of interest. Pulsing, prayers, and medicinal plants are always used as well, of course.

The Clinical Context

The Maya calendar, in addition to being a diagnostic tool, is also important in treatment. It is generally known that certain days are better than others for certain treatments and that some days should be avoided where possible. "Each day of the Maya calendar has different spirit and powers," says Francisco. "Every day is different and has a different meaning. It has different grades and energies." For instance, atonement for sin is best done on No'j, according to Francisco. He also tries to treat patients suffering from k'a'uxlak (excessive worry or anguish) on No'j. "You need a strong day to stabilize the mind, like 12 No'j," a day known to reflect the energy of the mind, "so that the mind would open and function good in order to achieve the goal that he wishes." Francisco and Emilio in particular use the Maya calendar to determine the best day to cure a specific sickness in the context of a patient's maatan (destiny linked to the day they were born).

The Greco-Roman tradition of a seven-day week is also invoked to some extent by all the iloneleb'. They know, for instance, that evil spirits are particularly active on Thursdays and Fridays, so extra precautions should be taken when treating or visiting patients. Saturday is recognized as a strong therapeutic day.

Time of day, in some cases, is important to consider when planning a treatment session. Many treatments that have significant spiritual involvement must be done at very particular times. Midnight is common. In his treatment of a case of kaanil (spirit loss), Lorenzo explains that night provides a cover for the returning spirit, which otherwise could be easily frightened by encounters with other living entities. Emilio uses a technique called *b'oqok mu* ("calling spirits") to bring back the lost spirit, and usually the treatment occurs at night, around eight or nine, when the patient is already asleep. He wakes the patient, to be bathed in a medicinal concoction from cacao, at three in the morning, "because that's when the red star is coming up, and only at that time you can do it."

Almost any locale can serve as the "clinic" where treatment is undertaken. Some treatments are typically done in the patient's home; some can be done anywhere the patient is found, especially if urgent attention is needed. The patient may also come to the home of the ilonel. Some more serious sicknesses, especially those involving evil spirits, may require a specialized, often isolated place, a special hilltop or a cave, for instance, where an altar has been constructed. Emilio and Francisco have several such places, where one finds evidence of long-standing use. Francisco explains that while he can do some treatments anywhere, some will contaminate the locale. "You should have a special place, because there are sicknesses that require too much power," he notes, "and when we do it anyplace, we leave some negative energy there that somebody can be damaged or affected by." Sicknesses that were caused by an incident, such as a fall, may require the patient and ilonel to return to that spot, where the patient's lost spirit is likely to be lingering. The iloneleb' are highly mobile then, except when experiencing their own mobility issues as they age, and do not have a set clinical space in which to work.

Clinical Empiricism

"What would happen if the sickness didn't go away?" I ask Lorenzo one day during an interview. He laughs. "Well, it's time to change to another bush doctor!" he replies. But then he grows more serious. "I will go and get other plant medicine to treat the problem." Picking up on his initial response, I push a little further. "So, you will still try to treat the problem?" He answers, "Yes, I have to treat a patient until he gets better." Turning a little pragmatic, he adds, "That makes the cost of the treatment go up, because you will have to go and obtain the plant medicines from very far. You will have to try your best so that the sickness goes out."

In a sense, the idea of treatment failure is not usually entertained by the iloneleb'. Emilio, when asked if he has ever been unable to cure a patient, explains succinctly, "No. I don't have any that I leave sick. All that we are asked to attend to get better." There is also a reluctance to admit that sometimes patients die under their care, despite their best efforts to cure them. In all cases where I have adequate information about such deaths, the patient was utilizing both biomedical and iloneleb' services, confounding the issue of jurisdictional culpability (see Waldram and Hatala 2015). However, sometimes cure is not easily or quickly achieved. The strength of the patient's blood or spirit is always important to treatment, for instance, and sometimes deficits here cannot be overcome. Francisco says that it is easy to cure a person with a strong nawal (gifted energy). But for an individual with a weak nawal, "it takes time. It's hard. Sometimes they never get cured." And, more pragmatically, the iloneleb' admit that sometimes a cure is not possible. Sicknesses of long standing, such as those related to witchcraft, can be vexing, especially if the patient has taken a long time to consult the ilonel. Sicknesses considered to be "new," such as HIV/AIDS, are considered by some iloneleb' to be beyond their expertise, as they have no traditional experience with them. This does not mean, however, that some will not try. As documented elsewhere (Waldram and Hatala 2015), they often understand a sickness, such as those related to HIV, to be related to other, more familiar sicknesses before they conclude that there is something more serious and unfamiliar going on.

The ilonel may need to adjust treatment strategies or plant medicines, and perhaps even reconsider the initial diagnosis, with difficult cases. It may be some time before progress, let alone total cure, is apparent. Manuel Choc, describing eet aj yajel (epilepsy; the "foolish sickness"), which the iloneleb' understand to be curable, explains, "Sometimes the sickness goes out completely. But sometimes, if it is not treated good, it comes back again." Thermal properties are of course important in how the iloneleb' approach treatment, yet they are rarely wedded to any particular interpretation of a sickness as hot or cold. For instance, in treating a case of *k'otakil*, or diarrhea, Manuel Choc assumed at the start that it was a cold sickness. So he used a hot medicinal plant mixed in warm water. When that was unsuccessful, he reinterpreted the sickness and used a cold plant and cool water, with success.

Although the iloneleb' have undergone considerable training by masters to practice medicine, to a significant degree their knowledge is shaped and expanded by actual clinical cases. "You learn as you go along," says Manuel Choc. They rely on practice-based evidence—that is, evidence based on real-world clinical experience—to refine their knowledge (Green 2006; Swisher 2010). In their quest to cure, they often find themselves changing treatment directions; adjusting the medicines, prayers, and other techniques used; and even changing the diagnosis in response to persistent disorders. They are unafraid to adjust accordingly and do not stubbornly cling to a diagnosis or approach that does not appear to be working or, even worse, dismiss the case as untreatable. As Lorenzo explains succinctly when detailing his treatment for waxk'ay (mild craziness), "if the waxk'ay doesn't cure with one medicinal plant, then you change it." His general approach to clinical empiricism is clear. "If the sickness doesn't stop," he says, "the ilonel has to find a way how to cure the sickness. He will go to look for medicines that he hasn't tried yet, give them to the patient, and treat the patient until the sickness is completely gone." Francisco, discussing his treatment of a case of q'an yaj (ulcer or stomach "sores"), remarks that if one treatment does not work, "I will have to look for another treatment, which will be with medicinal plants, because there are many plants to treat ulcer." The issue at hand is determining the best plant or combinations to use in each specific case. In this manner, practitioner clinical knowledge continually develops. Albino concurs with this approach. If a treatment is not working, he does not give up:

> I will continue the treatment and change the plant medicines. Sometimes a [single] treatment does not work, and you have to do another one, or maybe three or four times, or until the person gets better. If I give a patient one set of plants and it is not working, it might be a different sickness. I would use another set until I find which one would work.

About treating maa'us aj musiq'ej (sickness caused by evil spirits), Manuel Choc adds simply, "Well, what I do if the plant medicine does not work is I change it until I find the plant to treat the problem."

A good example of this willingness to change course is evident in a treatment by Lorenzo of a woman suffering from stomach pain and vomiting, with fever, chills, and headache. He initially diagnosed her with q'an yaj, or stomach ulcer, a common problem. He describes his approach: "I heated her body with medicinal plants at that time [warmed on the fire hearth]. She suffered abdominal pain, and the entire waist area is where I heated with plant medicine. I massaged [jilok] her and gave her medicine to drink." The patient recovered within a few days, but two months later she experienced similar symptoms, this time more serious. Lorenzo concluded that the first treatment had not been entirely successful and began to suspect that his initial diagnosis was not accurate, now judging the disorder to be xyajel maa'us, or sickness of the devil or evil spirit. This was a new sickness for him, one he knew about but had never actually treated. He decided to change the approach accordingly and use different plant medicines. "I was experimenting with plants for that sickness," he explains, "because I'm not sure which plant to use for that problem." The patient recovered again within a few days and several months later remained symptom free.

This is an excellent example of diagnostic rationality and empiricism. Typically, a less serious form of a sickness, such as q'an yaj, is assumed before a more serious one is entertained. Q'eqchi' iloneleb' "think horses, not zebras, when they hear hooves," as the expression goes. A sign and symptom constellation leads to a familiar or common diagnosis first, and only in the face of contrary information—a lack of proper response from the pulse or, more generally, a patient not recovering—does the ilonel entertain a more esoteric possibility. If prayer and plant medicines alone are ineffective, the ilonel may suspect that obeah or witchcraft is involved, leading to the use of an awas procedure involving an animal sacrifice. Treatment is linked to diagnosis, and both are understood in the context of the medicines, prayers, and techniques known to treat the specific sickness. The selection of plants, for instance, is not random but rather categorical. "Each sickness has its own set of plants," explains Manuel Choc. "If one plant does not work, I try another, until I find its [the sickness's] treatment." As noted above, biologists have documented the different species of plant medicines used for specific sicknesses by members of the MHAB and other Maya practitioners (e.g., Amiguet et al. 2005; Bourbonnais-Spear et al. 2005, 2007; Amiguet,

Arnason, and Maquin 2006; Awad et al. 2009; Heinrich et al. 1998), a set of sickness-specific options from which the ilonel can draw, like a biomedical practitioner diagnosing an infection and choosing from a set of known antibiotics. If one does not work, another one is tried. A smaller set of more generic and accessible go-to plants is often used first before more targeted plants are accessed. From the xyajel maa'us case, Lorenzo gained both diagnostic and treatment skills and knowledge, and he is better positioned to recognize and treat a case of xyajel maa'us in the future.

Clinical empiricism is at the heart of the training of Q'eqchi' iloneleb' and in many ways is at the core of the Q'eqchi' medical system more generally. "Medicine began by the ancestors," explains Manuel Choc. "What happened was that they experimented with different plants for different sicknesses. When a particular sickness was cured, then that plant was labeled for that sickness. Everybody exchanged ideas on the remedies." Francisco likewise suggests that the origins of Q'eqchi' medicine are found in experimentation on a sick person; some try different plants, others different forms of jilok. "Suddenly the sickness would go away," he explains. "When that happened, people would repeat the process any time another person got sick. This information was kept and passed on through generations and can be found today and practiced by traditional iloneleb' in all Maya communities." Francisco shares a story about the origins of known remedies for snakebite that highlights how medical knowledge was attained by humans. It involves a person observing a conflict between a snake and a vulture. When the vulture attacks the snake hoping for a meal, the poisonous snake bites it. The vulture goes to the edge of a nearby stream, eats some leaves, and seems fine. He tries a second time, is bit again, and eats more leaves. On the third try the vulture is successful and enjoys the meal. After the vulture flies away, the observer finds the plant that the vulture was eating. A new snakebite medicine has been discovered!

Francisco and Manuel Choc are referencing a source of knowledge that is often called the oral tradition. Yet it would be insufficient to refer to their medical knowledge as primarily oral tradition, as is often the case with Indigenous peoples, as this idea cannot accurately grasp how knowledge advances at the level of individual practitioner. Certainly, there is a need to propitiate the ancestors by acknowledging their role in the initial development of medical knowledge, but clinical empiricism is the true legacy that has been passed on, the inclination to learn about sickness and its treatment through apprenticeship, hands-on practice, and experimentation.

The practitioners in this study did not respond to a "calling," and their knowledge of medicine is not, directly speaking, a gift of God, as is suggested in some other studies of Maya medicine (e.g., Metzger and Williams 1963; Fabrega and Silver 1973). Qaawa' has provided everything that humans need to identify and cure sickness, and it is up to them to figure it out from there. The knowledge of the iloneleb' comes from deliberately applying themselves to learn under their masters and to develop their clinical expertise as practitioners. This is not a lecture-based educational system; while some aspects of treatment, such as the prayers, must be learned in advance, training involves hands-on clinical experience under the watchful eye of the master. Lorenzo explains how he was taught in this experiential way:

> It was hard. The hard part is when you're taken to do a treatment for the very first time. You'll not be sure what the sickness would be. Your master will ask you if you understand what the sickness is. If you don't understand it, your master can go with you for another time. But he will also ask you to check the patient's pulse to diagnose the problem. He will ask you again and again to feel it, so that you understand how the blood is flowing. If you still are not sure what the problem is, he will describe to you how it feels to him.

Francisco discussed learning in a similar way. His uncle, who was teaching him, started by taking him to treatments. "He asked me to pay attention keenly to the prayers used to do treatment," remembers Francisco. "Yes, he told me the prayers, and I would repeat them to do treatments. The lessons are all theory, and my uncle taught me step by step about the praying and to do the jilok [massage]. He showed me the techniques." Francisco was taken to many patients by his uncle, to first observe and then, like Lorenzo, to try diagnosing and using the jilok. It took several months to learn the technique and the prayer associated with jilok before he was allowed to move on to learn, in sequence, how to maneuver a fetus in the uterus for proper birth position, and then how to treat back pains, menstrual problems, snakebite, and ulcer. Only then did he graduate to more complex problems involving meta/material forces, such as kaanil (spirit loss).

The Clinical Experience

In a paper published with my colleagues Andrew Hatala and Tomas Caal (Hatala, Waldram, and Caal 2015), we suggest that Q'eqchi' nosology for mental disorders could be meaningfully understood to constitute a narrative with several "genres" of disorders. As narrative theorists know, narrative is essentially about experience. Hence these genres represent categorical kinds of patient experiences or, more properly, patient–practitioner interactive experiences of diagnosis and treatment. Perhaps surprising is that this narrative structure seems to exist without significant input by the patient. The clinical encounter typically is not one in which the patient relates a detailed story of the emergence of symptoms in the context of a life being lived and reflected upon. There is little effort or need to develop a "shared narrative" (Mattingly 1994), and there certainly is no polyphonic merging of voices of patient, practitioner, and others, as Harvey (2013) has described. Rather, as I argue (Waldram 2015b), the patient is somewhat dialogically passive.[6] The narrative structures of which we wrote are the product of a variety of experiential and diagnostic inputs in which the patient plays a role that is rarely if ever the dominant one.

As I noted earlier, in the chapter on diagnosis, typically, when an ilonel is initially consulted by patient or family, some information regarding the patient's disorder is provided. While the patient or family member is likely to relate something of the signs and symptoms that are being noticed—these may be physically embodied or behavioral—they are unlikely to tell a story of the sickness. Since some sicknesses, as we have seen, are inherently narratological insofar as they are best diagnosed through the understanding of an experience (for instance, falling in the river), it is sometimes necessary for the ilonel to ask a few questions at the outset of treatment. "I ask the patient what happened, either falling or getting frightened in a river," Albino relates. In other cases, the ilonel may feel the need to obtain more information. "I ask how they feel," notes Emilio. This is of greater importance to Emilio especially because of his use of the Maya calendar. "It is necessary to ask questions—for example, when did this start or how do you feel? On which day the sickness started?" This interaction with the patient precedes the treatment and is mainly for purposes of diagnosis.

During the actual treatment, there is virtually no dialogue between the patient and the ilonel, with the exception of instructions regarding bodily position (for instance, asking the patient to roll over) and, when the treatment is over, instructions about the use of any plant medicines. Unless directed to pray, which is typically done as an independent, simultaneous, and unsynchronized act with the ilonel and others present, the patient typically says nothing and remains passive. The dialogue that characterizes the treatment session is primarily between the ilonel and the blood, the sickness, Qaawa', or other meta/material entities understood to be involved. As we have seen, this prayer dialogue is often uttered at a very low, inaudible volume, rapidly, and it sometimes involves an esoteric form of the Q'eqchi' language that is unfamiliar to almost all patients. "I don't know the words he uses" (Waldram 2015b) is a typical response of patients to my query about if they understood what was happening during treatment. The iloneleb' are blunt when they say that it is often not necessary to talk to the patient to diagnose a problem, and this disinclination continues throughout treatment. Nor is it important that the patient understand what is being said by the ilonel, who is busy engaging the relevant meta/material forces. "No, it is not necessary," explains Emilio, suggesting that the patient has no real role to play. "It is us that prepare the treatment." A few even suggest that patients are not capable of using such knowledge safely, so it is best that they not be informed. "No, I don't tell them [about their sickness]," says Emilio, "because many times people would take things very seriously. Some people might not understand the disorder and would start to say [it is] something else. This can cause a problem for him and for me as well. I just tell them their problem is a minor case, so let's do our best to treat it." This is especially the case when witchcraft is suspected, as we saw earlier, but it is also an issue when medicinal plants are left for the patient; patients may overdose if they know what is being used and are able to find it themselves. "No, I don't know what plant he gave me," says one patient after a treatment. "I only know that it can help to cure the sickness." Patients seem unconcerned that they are not informed about the treatment. As Francisco reminds us, "People are used to this tradition."

Despite treatment rich in symbolism—as all medical treatments are—interviews with patients show that they rarely understand the symbols, and the iloneleb' never explain them. This means that anyone from any cultural or linguistic background can be effectively treated; the patient need not be Q'eqchi'. The meaning and therapeutic force of the symbols are the domain of the medical practitioners and their interlocutor meta/material forces and entities. In a sense, then, the shared symbolic system is between the ilonel and these meta/material forces. The ilonel, of course, represents a powerful symbol, but one for which the meaning is somewhat obscure for patients beyond a connection with the past and a rich cultural heritage. It would therefore be tremendously misleading to suggest that Q'eqchi' medical practice is fundamentally symbolic or transformative, despite the popularity of this interpretation of Indigenous medical systems, as I argue earlier in this book. There are few purposive transactional symbols used (which is not to say there is no symbolism), and post-treatment interviews with patients uncover that language is not the only thing they do not understand about the treatment. They rarely understand what the ilonel is doing or why. How pulsing works, what jilok is, what the eggs and tortilla are for—none of this is explained, and they do not ask.

There is also little use of "talk therapy," in which the ilonel entertains a conscious dialogical process, allowing the patient to speak about his or her concerns and receive counsel from the wise practitioner. The Jerome Frank multifactor model (Frank 1961; Frank and Frank 1993) for a successful therapeutic relationship does not hold here. A few other studies—most notably the work of Kaja Finkler (1985, 1994) and, more recently, Sienna Craig (2012)—have noted the relative lack of dialogue during the clinical encounter and, in Finkler's work in Mexico, a disinclination on the part of the practitioners to learn anything about the patients, even their names. In the Q'eqchi' case, psychosocial issues are usually medicalized as medical disorders and are treated with pulsing, prayers, plants, and jilok, just like other disorders. Mental signs and symptoms in the absence of a behavioral component are often not seen as sicknesses at all. Interpersonal stresses and strains, such as problems between a husband and wife, are not treated with a Q'eqchi' form of psychotherapy or family therapy but with medical therapy, and both partners need not be involved. When I tell Francisco about how psychologists and psychiatrists might try to treat a patient by talking with him or her only, he replies respectfully, "I have no doubt that can cure, but we have our way. That is how we understand life and how we hope to help the people. . . . Because we do not convince the person through the words. We make the person feel it through the energy."

As an example, I observed a session involving Emilio and a couple who came to see him about troubles in the family related, in effect, to their poverty. They wished to have the lot of their lives improved and asked Emilio for help. The problems between the husband and wife resulting from their disagreeable situation were not detailed for me, and Emilio notes only that such "troubles" existed. "It is only a problem with financial resources, and that is what we're helping with. His [the husband's] main problem is a not very good relationship with his wife." But rather than using talk therapy, Emilio approaches the problem as he would other medical disorders, by linking it to the husband's maatan, his destiny or luck (or, more properly, his lack of luck), which is inhibiting his ability to get ahead and properly provide for his family. Emilio's treatment for this is quite elaborate, and with the assistance of Francisco, he uses a broad range of approaches and techniques, including candles, pom, turkey, agua florida, and extensive prayer. He even provides plant medicine to "cool down" the family. At certain points all those present—the iloneleb' and family members—engage in simultaneous yet individualized prayer in a cacophony of tangled voices. But at no point does either ilonel provide any advice or direction for the couple to help them work out their problems.

This approach is typical when dealing with psychosocial issues, be they individual or group in origin. Spousal therapy, as described above, is a good example. "Let's say a husband and wife had some problems between them," I ask Emilio one day. "How would you treat that?" "That can be treated by me praying and asking for blessing, for that particular household, from Qaawa' and the air, using candles," Emilio replies matter-of-factly. "This would help treat the problem." Manuel Choc describes how he treats issues between a husband and a wife where one is clearly the problem, having left the household. Interpreter Pedro Maquin explains:

> What he does to them, with the knowledge and the prayers he has, is

> to bring couples together again. He prepares either a drink or bread for the person who is bad in the family. Whenever the person eats that, it remedies the mind, and they come back together to live. The person who causes the problem most is the one that is treated. The prayer calms down the mind whenever the person eats that item.

This medicalized approach is sometimes what the family requests. "They don't have a very good relationship in their household," Emilio explains, discussing a recent treatment. "The woman always thinks of leaving her husband. Her husband told us that whenever he goes somewhere, she blames him with having another woman. He thought maybe she was given a spell [through witchcraft], so he asked us to help her with plant medicine." The wife consented to treatment. "Well, the woman admitted that she has a problem," Pedro interprets Emilio. "She feels that there is a problem that is affecting her, and she agreed to the treatment. She has children and doesn't want to have this problem and separate." The treatment was reminiscent of many I observed: "We burned an offering and had a ceremony and used plant medicine for her treatment," Emilio explains.

The absence of patient interviews by the practitioners, including a lack of case histories, and anything resembling counseling in treatment have a profound effect on the length of treatment sessions. They tend to be quite short. The average length of treatment sessions that I video recorded was six and a half minutes. This is actually not all that unusual with so-called traditional treatments: Craig (2012) describes sessions of seven to eight minutes among Tibetan practitioners, Langford (1999) some five minutes among Ayurvedic practitioners in India, and Finkler (1994) less than ten minutes with Mexican spiritualist healers. Compare this with the average of sixteen and a half minutes for visits to primary care physicians in one US study (Mechanic, McAlpine, and Rosenthal 2001). A more recent study (Peckham 2016) of physicians across a wide range of specializations determined that most had between thirteen and sixteen minutes of "facetime" with each patient; the next most common time block was seventeen to twenty minutes. Only a small minority spent less than nine minutes. Of course, the type of treatment needed is the key factor in the actual length of Q'eqchi' clinical sessions, and the more it is necessary to engage the meta/material aspects or use medical technology, the greater the length of the session. And what constitutes a "treatment session" is also an important issue. In some documented sessions, I mark the start when the ilonel renders his opening prayer and the conclusion when he makes the sign of the cross over the patient and ends the prayer. With more elaborate ceremonies, I still use the start of the opening prayer, not the elaborate process of organizing and setting the needed items in place. I also exclude the time needed to explain the use of any plant medicines being left for the patient. These additional time periods would not add significantly to the overall average time, perhaps no more than a few minutes if there is no elaborate procedure or spiritual ceremony involved. Spiritual ceremonies are a different thing entirely, and some go several hours, with breaks, where there is often much dialogue. However, this is more social talk than it is therapeutic. The key point here is that the clinical demeanor and approach of the ilonel is professional, efficient, and somewhat detached from the patient.

Assessing Treatment Effectiveness

In this research, "effectiveness" of treatment means the extent to which intended outcomes are achieved; I reserve the term "efficacy" for references to clinical trials within the biomedical system (Young 1979, 1981, 1983). Both iloneleb' and patients (including their families) make assessments of effectiveness and act accordingly. Iloneleb' often state, or imply, that a cure has been achieved at the conclusion of treatment. Patients do not challenge this assertion, but if they feel there has not been sufficient improvement in their disorder, they are likely to quietly seek out another option.

Iloneleb' assess the effectiveness of their treatments clinically in several ways. The most immediate means is through pulsing. Not only will the pulse react when the correct sickness is mentioned (and there is a certain assuredness that once the sickness is known, cure will follow), as treatment ensues, the pulse should start to react accordingly, calming down and reassuming its normal flow and feel. The ilonel monitors the pulse throughout the treatment session and may check at all four pulsing points in sequence. Describing a case of xiwajenaq (frightened spirit), Manuel Baki explains that "by touching the blood pulse, if it is not flowing, she is not getting better."

But when cure requires several treatments, often over several days, the pulse is still the key barometer in the clinical assessment of effectiveness and prognosis. States Francisco with respect to his treatment of eet aj yajel, "The pulse of a person jumps very fast. You will have the patient bathe with plant medicine. Then you check the pulse in a week's time. If it is still jumping very fast, you need to provide more plant medicine until it calms down." In fact, Francisco is willing to acknowledge that treatment can take weeks, even months, but not "years" and that while effective treatment serves to calm the patient, strengthen the body, and reduce seizures and other related problems in the interim, the ultimate goal remains to cure the individual of the disorder.

Most serious sicknesses require a course of treatment, and this is especially true of disorders of mental states. Emilio describes a patient with wax ru (severe craziness) who had been tied up by family members because of his erratic, threatening behavior, including running off into the bush. Six treatments on consecutive days, all somewhat different, were necessary. "On the first day of the treatment," Emilio explains, "he was not better. The second day he was like an intoxicated person [an improvement], and on the third day he was able to talk and recognized who we were." The patient was then untied, but the treatment continued, and on the sixth day, "he became normal." At this point, the treatment was declared a success. There was no predetermined course of treatment; Emilio committed to curing this individual, and in this case, it took six days. "I would have continued the treatment until the patient fully recovered, because that was my task," he adds.

Self-reports by patients and observations by iloneleb' and significant others are also very important in assessing effectiveness. Symptom relief is key, but so too are signs noticeable by the ilonel or family members. Pain subsides, rashes disappear, normal thinking patterns return, and the patient becomes more active, resuming normal roles; the proof is empirical and self-evident. "It is based on the way the patient feels," explains Emilio. "If the patient says I am feeling much better, then the medication has worked." Treating a child with xyajel maa'us (sickness of the devil or evil spirit), Manuel Baki notes that the patient's behavior is a key indicator; if the child becomes more mobile and regains an appetite, the treatment is working. Emilio, treating a little boy with choql (sickness caused by exposure to clouds or mist) who is experiencing eye distress, including excessive twitching and blinking, looks for the eyes to calm down. Manuel Choc details the multifaceted approach to determining effectiveness common to all iloneleb' in the MHAB: "There are two things to look for when a patient has gotten better," he says. "First of all, the blood pulse becomes normal; the blood will be flowing properly. It is not really running that fast. And the second one is the physical appearance of the person himself. Like maybe the facial appearance . . . the person would look better, more color in the face, and so on." He concludes, "The patient feels better too."

Follow-up is common but not characteristic of all sickness treatments. In some cases, cure is achieved unequivocally after treatment is concluded. In other cases, the ilonel may check back some time later to see how the patient is doing and, if necessary, undertake more treatment. Manuel Choc details his approach:

> After I have told the patient that he has gotten better, I would wait like, maybe, a week, then go back to see how he or she is doing. A week is a good wait because most sicknesses will come and go, and after I go back after this week, and then if the patient says that he has gotten better, then that would be the last visit.

This is often the case when the patient has been provided with plant medicines to use at home. The ilonel is likely to look in on the patient to ensure they are taking the medicines properly and, if necessary, provide more. For Emilio and Francisco, who often travel great distances to treat patients, follow-up can sometimes be tricky: "Well," says Francisco, "if a patient lives far away, maybe it takes three days or a week for me to go and ask how she is feeling. Yes, I have to go and ask if the medication worked well or if the sickness is cured." Follow-up may involve simply asking the patient how they are feeling, but it may also require a combination of prayer dialogue, pulsing, and jilok to determine if any sickness remains.

Sometimes the initial sickness gives way to other issues that must be addressed. With a snakebite, for instance, the patient may fear death, and this creates much worry, which can become a serious problem itself. In such circumstances, the ilonel "has to treat them both" [the snakebite and the anxiety], explains Francisco. "But first, he has to make sure to cure the sickness. And then, yeah, when it is a long-term sickness, that is where we have different activities for treating, because we have to treat the worries now." Worry, medicalized, is typically treated with plants and prayers, not psychotherapy and counseling.

The Four Pillars in Action

Francisco was involved in the treatment of a young woman with xyajel maa'us (sickness of the devil or evil spirit), which highlights the integrated nature of the four pillars. This woman was experiencing fainting, falling to the ground in convulsions while in the throes of seizure. Francisco identifies the proximate cause of the "epilepsy," that which causes the fainting and seizures, as a problem "with the blood circulation by the heart. If it stops circulating, the person falls." The distal causes relate, in part, to genetics: "Epilepsy comes or affects a person many ways. Sometimes it is passed on to children through the genes. Maybe a parent does not suffer greatly from it, but if it is inherited by a child, it would cause more danger and suffering from it." More specifically, xyajel maa'us is inherited "through the blood, from the development of a child [in utero]. It is in the parent, but they are strong [enough] to live with it. But in a child, when she is born, since she got it from the developing state and grows up, the sickness gets worse." This material explanation is supplemented by a meta/material one, as the parents may have acquired the xyajel maa'us in a different manner, involving evil spirits. "Yes, the parents got it through the air," says Francisco, "which is then brought to the child. This means that the evil spirit enters the person. It affects the blood, the spirit, the heart. This evil spirit is able to penetrate into the heart and mind, and it is this powerful spirit which can enter people." Treatment, logically, will require both material and meta/material approaches.

This was a problem the patient had been experiencing for more than a decade, and she had seen many medical doctors and traditional practitioners without a cure. A family member contacted Francisco to see if he could help and offered a small amount of money, fifty dollars, "to start the treatment." He began with pulsing and prayer dialogue to confirm the diagnosis. "First, I asked Qaawa', that in his name I will tend to this sickness. And then I started to feel the blood pulse, and in the name of God, I asked what she has encountered or what is happening to her. Then I started to feel how the blood is reacting to my question." He continues, "It is what you determine in her pulse. Her blood was flowing rapidly and seems as if it is scared and moves rapidly again." Diagnosis confirmed, he moved to the next step. "First I used my prayers for the jilok. That sickness, it requires that you start the jilok on the head, then going down, because the whole body is suffering from this sickness." Jilok with prayer was meant "to cool or ease down the problem in the person." He continues, "These prayers were learned to treat these problems. We start by asking Qaawa''s blessing, and through him this sickness would leave this person. It is in the prayer that [the sickness] is ordered to leave the person, calming her down." Jilok "restores" the patient, he adds. This he followed with sib'te'enk, "smoking" the person using the pom, to cleanse and offer a sacrifice on her behalf, while praying to the Tzuultaq'a. At this point, understanding the complexity of the case, he went off to look for the appropriate plant medicines. Upon return, he gave her the "medicinal treatment. I treated her with medicinal plants [intended] to treat epilepsy."

It took a long time to treat this young woman. Francisco worked for six months and used many different medicinal plants over that period. "I treated her every day. Every morning she would drink and bathe with the plants, and she would repeat this the following morning. Only one treatment per day. Any time it ran out, I replaced it with new medicine." Sometimes a family member would pick up the new medicine supply, but other times Francisco brought it and checked up on the patient. He estimates that he used the pulsing/jilok/prayer dialogue/pharmacology combination more than one hundred times over this period "until she got better." He watched her progress carefully: "If she is getting better, she does not fall. Slowly it started to go away, and after two months, nothing happens to her again. But I did not stop giving her medication, I did not want to let this sickness come back again." How was he certain that the patient had recovered? "She told me she got better. She does not experience any more problem as before, and that's how I knew that my treatment worked, because the medicines that we used is not only one but hundreds."

Treatment completed, he was paid another fifty dollars. One hundred dollars for six months of ongoing treatment might seem slim, but

Francisco, like the other iloneleb', does not complain. At the outset, he did not know that he would be involved with this patient for so long, but the imperative to cure was strong. "I didn't know it was going to last six months, but I told them that, together, we'll try our best until she gets better. We were grateful that within six months she got better." The family had for many years been trying to cure their daughter, and Francisco is compassionate. "I understand that for eleven years, they spent a lot of money on pharmaceutical medicines, healers, and other medications. I know for sure they feel very sorry for themselves. Even if it is not enough [money] for me, I cannot expect anything more because they spent their money." He continues to check in on her, more than a year later, and she is doing well with no reported relapses.

Conclusion

Members of the MHAB are well-trained, experienced, and knowledgeable medical specialists whose knowledge is closely tied to ongoing clinical experience. Their willingness to question their diagnoses and respond to difficult cases by altering directions represents the best of clinical patient care. With an imperative to cure, their approach to treatment reflects a highly developed system based largely on restorative processes. They are not always completely successful, of course, and they appreciate that improvement in a patient's disorder is better than no change at all. They also understand that the medical doctors at the hospital have better medicines and techniques for diagnosing and treating certain kinds of sicknesses, and they will readily refer patients to them. They themselves will occasionally go to the hospital or clinic, and with any disorder requiring surgery, there is no question. In this sense, they represent a powerful resource in a Belizean health system characterized, as are most national systems, by pluralism (Reeser 2014).

The analytical perspective that I have taken here is designed specifically to explain what the iloneleb' do when they treat patients, why, and what outcome they seek. As ethnographers understand, representations of experiential knowledge are flattened by the medium of text, and here the various aspects of Q'eqchi' medical treatment, dissected and teased out, inevitably offend the integrated approach to treatment that they actually employ. Just as both apprentice iloneleb' and Western medical students learn some aspects of their medicine from oral and written text, the really valuable knowledge comes from experience gained in the clinical setting—first watching, then doing. The documentary film *Healthy People, Beautiful Life: Maya Healers of Belize*, referenced in chapter 2, augments this text by visually demonstrating the approach and techniques used by the iloneleb'.

CHAPTER 7

Principle and Practice in Q'eqchi' Medicine

IN THE INTRODUCTION, I ask what is lost when we confine Indigenous therapeutics to the realm of symbolic "healing" and treat Indigenous knowledge as "beliefs" rather than as representative of a rational, empirically based, and detailed understanding of the material and meta/material aspects of the world and human life. One main argument of this book is that Q'eqchi' Maya therapeutics are best understood as a form of restorative medicine rather than transformative healing and thus there are some obvious and striking parallels with biomedicine. Rather than suggesting simply that biomedicine is the comparative standard for the truth value or robustness of knowledge claims, a suggestion that is typically criticized by medical anthropologists (e.g., Good 1994), I suggest that these similarities speak to a commonality in medical treatment that has survived the positivist science tradition of modern medicine and that speaks to clinical practice cross-culturally as founded on certain similar principles and approaches that emerge from an empirical engagement with bodily sickness and distress. As Good (1994:24) suggests, all medical systems harbor both "rational and deeply irrational elements" and "an attention to the material body" as well as a "concern for the moral dimensions of sickness and suffering." But why treat those moral aspects as largely religious, symbolic, and irrational or, in a word, immaterial and not as material and empirical? In a sense, the evidence-based practice movement in biomedicine represents the most recent attempt to dismiss this more universal approach to clinical therapeutics, what some advocates now call practice-based or experience-based evidence (Cassell 1991). In this concluding chapter, I want to first elucidate the main points of Q'eqchi' Maya principles and practice of medicine and then turn my attention to an equally significant issue: why it matters that we see this as medicine and not "healing."

On Principle and Practice

The "Principles of Medicine," according to the twenty-second edition of Davidson's well-known text (Walker et al. 2014:v), are "the mechanisms of health and disease, along with the professional and ethical principles underlying medical practice." The Q'eqchi' iloneleb' in this research clearly articulate these mechanisms and the broader professional and ethical principles within which they are embedded.

The iloneleb' have an imperative to cure their patients of the various diseases, disorders, and malign conditions that afflict them. In this, they engage an understanding of the material aspects of the world more broadly, one that includes tangible things you can touch and those things that are assumed real by virtue of consequence—that is, the virtual. "The practice of medicine . . . is irreducibly material," writes Montgomery (2006:26). "The body is there: alive, beyond construction or representation, although unknown without those human acts." The Q'eqchi' iloneleb' seek to know the body, using the best tools and knowledge available to them, including a willingness to learn from biomedicine. Part of that understanding involves the existence of certain other-than-human forces that affect humans in both positive and negative ways. I have referred to these less tangible aspects of the world—as understood within Q'eqchi' cosmovision—as the meta/material, and together with the material, they point toward efforts by these iloneleb' to comprehend, in a very practical sense, what makes people sick and what they can do about it. Another way of thinking about this is to appreciate that meta/material forces have material consequences, in that the body or mind becomes sick, and that those forces are susceptible to human intervention through ethical action. Even maatan ("destiny") is not without amenability to human agency. Maatan is not simply a fate ascribed at birth over which the person is powerless. Q'eqchi' iloneleb' suggest that there is some possibility to affect destiny positively, altering one's diathetic prognosis, through human action. In this sense we can say that the forces that affect human lives that exist beyond the material are still thought of as material-like, or virtual;

are subject to varying degrees of knowing and being known; and can be engaged.

This represents a form of phronesis in the Aristotelian sense, a practical and virtuous wisdom and knowledge that is based on a long tradition of empiricism. This is not simply the rote application of previous knowledge—that is, latent empiricism—to new cases. This is not "recipe knowledge" (Hausmann-Muela and Ribera 2003), although there are certainly times when the iloneleb' can go no deeper in explanation than "because that is how we do it" or "that is how we have always done it." Further, the meta/material is not simply magical in the sense of irrational thinking. Robert Thornton (2015) refers to magic not as a "deficient medicine" but positively as "a set of practices, including knowledge practices, that envelope and situate pragmatic and empirically grounded acts in an appropriate emotional—or 'spiritual—context." Thus defined, "magic" is a key component of biomedicine as well as Indigenous medicine (Gordon 1988; Thornton 2015), and it references both material and meta/material knowledge. For both Q'eqchi' and biomedical practitioners, this "magic"—initiated in the clinical encounter—provides the patient with the broader context beyond the clinic with which to make sense of the lived experience of sickness and to address existential issues. Q'eqchi' cosmovision provides this context.

What the Q'eqchi' iloneleb' engage in is manifest empiricism, the application of learned knowledge and experience to new cases of sickness, which requires them to identify and employ relevant diagnostic and treatment knowledge from a much larger pool of knowledge. This is not a random process, as Q'eqchi' medical knowledge is inherently categorical. As I show in chapter 4, medical knowledge is distributed through a nosological system that is largely shared among the iloneleb', even though there is no sanctioned body of medical knowledge and no textbooks or regulatory mechanisms that systematize and scrutinize that knowledge, no centripetal or involutionary force of conformity to standard. Both biomedical and Q'eqchi' therapeutics are based on "clinical empiricism"—that is, "the observation of patients and on the reflective appreciation of the physician's experience with illness and the care of patients" (Cassell 1997:59)—and on "clinical judgement"—that is, "the ability to work out how general rules . . . apply to one particular patient" (Montgomery 2006:5). Such practical reasoning—common to biomedicine as well (Saunders 2000)—is fundamentally about finding the best answer in a given context. It is neither exclusively inductive nor deductive; Montgomery (2006:47) suggests that this clinical approach is abductive, a "circular, interpretive procedure [that] moves between generalities in the taxonomy of disease and particular signs and symptoms of the individual case until a workable conclusion is reached." This is the interplay between latent and manifest empiricism and represents Q'eqchi' "best practices" of clinical medicine.

Like biomedicine, this is not a perfect system; nor does it have all the answers. Both are "messy" in the application of general knowledge to specific cases (Mol and Berg 1998), both are interpretive practices (Montgomery 2006), and both demonstrate a high degree of variability in what knowledge is accessed and applied. Clinical biomedicine is hardly the simple application of scientific knowledge, and the personal experiences and abilities of individual physicians loom large in the diagnostic and treatment processes (Berg 1998), as does personal morality (Montgomery 2006). Variability in knowledge and its clinical application, including varying degrees of consensus (Eddy 1990a, 1990b), should be no more surprising in either the Q'eqchi' medical system or biomedicine. But Q'eqchi' medicine does have sufficient answers that make sense, that are rational within the context of Q'eqchi' cosmovision and understanding of the material and meta/material aspects of the world. While it is true that such knowledge systems have "matured over a long period of time . . . under conditions which have permitted a gradual, spontaneous 'weeding out' of imperfections" (Richter 1972:46), as Allan Young (1979) and Robert Edgerton (1992) caution, longevity per se is no guarantee of effectiveness or even harm-free practice. Indeed, even biomedicine, with its current emphasis on "evidence-based medicine" (Eddy 2011), cannot escape the bounds of tradition in knowledge translation, as much clinical knowledge admittedly still "reflect[s] wisdom and understanding distilled over hundreds of years and passed from generation to generation of doctors" (Cumming and Noble 2014:2). Daily clinical empiricism is what maintains the status of such knowledge as useful.

This research demonstrates that we should not assume that practitioners and patients share broad cultural symbolic systems or worldviews, desired goals of treatment, or even understandings of the objective of medical intervention. Health, for the Q'eqchi', is a multidimensional concept that engages the idea of the absence of disease or infirmity—the perspective of the iloneleb'—as well as one's ability to work or function socially—the perspective of the patients. Sickness represents for the patient a disruption in the ability to fulfill roles and responsibilities. The Q'eqchi' medical system, therefore, is both externalizing and internalizing (Young 1976b) in seeking the cause of sickness. There is attention to both external events and social relationships and to internal physiological processes, each born of the material world but governed by meta/material principles.

The mechanisms of health and disease within the Q'eqchi' medical system are bound to the idea of balance, as is well known not only in Maya ethnography but also more generally among Indigenous populations. Perhaps this has become too much of a mantra in contemporary scholarship and pop culture, however, as it has become all too convenient to say that sickness is caused by imbalance in the mind-body-spirit human system. A closer look reveals a far more complex and nuanced system at work.

The Q'eqchi' are not simply holistic in their thinking, and there is much evidence that they appreciate the role of mind and body, and the body's constituent parts and systems, as separate contributors to health and well-being, as well as how they work together. Specific organs and body systems can be affected by sickness. The mind-body-spirit is not typically treated as an integrated whole, and although the connections between the parts are understood, the iloneleb' often treat them separately. The mind is not necessarily involved in all sicknesses, and mental and social problems are medicalized more than psychologized or socialized—that is, they are treated as medical problems divorced from the social context in which they may be embedded. While "the reduction of problems in the patient's life world to disordered physiology" (Hahn and Kleinman 1983:312) is understood as a characteristic of biomedicine, the research here challenges the enduring assumption that Indigenous medicine is not reductionist, that it is in essence holistic (e.g., Erickson 2008). In many ways, the Q'eqchi' medical system is an allopathic one, working "against pathology" (Gaines and Davis-Floyd 2004:95), "to oppose or attack the disease as directly as possible," just like biomedicine. Rather than thinking of Q'eqchi' medicine as a holistic system, in the typical sense of this word, it is better to characterize it as an integrated system striving to understand how the various parts and systems work both separately as distinct entities and as part of the integrated, functioning whole.

Q'eqchi' diathesis postulates a role for one's maatan, or destiny, tied to the day of birth in the Maya calendar, which, while not rigidly directing one's life, shapes one's symbiotic engagement with the challenges that life will bring. And those challenges are many. The Q'eqchi' body can be easily attacked or invaded by agents of sickness, so having a strong nawal and maintaining one's positive relationship with other people and forces is essential. Q'eqchi' public health discourse underscores the need to live a humble, social, and moral life; to understand the need to maintain relationships in the material and meta/material world; and to learn and invoke certain practices designed to maintain health and well-being. This is a moral cosmovision, within which improper or unethical behavior has consequences. Such a moral ontology is well known globally (e.g., Shweder 2003) and is the bane of some commentators of contemporary medicine who critique the tendency to invoke the idea of sickness caused by bad or immoral personal behavior (e.g., Lock and Nguyen 2010). While it has been argued that the focus on the material aspects of sickness is important to avoiding such moralizing discourse (e.g., Sontag 1978), Q'eqchi' medicine demonstrates how difficult and unlikely it is to separate morality from materiality when the meta/material is considered a core element of health ethos.

So a sudden threat to one's bodily balance, such as plunging in a cool stream after a hot day in the fields, will not necessarily cause an imbalance leading to sickness. By the same token, some sicknesses just happen. And while the iloneleb' employ a diagnostic and treatment system that is based on ideas of balance, such as thermal regulation, this is one area where consensus is less evident, suggesting that as a therapeutic principle, the idea of balance is suggestive, not directive, of sickness and that there are other, more relevant matters to which to attend. Balance is a key principle, but it is understood (including how it is achieved and disrupted) in different ways.

Q'eqchi' medicine, framed within Q'eqchi' cosmovision, is an ethics-bound system that engages both the material and meta/material aspects of sickness. The imperative to cure is the first and paramount ethical principle of virtue; the iloneleb' have a responsibility to see treatment through to the end, inevitably a cure, or to refer the patient to a better-qualified practitioner (including within biomedicine). While custom dictates that a fee should be paid, in practice no patient is turned away; the iloneleb' accept without complaint what is offered to compensate them. Set fees, of course, are prohibited. As a result, the iloneleb' live an impoverished life, enriched by the rewards of helping others but wanting in a material sense. They do this work because it is needed, a noble calling for sure.

The imperative to cure, while patient-focused, also brings into play a whole range of meta/material forces that at times may render the patient somewhat tangential to the treatment process. That many treatments are quite quickly rendered, that the ilonel may undertake a patient interview only minimally, and that rarely is there an effort to develop a patient or joint narrative of the sickness in any detail may on first blush resemble the worst of biomedical clinical practice. But as I have shown, the Q'eqchi' clinical encounter is rife with communicative symbolism; it is an inherently dialogical process in which the ilonel consults extensively with the patient through the blood pulse, and with the meta/material forces implicated in the sickness or its treatment through prayer dialogue. The patient may not be informed of the diagnosis in any detailed manner. This idea of selectively informing the patient represents perhaps the greatest ethical principle, as it is done solely out of interest for the patient's well-being. The patient also may not understand a great deal of what is happening in treatment, as the symbolism is not directed to him or her, and such understanding is not essential to therapeutic success, with the exception of the need for the patient to understand the use of prescribed plant medicines or any other post-treatment care instructions.

The patient's subjectivity and meaning-making capability here is largely subservient to the ideas that a body is indeed a body; that all bodies are essentially the same and are subjected to the same sickness-making processes as material entities and not as persons or individuals; and that all can be treated successfully, even if the patient is not Q'eqchi'. Even the use of the Maya calendar to determine a patient's maatan as a step toward diagnosing and treating is based not on individual characteristics but rather on a historical event, although one that does allow for some understanding of individual variability. Sidestepping patient subjectivity in favor of the universal body, and especially a focus on the body "in disease" rather than "general well-being," is a fundamental principle of biomedicine (for which it is often criticized) (Hahn and Kleinman 1983:312) and is counterintuitive to the mantra of holism ascribed to many traditional medical systems by medical anthropologists (e.g., Lock and Nguyen 2010:56). Yet this is precisely how the Q'eqchi' iloneleb' approach sickness and its treatment. Well-being is a consequence that follows logically from the removal of pathology and the cure of the patient; it is not an immediate concern for these practitioners.

Although they do not articulate it as such, the iloneleb' follow a principle akin to "do no harm." Their knowledge and abilities render them quite capable of creating sickness and misfortune—a kind of iatrogenic malpractice, also seen in biomedicine—a fact that vexes them in their ability to promote the work of their association. Constant rumors and allegations tell of their powers to use witchcraft, which they avowedly eschew as members of the MHAB. They are dedicated to practicing only positive medicine, and while they will treat patients who are victims of witchcraft, they deny employing it and will turn away any who request this service. Since witchcraft accusations can lead to feuds, they also often mislead patients as to the actual diagnosis. They remain vocally critical of those who charge high prices for the treatment of witchcraft-related problems (often in the thousands of dollars) and charlatans who pretend to diagnose such problems and pretend to treat them at such a fee.

"Do no harm" also comes into play with sicknesses that are beyond their expertise. Their imperative to cure does not mean at any or all costs to the patient. They will refer patients to other iloneleb' if the sickness is beyond their expertise, and to the hospital when they know that biomedical technology and practice are superior for a particular problem. No damage to ego ensues when referrals are needed. They do not bind the patient to their practice with threats of negative consequences should the patient go elsewhere.

The ethical demand to help in Q'eqchi' medicine is also evident in the willingness of the iloneleb' to accept medical ideas and practices from biomedicine, and anywhere else it seems better answers can be found. As I note throughout, they are acutely aware of the political and curative powers of biomedicine and have chosen to work with it, attempting not only to learn new ideas but to find points of compatibility that will open doors for better collaboration, perhaps even integration. This pragmatic, "whatever works" approach has been noted among other traditional medical systems (e.g.,

Quah 2003). Recasting their medicine, to some degree, to address explicit and implied concerns of biomedicine and its practitioners is inevitable if they wish such collaboration, as has been documented elsewhere in the world (e.g., Langwick 2011). Declaring such medical knowledge to be "scientific" despite no connection to scientific methodology is another means to assert validity (e.g., Adams 2001). The Q'eqchi' iloneleb' do not make such an assertion, appreciating that their empiricism has roots in a different way of knowing, but they do assert the validity of their knowledge and see science as a means of applying another lens, a different way of knowing, to affirm what they know to be true, what I refer to as a triangulation. To a considerable extent, their request that this research be undertaken reflects a concern to talk with, rather than against, biomedicine by using a language and framework that biomedicine can understand. And recognizing as well that there is much still to learn within their own medical tradition was one impetus for the formation of their association. The imperative to cure includes the imperative to keep learning.

I argue here that Q'eqchi' therapeutics are a form of medical practice. But is there a system or simply a somewhat incoherent set of practices with a loose, common cultural foundation? As I have noted above, there is all kinds of evidence that biomedical clinical practice, and the science behind it, is inconsistent if that is your comparator. Ideals of medical science and practice clash with the realities, and there is much magic and symbolism involved. Murray Last (2007:5) provides an excellent review of the concept of "medical system," arguing that it must meet three criteria. First, there must be "a common, consistent body of theory" and practitioners must "base their practice on a logic deriving from that theory." Chapters 3 through 6, the core of this book, detail the ways in which this test is met while recognizing the limitations that such a test imposes on an oral and experience-based medical system. Second, patients must recognize these practitioners, their theory, and their logic. Chapter 6 in particular discusses this test. The iloneleb' are clearly recognized as medical practitioners in the villages and to some extent by government, and even those who on the surface may reject their knowledge, including church officials, may utilize them when sickness strikes. Patients seek out the iloneleb' in part because they subscribe to the broader principles of Q'eqchi' medicine even while being somewhat ignorant of the specific medical knowledge and clinical practice. In this, they are no different from patients of biomedicine. Third, "the theory is held to explain and treat most illnesses that people experience." As I have shown, most sicknesses, even new ones, are accommodated within the Q'eqchi' medical system, and the iloneleb' employ an abductive approach to determine and treat specific sicknesses from a broad, categorical set of afflictions. Q'eqchi' medicine thus represents a more or less coherent set of theories and practices, with associated techniques, to treat most of the sicknesses people are likely to encounter, and this includes an accommodation with biomedical practice, which is seen in some instances to be better, and in others worse, than what they offer.

In general, then, the Q'eqchi' medical system is essentially restorative; like biomedicine, it seeks to cure, "to fix malfunctions" (Gaines and Davis-Floyd 2004:101). It does not work "to effect long-term beneficial changes in the whole somatic-interpersonal system," even though so many medical anthropologists and others want desperately for such Indigenous systems to be inherently transformative. This expands our understanding of what constitutes "medicine," especially Indigenous medicine, and challenges the many stereotypes that have, at their base, a denigration of Indigenous medical knowledge even while being couched in positive, romantic affirmations of holism and transformation. Certainly, there have been voices arguing against the idea that Indigenous medicine is essentially holistic (Thornton 2015) or that mind-body dualism is not inherent in their epistemologies (e.g., Kohrt and Harper 2008). Some even argue that traditional medical systems and biomedicine are not all that different when you cut away the ill-informed stereotypes (Kleinman 1980; Singer and Baer 1995), a task I am engaged in here. These voices, attempts to allow Indigenous people to be real as opposed to caricatures developed from Western romantic and primitivist thinking, are too few. It is time to reclaim "medicine" as a meaningful concept with which to interpret Indigenous therapeutic practice, such as that of the Q'eqchi'.

Why "Medicine" Matters: Resistance and Revitalization

Why does it matter if Q'eqchi' therapeutic intervention is understood as "medicine" and not "healing"? Why does it matter for Indigenous therapeutics more generally that, alongside its ability to engage in psychosocial healing processes of transformation, there remains a capacity to offer medical, restorative treatment?

First, a simple statement. The iloneleb' argue that they practice medicine (although "medicine" is typically glossed as "healing" in translation). The research here suggests that "medicine" is a more apt description than "healing," with the latter's focus on symbolic transformation, holism, well-being, and psychosocial repair. I refer to what they do as restorative practice, in contrast to the transformative practice ascribed to much contemporary Indigenous healing. The imperative to cure is an ethical demand of the profession, deeply rooted in Q'eqchi' notions of morality, especially the necessity to help others when it is within your power to do so. The imperative to cure, for the iloneleb', combined with supreme confidence in not only their own knowledge but also that of their medical tradition, is in part what has driven them to request this research. So this research matters to them, as an expression of their will and a global pronouncement on the nature and effectiveness of their practice. They want their practice to be seen and evaluated as medicine.

To this end, the formation of the MHAB represents an effort to mimic certain aspects of biomedicine's regulatory environment. The association represents a new, and somewhat controversial, way to organize Q'eqchi' medical services in a manner that would demonstrate its inherent professionalism (Waldram, Cal, and Maquin 2009). The examination of potential new members (involving a walk through the forest to identify medicinal plants and their uses) and the development of a code of conduct are essential ingredients to seeking recognition of their professional status. Symbolism is important too, and the iloneleb', through interlocutors, have produced certificates of qualification (Figures 27 and 28) and even identification cards (Figure 29), the latter proving to be especially valuable when they are challenged by the police over the contents of their medicine kits. The point of all of this is to use the tools of the dominant society to apply a kind of bureaucratic visage over the top of their existing practice such that it is more readably understandable by others. The MHAB is not a radical change in how Q'eqchi' medicine is learned or practiced; it is an effort to translate that medical learning and practice for those with power.

Then there is the obvious: the botanical medicines. So much attention has been paid to "ethnobiology" and "ethnopharmacology" by researchers that it almost seems unnecessary to emphasize that Indigenous peoples such as

FIGURE 27. Albino Maquin holding membership certificate for the Kekchi (Q'eqchi) Healer's Association of Belize (now the Maya Healers Association of Belize). Indian Creek, 2009. Photo by author.

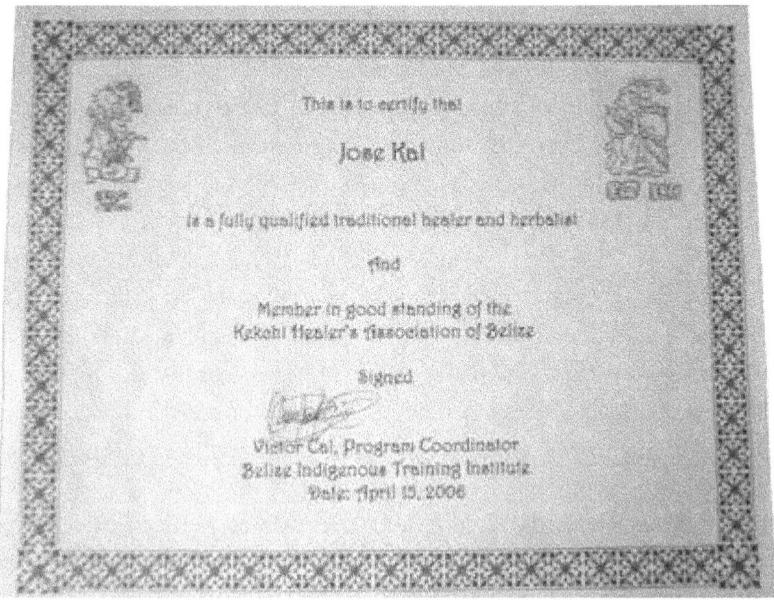

This is to certify that

Jose Kal

is a fully qualified traditional healer and herbalist

And

Member in good standing of the
Kekchi Healer's Association of Belize

Signed

Victor Cal, Program Coordinator
Belize Indigenous Training Institute
Date: April 15, 2006

FIGURE 28. Membership certificate for Emilio (José) Kal. Jalacte, 2015. Photo by author.

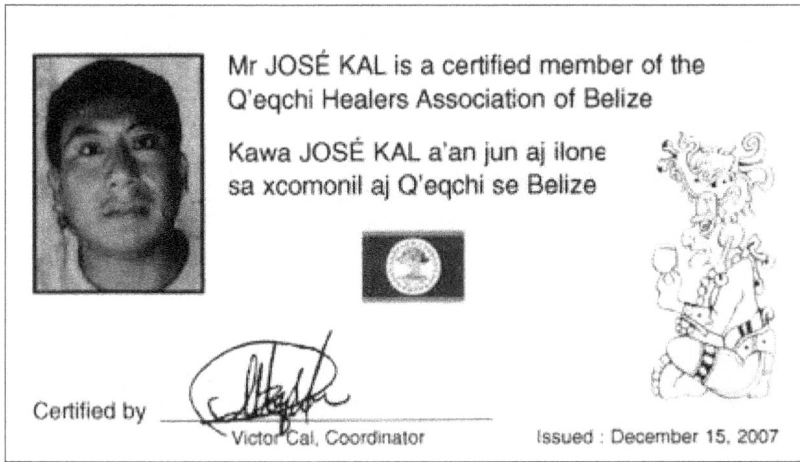

Mr JOSÉ KAL is a certified member of the
Q'eqchi Healers Association of Belize
Kawa JOSÉ KAL a'an jun aj ilone
sa xcomonil aj Q'eqchi se Belize
Certified by
Victor Cal, Coordinator
Issued : December 15, 2007

FIGURE 29. Card identifying Emilio (José) Kal as a member of the Q'eqchi Healers Association of Belize (now the Maya Healers Association of Belize). Punta Gorda, 2011. Photo by author.

the Q'eqchi' have well-developed pharmacopeias based on the use of plants and that this knowledge has, in past as well as today, greatly informed biomedical treatment. What the iloneleb' use as medicines, and what they treat with specific plants and combinations, provides excellent empirical evidence that some compound contained therein is worth discovering by Western science. As I note in this book, there has been some research done with the iloneleb' in this study, with some insightful results, but more can be done. Such research is expensive, and university-based researchers have considerably less access to research funds than pharmaceutical companies. In the meantime, members of the MHAB engage in public education among their own people regarding their use of botanicals.

Any discussion of Indigenous botanical medicines conjures up the incredibly complex area of intellectual property rights for Indigenous peoples. The United Nations *Declaration on the Rights of Indigenous Peoples* (2008) states that "Indigenous peoples have the right to their traditional medicines and to maintain their health practices, including the conservation of their vital medicinal plants, animals and minerals" (Article 24); the "right to maintain, control, protect and develop their cultural heritage, TK [traditional knowledge] and traditional cultural expressions, as well as the manifestations of their sciences, technologies and cultures, including . . . medicines" (Article 31); and the "right to maintain, control, protect and develop their intellectual property over such cultural heritage, traditional knowledge, and traditional cultural expressions" (Article 31). The WHO (World Health Organization, World Intellectual Property Organization, and World Trade Organization 2012) cautions that such traditional knowledge, while not codified, is not therefore necessarily in the public domain and that source communities should share in the benefits of research development based on that knowledge. How this might be done, however, is admittedly quite complicated. Whether or not reference to "health practices" extends beyond the beliefs of a citizenry to include traditional medical practice of specialists is unclear. It is one thing to recognize the rights of Indigenous individuals to seek care from traditional practitioners and to use traditional medicines; it is quite another to recognize the rights of practitioners to practice, and especially to practice medicine. The latter remains an ill-defined right. In many nations, "medicine" remains a legally defined, scientifically informed biomedical practice that is highly regulated, with penalties for those who practice unlicensed and/or without the proper training. This hegemony is a fundamental issue in the meaningful implementation of the declaration.

Contemporary intellectual property rights law was built upon a Western philosophy that allows individuals or groups of individuals to claim creative and ownership rights over things and ideas (Oguamanam 2006). Indigenous knowledge, in particular what the WHO (World Health Organization, World Intellectual Property Organization, and World Trade Organization 2012) refers to as "non-codified" knowledge, is not a product of this Western and highly individualist approach, and much of that knowledge is considered communal, to be shared. There is a risk that this form of knowledge can be easily exploited by the assignment of copyright to others. Further, the kind of empiricism that leads to the development of new medical ideas emerges so slowly that it is not possible to identify a specific creator of that knowledge, or even a specific group. As anthropologists know, culture—in the manifest form of both ideas and objects—is not constrained by political borders. So geopolitical issues are also relevant.

The Q'eqchi' iloneleb' in this research share much plant knowledge with

Q'eqchi' who are not in this study; with other Mopan and Yucatec Maya in Belize, Mexico, Guatemala, and Honduras; and likely with other Central American Indigenous groups. The plants, and the knowledge of their medicinal properties, do not respect national or cultural boundaries. While the iloneleb' have invited the scientific laboratory study of their plant medicines, they would not suggest that they own these in the copyright sense, even though the specific knowledge they have as individual practitioners is considered proprietary. This is a complex situation. The knowledge of medicinal plants is shared throughout the community, but the iloneleb' have much greater knowledge—not just about plants but also about how to use them—for which they must pay as part of their training; that knowledge becomes their property. But this is understood in a broader context, in which the plant medicines can work only when applied in the right manner, to the right sickness, with the right diagnostic procedures and treatment prayers. It is *this* integrated knowledge that is proprietary, and this explains why they are happy to share their plant medicines with scientists. While the scientists are expected to find the compounds within the medicines that have the effects the iloneleb' indicate, this is to prove the validity of one small part of their overall knowledge of medical treatment, an integrated knowledge of the material and meta/material that is largely beyond the reach of the scientific method. As I have argued before (Waldram 1997, 2000) and as Craig (2012:248) observes, "Materialist methods are hard-pressed to evaluate what could be considered metaphysical acts." It is important to the iloneleb' that science validate aspects of that knowledge, for reasons I detail below. But, simply put, science is a vehicle of cultural resistance for the Q'eqchi' and not a threat per se.

The rapid cultural change occurring in the Toledo District is challenging Maya culture and identity in unprecedented ways. Young people, learning English and science in schools, are less interested in the traditional ways. They tend to see Q'eqchi' medicine not as an empirical system but as a system based on antiquated superstition. They are learning in schools that science has the "truth." But there is another "truth" in Toledo as well, one that threatens to do even more damage, and that is US-based evangelical churches and missions (Kukul 2013), including medical missions, which seem to have no problem frightening the people with mental images of the iloneleb' as devil worshippers or witches. These churches sometimes use biomedicine as a cover to proselytize, dividing families and villages if necessary. If scientific research can confirm certain aspects of Q'eqchi' medicine, the iloneleb' thinking goes, it will help in the resistance movement. This is an urgent matter; none of the iloneleb' in this study have apprentices, and several have now passed on.

While the World Health Organization's *Traditional Medicine Strategy* (2013) seeks to build on earlier efforts to promote the integration of traditional medicine into health care systems "where appropriate" (13), the science emphasis of its policy is on research and regulation, with a focus on determining "efficacy" (13), promoting safety, and "evidence-based" use (16). Surprisingly, the WHO definition of traditional medicine has changed little over the previous few decades and remains "the sum total of the knowledge, skill, and practices based on the theories, beliefs, and experiences indigenous to different cultures, whether explicable or not, used in the maintenance of health as well as in the prevention, diagnosis, improvement or treatment of physical and mental illness" (15). The WHO does not make the crucial distinction that I make here, between medical and healing practice.

To deal with the issue of traditional medicine on a global scale is no small matter, and therefore the tendency of the WHO to focus on the major systems found in Asia and Southeast Asia (such as traditional Chinese medicine and Ayurveda) and practices that themselves are now more global (such as chiropractic, acupuncture, and naturopathy) is understandable. There is a privileging of systems that are teachable in or certifiable by institutes of higher formal learning that emulate Western colleges and a subtle affirmation of the ways of knowing of these major knowledge systems. Further, there is an effort to expand the idea of research beyond the controlled clinical trial to include other evaluation methods. "These include outcome and effectiveness studies," the document states, "as well as comparative effectiveness research, patterns of use, and other qualitative methods"—that is, "'real world experiments' where different research designs and methods are important, valuable and applicable" (39).

Does the policy have much to offer the Q'eqchi'? To a certain extent, yes. The imaginative capacity to envision alternative, nonscientific ways to study traditional medicine is perhaps the most valuable but will prove complicated to operationalize and implement. Belize has recently acted on the WHO's encouragement to develop a national policy that promotes integration of traditional medicine and biomedicine, as I discuss below. Unfortunately, however, the WHO examples presented are not those of "noncodified" systems like Q'eqchi' medicine but rather those that most emulate biomedicine (in theory, practice, training, and/or regulation/certification). While the members of the MHAB have themselves developed regulatory policies, this act has created some opposition from other iloneleb', who feel either left out or threatened. More formalized, especially government, regulation and standardization, as called for by the WHO, will not likely be met with favor by the Q'eqchi' medical practitioners in this study, whose medical system is firmly ensconced in broader, culturally based standards that are seen as integral and largely beyond regulation. The often-strained political relationship between the Q'eqchi' and the national government over land and other Indigenous rights renders opposition to government control inevitable.

"Traditional medicine" did receive important government attention as Belize recently worked through the development and adoption of a national cultural policy, with some positive results.[1] The overall emphasis of the policy is to protect, study, and integrate "best practices" of traditional medicine with Belize's "modern health system." A draft policy (Government of Belize 2013) gave way, after consultations, to a final policy document that speaks almost entirely of "traditional medicine" rather than "healing" and that acknowledges the "vast knowledge for effective health practices" of the ancestors of all of Belize's "cultural groups" (Government of Belize 2016:10). There are some very progressive aspects to this policy, including committing the government to ensuring "that the knowledge and practice in traditional medicine are safeguarded through the evaluation of the philosophy, knowledge and health practices of previous generations and the ascertaining of the degree to which this knowledge and these practices can be applied in Belize's modern health system" (10). The accentuation of "knowledge" and the complete absence of reference to "beliefs" in the policy are major developments, as is the emphasis on practice as well as knowledge. The lack of a definition of what constitutes "knowledge" and "practice," and of course "traditional medicine," is problematic, but the policy is national in scope and necessarily broad. One hopes that specific aspects of the policy will be operationalized moving forward. Also included is recognition of the need to develop systems to protect intellectual property rights of traditional medicine knowledge, although, as discussed above, this is not an easy task.

The emphasis of the policy, perhaps not surprisingly, is on "knowledge of flora and fauna" in Belize's "nature-based traditional medicines" (Government of Belize 2016:10). As I show in this book, and as the iloneleb' argue, there is considerably more to Q'eqchi' medicine than flora and fauna, and the extent to which the meta/material as well as the material aspects of Q'eqchi' medicine will be included for research, protection, and integration remains to be seen.[2] Since no specific cultural groups are identified in the policy, there remains a risk of conflating Q'eqchi', Mopan, and Yucatec Maya medicine with that of the Creole, Garifuna, East Indian, Chinese, Mestizo, and other groups with very different approaches, and in some cases more globally recognized medical systems. These groups also have a greater political and economic presence and influence in the country. The Maya people remain largely powerless in Belize and have little presence at the federal government level.

The policy that calls for the protection, evaluation, and integration of traditional medicine therefore risks continuing to render Maya medicine largely invisible because some of the other traditional or alternative medical systems will be more amenable to and compatible with the biomedical system at the core of the nation's health care delivery. Further, while the iloneleb' would welcome inclusion of their medical tradition in the national policy, because any formal acknowledgment is appreciated, its inclusion in a "culture" policy supports the dominant notion that Q'eqchi' (and, indeed, other "alternative") therapeutics are primarily symbolic and not material in orientation (outside of specific plants whose properties can be scientifically determined), which could lead to further marginalization. A parallel national health policy that includes Q'eqchi' and other medical systems is needed if they are to be taken seriously as meaningful providers in the national health care system. Unfortunately, the recent strategic health plan for the country, while noting the shortage of biomedical professionals, fails to mention any type of traditional, alternative, or Indigenous medical services (Government of Belize 2014). The incompatibility of these two policies is telling of the government's view—one not uncommon in much of the world—that Indigenous medical systems remain remnants of cultural traditions that have little to offer the modern, science-based practice of medicine.

The iloneleb' remain open to the scientific study of their treatments as a means of proving that they "work," if such study could ever be designed according to Q'eqchi' medical principles. The iloneleb' understand science to be the politically powerful way in which the national Belizean society at large, and Westerners and "modern" people, "know." They accept that there are different ways to "know" material and meta/material phenomena in the world and different ways to act on what is known. But at the core, they implicitly accept that all peoples essentially have the same material reality and that these different ways of knowing point to that shared reality. For them, the lens of science, properly applied, will affirm the material and meta/material world that they know to exist; in the past, science simply did not bother to look. Science, however, is not the only "true" way to know, and fears of the application of inappropriate research methods are legitimate.

Is there a risk, then, for Indigenous medicine such as that of the Q'eqchi' to welcome the gaze of science? It might seem that insisting that some Indigenous therapeutic approaches represent medical, as opposed to healing, practice legitimately opens the door for scientific scrutiny and the use of scientific methods to test the validity and reliability of that knowledge. The Belize cultural policy implies just that. Interdisciplinary researchers have in the past been somewhat frightened away from directly addressing the effectiveness of Indigenous medical practice out of concern that it would not measure up and therefore be ridiculed and dismissed. As I argue in chapter 2, the shift away from studying Indigenous *medicine* toward the study of Indigenous *healing* was, in part, a response to such concerns, as anthropologists in particular became sensitive to allegations that their research often portrayed Indigenous peoples in a negative light. It's better to focus on symbols than to ask the difficult question: Does it work?

To understand the nature of the risk involved in viewing Indigenous therapeutics as medical practice, we have to appreciate that the broader knowledge systems within which they are embedded likely developed in the context of local understandings of what constituted effectiveness, and this did not involve an aggressive process of reductionism to isolate the exact aspect of treatment that led to the exact, desired effect. The iloneleb' are content in knowing that specific prayers, pulses, and plant medicines, used together, achieve the desired outcome. While botanists may focus on identifying the chemical compound in a plant that produces a specific effect, the iloneleb' will tell you that, while this may satisfy science, it is the whole package that is effective and that any given element in isolation cannot possibly work. There are many reasons why scientific research—especially the double-blind controlled clinical experiment—is inappropriate to assessing Indigenous medical knowledge (Waldram 2000, 2013), and we must be vigilant in our appreciation that in science, as in all knowledge systems, there is an epistemological and ontological coevolutionary process in which what is knowable, what is worth knowing, what is known, and how it is known are intertwined (cf. Young 1982). Acknowledging that scientific knowledge, like Indigenous knowledge, is also the product of a "cultural process" (Richter 1972) frees us to appreciate the Q'eqchi' medical system as a distinct knowledge system that, as I have shown, has many similarities to biomedicine but that must still be appreciated on its own terms. These terms include an openness to new ideas and a willingness to collaborate with biomedicine; they do not include a capitulation to biomedicine as a superior system. There are "windows of compatibility" (Dickinson 2008) that provide opportunities to make the best of both systems available to the Q'eqchi' people, not as fully integrated systems, as these tend to marginalize the Indigenous system, but as parallel systems that allow patients to move freely to options of their choice, to construct their own integrative medicine. Not only would this be very pragmatic in a nation with limited wealth and biomedical resources, it would be in harmony with many global Indigenous initiatives to ensure the continued viability of their knowledge systems.

In this, the Q'eqchi' iloneleb' are showing us the way. Their initiative, and those of other Indigenous peoples throughout the world, will benefit when scholars, medical professionals, scientists, and policy makers learn to take Indigenous knowledge systems and ways of knowing seriously, when they accept that Indigenous peoples had, and still have to varying degrees, medical systems focused on restorative principles and practices. It is my hope, and that of the Q'eqchi' iloneleb', that this book will positively support that initiative.

Afterword 2020

The iloneleb' typically signal the conclusion of a treatment session by uttering "*us*," a Q'eqchi' word meaning "good"—as in, "Finished. We are done." But while a session may end, the knowledge gained by the ilonel in that session carries on to the next patient, contributing to the dynamic empiricism at the heart of the Q'eqchi' medical system. Treatment ends, but knowledge grows.

More than fifteen years have passed since I started work with the members of the Maya Healers Association of Belize. Associations such as theirs are hard to maintain in the long term. Funding is almost always precarious and tied to foreign entities. The Itzamma Medicinal Plant Garden is the centerpiece of the association's work, largely funded by Canadian botanical researchers whose resources ultimately dried up. The garden, located just north of Indian Creek Village, has always felt pressure from competing villager interests in the land for farming and settlement. Over the years, new homes have sprung up closer and closer to the garden site, threatening to subsume it. By 2020, in the absence of continued funding, it seemed as though prospects for the association's viability were slim. Meanwhile, three of the iloneleb' had passed away.

The MHAB is not a failed experiment. Its legacy lives on in the form of a well-documented model for the contemporary organization of Q'eqchi' medical services within the evolving governmental landscape of medical and health service delivery in Toledo. As the Maya leaders of southern Belize actively continue to plot their future, they have become increasingly aware that the Q'eqchi' medical system is their canary in the coal mine. The loss of their medical system signals a dangerous loss of Q'eqchi' knowledge and heritage, as well as autonomy, and will reverberate throughout all aspects of Q'eqchi' life in the future. A broadly based Toledo association of Maya medical practitioners is being considered. This proposed association would work to not only protect Q'eqchi' medical knowledge but also to reinvigorate and advance it. A massive archive of data—interview transcripts, audio and video of interviews and treatments, still photos—has been produced through this research and is being prepared for return to Toledo as a resource to assist in this process. And the research continues. There is hope, therefore, for the future of the Q'eqchi' medical system, not just as a legacy but also as a compass pointing toward the great possibilities ahead. The MHAB may ultimately come to an end, but the lessons of the association will not. The imperative to cure remains a deeply embedded principle. *Us.*

Glossary of Local Q'eqchi' Terms

The terms presented here in many cases are localized expressions used among the iloneleb' and their patients in this research. While spellings and meanings have been cross-checked with two Q'eqchi' dictionaries (Juárez et al. 2003; Frazier 2015), written forms of Q'eqchi' are still evolving, and precise definitions and spellings here may vary from Q'eqchi' dictionaries and usage in other areas. There are also idiosyncrasies in the way the iloneleb' refer to sicknesses, signs, and symptoms: in some cases, short forms are used; in others, alternative but equivalent names, words, or descriptors are used. Q'eqchi' language expert Tomas Caal has worked closely with me to refine the spelling and definitions as locally expressed.

aam: Heart
awas: A procedure involving a sacrifice (usually of an animal) to remove sickness; also known as isink awas
awas: A condition of an infant caused by behavior of the mother while pregnant
b'ak'ok: To bind or tie
b'ak'ok b'aqel: To bind the bones for bone, skeleton, or joint pain
b'ak'ok kub'sa': To tie the uterus to alleviate pain and bleeding after birth
b'an: Medicine; used as a euphemism for "cure"
b'anok: To cure; to heal
b'oqok mu: A technique for "calling spirits" back to a person
cha'al: Body parts
chaab'il wank: To be good or content; well-being; good living
chaab'il yu'am: Good life; good living
ch'e'ok kik': Feeling or touching the blood (metaphorically); pulsing

ch'oolej: Soul or spirit; "heart," as a euphemism for emotions
choql: Sickness caused by exposure to clouds or mist; sometimes glossed as pneumonia or a persistent cough
eek'ank: Emotions; understood locally as feelings; to feel emotions
eet aj yajel: Epilepsy; "the foolish sickness" (a reference to the person's behavior)
ha'sa'il: Diarrhea (often caused by contaminated water)
ilok: To see or examine; to take care of someone who is sick; to treat the patient; the practice of medicine. (See also *remeerik*.)
ilonel: Medical practitioner; healer; one who "sees." (The plural form is *iloneleb'*.)
jilok: To massage
jilok yaj aj ixq: Massage for a pregnant woman
jolomb'ej: Common head cold; cough due to the common cold virus
jun xaaqalil: Entire body
jwal nak'a'uxlak: Worrying too much
jwal naxik xk'a'uxl: Thinking too much
kaanil: Spirit loss; sometimes glossed as a form of susto
kaq jolomb'ej: Flu
katzkatz xox: Itchy sores or rash
k'a'uxl: Mind
k'a'uxlak: Excessive worry or anguish
kaw: Strong; healthy
kawilal: Health
ke: Cold
ke aj muchkej: Cold body cramps or chills
k'ehol yajel: Witchcraft sickness
kik': Blood
k'irtasink: Cure
Kojaj: A local name for one of the Tzuultaq'a
k'iraak: To be cured
k'ochob'anki: A healing procedure to promote harmony in a relationship
k'otakil: Diarrhea
k'ub' sa': Uterus
look aj k'a'uxl: A mixed Spanish–Q'eqchi expression meaning "crazy thinking"; same as waxk'ay (mild craziness)

lukum: Ascaris or roundworms that live in the stomach and intestine
maak'a' xmaatan: Bad luck or no luck
maatan: Gift; destiny
maa'us: Evil or devil; a term derived from Christianity
maa'us aj musiq'ej: Sickness caused by evil spirits
maa'usat: Evil spirit intrusion
may: Pain; body aches
mitz' aj xul: Virus
mosque chicler: Leishmaniasis
mu: Spirit
muchkej: Body cramps
musiq'ej: Spirit; breath (alternative form of *mu*, used locally)
na'leb': Knowledge; customs; tradition
nawal: Gifted energy linked to spirit
nume' sa': Diarrhea; expulsion of fluids from the body; hemorrhage (especially by women through menstruation or after giving birth)
obeah: Witchcraft
ojb': Cough; flu; phlegm
oksinb'il xjolom: Disturbed mind; same as *po'b'il k'a'uxl*
pim: Bush plants used for medicine
po'b'il k'a'uxl or po'ol xk'a'uxl: Disturbed mind; an obsession that creates mental problems such as depression
po'ol kik': Disturbed or corrupted blood; blood that has "gone bad"
po'ol xch'ool: Disturbed soul or spirit; depression; a variation of *po'b'il k'a'uxl*
po'ol xk'auxl: Disturbed mind
pom: Incense made from resin of the copal tree
Qaawa': God
q'an yaj: Ulcer or stomach "sores"
q'an yajel: Yellow fever
q'eq pojink: Dark complexion due to strong blood
q'un ch'oolej: Weak soul or spirit
ra ch'oolej: Hurt heart (in an emotional sense); sad
rahilal: Suffering; pain
rahil ch'oolej: Being sad
rahil ch'oolejil: Sadness
rajlal po nat'ane'k: Always falling; falls every month; a symptom of epilepsy

rax kehob'l: Malaria; chills
remeer: Opening or diagnostic prayer used in medical treatment
remeerik: To treat using remeer; to treat the patient
rilom tzuul: Sickness caused by the mountain spirit; sometimes glossed as a form of epilepsy
sahil: Happiness
sahilal: Happy heart; happy and healthy; a variation of kawilal, or health
sahilal yu'am: Happy life; well-being
sib'te'enk: To smoke, smudge, or cleanse the patient to take away the bad spirit or sickness
sutam: Environment
t'anenaq se' ha': To fall in the water, causing fright; sometimes glossed as a form of susto
Taq'a: Valleys
taqenaq kik'el: High blood pressure
taqenaq tiqwal jolomb'ej: Headache or high head pressure
tib'l: Pain
tib'l aam: Heart pain or ache; heart attack
tib'l sa': Stomach pain
tij: Prayer (in general)
tiq: Hot
toj: Payment
tont aj yajel: A mixed Spanish–Q'eqchi' expression meaning "foolish sickness"; same as *waxk'ay* (mild craziness)
tuul: Witch; magic
Tzuul: Mountains
Tzuultaq'a: Spirits of the mountains and valleys
ulul: Brain
us: Good; done or finished
usaak: To get better after a sickness
waxk'ay: Mild craziness
wax ru: Severe craziness; schizophrenia
xa'ank kik': Sickness involving vomiting blood
xchiq'e' xsa': "Shaken insides" from a fall, typically happening to a pregnant woman

xjilb'al ich'mul: Checking the artery

xjilb'al xkik'el: Checking the blood pulse; pulsing; same as ch'e'ok kik' (feeling or touching the blood)

xiwajenaq: Frightened spirit; sometimes glossed as a form of susto

xk'eeb'al toj: An offering or payment

xmay xul: Infection; poison injected into a human and subsequent pain; caused by an animal or insect bite

xyajel maa'us: Sickness of the devil or evil spirit; sometimes glossed as a form of epilepsy

yajel: Sickness

yoob'tasinel: God prayer

Notes

Prologue

1. "Don" is an appellation that denotes a certain status of respect. Derived from Spanish, it translates essentially into "mister." Q'eqchi' convention—as is the case in many parts of the world—is to refer to individuals by their first name, such as "Mr. Jim" or "Miss Pamela" (regardless of marital status). However, to streamline this presentation, I will not use these titles after the initial introductions to the practitioners in this research.

Chapter 1

1. In this book I capitalize "Indigenous" when referring to Indigenous peoples but use the lowercase "indigenous" when referring to the idea of originality.
2. My reference to "phronesis" accentuates the kind of practical wisdom that comes from experience, a key element in Q'eqchi' clinical practice. I use "gnosis" in the general sense to refer to a kind of received knowledge linked to cosmology or "divine authority," one that accentuates the role of tradition and the unique status of "knowers" as an elite group (Bates 1995:4). Gnosis represents a concern with "how the world works" in a broad sense (Bates 1995:6), including what I refer to here as material and meta/material forces enveloped within Q'eqchi' cosmovision.
3. I use the term "sickness" to reference the Q'eqchi' perspective of disease, disorder, and experience. It is the best available English concept that approximates how they view it, and best reflects the Q'eqchi' term typically used, *yajel.* Sickness always entails context and relationships. Since I am working mostly at the level of the medical system and with the expert practitioners of that system, and not the individual patients, a concept that centers patient experience would be misleading. Further, I refer to disorders and avoid use of the expression "idioms of distress" to affirm the fundamental materialist nature of Q'eqchi' medical epistemology.
4. Ingold (2014:215), drawing on the work of others, distinguishes "objects" and "things." Going beyond his descriptions somewhat, I think of the former as being

about shape, physical substance, or appearance, and the latter as being about interactive potential and the ability to be something for someone—in other words, to entail an ascribed meaning.

5. The English term "cosmovision" is used locally, unlike the analytical term "cosmology" as articulated by Wilson (1993).

6. Elizabeth Grosz (2017:5) has advanced somewhat similar ideas in her definition of the "incorporeal"—that is, "the subsistence of the ideal *in* the material or corporeal"—in an effort to escape both dualist and monistic philosophies by highlighting the relationship between the ideal and the material, or the mind and body if you will. She employs a similar concept to mine, "extramaterialism," to mean "the inherence of ideality, conceptuality, meaning, or orientation that persists in relation to and within materiality as its immaterial or incorporeal disorders" (5). While this emphasis on imagination and meaning is well suited to understanding human cognition and human relationships with the world, the fact that people may understand the immaterial as "real" and not imaginary, different from human corporeality but nonetheless real in other ways, is also significant to stress.

7. References to "traditional medicine" abound in the literature and popular discourse, its authority derived from its temporality, its connection to the past, its historicity (in contrast to science, where authority is based primarily on method), and especially its position of resistance vis-à-vis colonial power. In many ways, the term "traditional" as used today is about neither knowledge content nor ways of knowing; rather, it is about the authoritative stance of knowledge; "tradition" empowers knowledge. Employing the term "traditional knowledge" is fraught with problems, however, as it also encourages the false understanding that such knowledge is static and anachronistic. So-called traditional systems are not sealed and impervious to new ideas; indeed, many have proven to be very dynamic and resilient in their adaptation to emerging circumstances.

Chapter 2

1. See Anthro*In*Sight, https://www.youtube.com/watch?v=k2clzMhNM3E&t=2s.

Chapter 3

1. Permanto (2015) provides an excellent detailed description of the nature of the Tzuultaq'a among Q'eqchi' in Guatemala.

2. Orellana (1987:29), in research on Nahua people in the pre-Hispanic and early colonial period, referred to a similar notion of "tonally," which she characterized as "a life force received by each individual depending upon the day of his or her birth . . . essential to an individual's vigor, heat, valor, and growth."

3. While typically iloneleb' will suck the venom out with their mouths, they recognize the risk of doing so, especially if they have cuts in their mouths. So they would

prefer to use commercially available snakebite kits and suction devices, but these are difficult and expensive to acquire.

4. See http://www.phac-aspc.gc.ca/ph-sp/determinants/index-eng.php#determinants; accessed January 11 2017. At the time of this research the government of Belize did not have an articulated set of health determinants available, so the Canadian ones were used. These determinants are: income and social status; social support networks; education and literacy; employment/working conditions; social environments; physical environments; personal health practices and coping skills; healthy child development; biology and genetic endowment; health services; gender; and culture.

5. See https://www.merriam-webster.com/dictionary/diathesis; accessed January 18 2017.

Chapter 4

1. Sicknesses not included in the pile sort exercise could likely be placed in this category. For instance, *mosque chicler*, or leishmaniasis, is known to be caused by sand fly bites. Xmay xul, or general infection, results from bites or wounds. HIV/AIDS, referred to as *mitz' aj xul* (meaning "small animal" or simply "virus"), is known to be sexually transmitted.

Chapter 5

1. While I suggest here that Q'eqchi' patients do not typically make use of extensive narratives to explain their predicaments, as Andrew Hatala, Tomas Caal, and I have suggested (Hatala, Waldram, and Caal 2015), it is certainly possible to understand the knowledge of iloneleb' from a narrative perspective, in which they fill in the narrative context of the signs and symptoms in order to better understand the problem.

2. Abstinence is important in the treatment of specific sicknesses involving powerful and evil forces. Q'eqchi' iloneleb' understand that sexual activity weakens the blood, rendering them more vulnerable to these strong meta/material forces while working with patients. Strong blood is a preventive factor.

Chapter 6

1. Much of what is referred to as Indigenous "healing" in North America today is about transformative processes. Elsewhere (Waldram 2012a) I suggest that part of the reason for this is that biomedicine and related colonial processes have successfully colonized Indigenous medical systems, taking over much of the medical function, but they have not had as great an impact on therapeutic aspects dealing with psychosocial issues and issues broadly understood as mental health. This has left an opening for Indigenous medical systems as they themselves transform into "healing" systems

intended, in part, to ameliorate the consequences of those very colonial forces. The associated pathologies are so deep and typically intergenerational that any notion of recovery or return to a previously healthy state is nonsensical; most individuals have never experienced that. Further, a "return" to a previous state, before the emergence of these post-colonial disorders, is also not realistic, as these colonial processes remain in effect. So the therapeutic emphasis has shifted toward transformation and adaptation, because "cure" is not feasible within this context and with these disorders.

2. I suggest that many Indigenous peoples likely retain aspects of their restorative medical tradition but have fallen victim to the romanticized, Jerome Frank–influenced gaze of researchers who seek only "healing" in their research, as I discuss in chapter 2.

3. Francisco also used the Spanish terms *limpio* and *limpieza*, explaining that the procedure is an internal "cleansing." While there are some similarities between this procedure and that recorded for other Maya groups as limpio (Kunow 2003), the Q'eqchi' jilok described here has a more integral function in the treatment process. The Q'eqchi' practitioners in this research do not employ the sweat bath therapeutically for purposes of cleansing, as is reported in the highlands of Guatemala (e.g., Orellano 1987; Groark 2005; Hinojosa 2015).

4. Manual palpation or "massage" of pregnant women, to "position" the fetus, for instance, or to stem excessive menstrual or postpartum bleeding, is a different procedure altogether (De Gezelle 2014; Hinojosa 2015), one that all iloneleb' practice. It is known as *jilok yaj aj ixq* ("massage for women's health problem"); this conflation further underlines that "massage" is an unfortunate gloss for jilok.

5. The iloneleb' in this study do not use the *sastun*, a diagnostic crystal or stone known among some Maya groups (e.g., García, Sierra, and Balám 1999) and given some notoriety by a popular book of the same name (Arvigo 1994). It is not the ubiquitous item of Maya medical technology that these sources might imply.

6. See Harvey (2013) for a different perspective on the significance of silence in Maya clinical encounters.

Chapter 7

1. There was no policy, cultural or otherwise, in place during the period in which much of this research was undertaken. However, during the research, the iloneleb' were made aware that a policy was in the works and that traditional medicine might be included. This is one of the reasons they requested this research, hoping to influence that policy.

2. On the other hand, as development continues in Maya territory and as Maya peoples continue to assert their rights over traditional lands, supported by court decisions and international Indigenous rights groups, conceptualizing their therapeutic practice as "nature-based" with a focus on plant medicine may further bolster their broader claims to land and resources.

REFERENCES CITED

Ackerknecht, Erwin H.

1942. Problems of Primitive Medicine. *Bulletin of the History of Medicine* 11:503–21.

1943. Psychopathology, Primitive Medicine and Primitive Culture. *Bulletin of the History of Medicine* 14:30–67.

1945. On the Collecting of Data Concerning Primitive Medicine. *American Anthropologist* 47:427–32.

1946. Natural Diseases and Rational Treatment in Primitive Medicine. *Bulletin of the History of Medicine* 19(5):467–97

2016 [1968]. *A Short History of Medicine*. Rev. edition. Baltimore: Johns Hopkins University Press.

1971. *Medicine and Ethnology: Selected Essays*. H. H. Walser and H. M. Koelbing, eds. Baltimore: Johns Hopkins University Press.

Adams, Vincanne

2001. The Sacred in the Scientific: Ambiguous Practices of Science in Tibetan Medicine. *Cultural Anthropology* 16(4):542–75.

Agrawal, A.

1995. Dismantling the Divide between Indigenous and Scientific Knowledge. *Development and Change* 26:413–39.

Amiguet, Virginie. T., John T. Arnason, Pedro Maquin, Victor Cal, Pablo S. Vindas, and Luis Poveda

2005. A Consensus Ethnobotany of the Q'eqchi' Maya of Southern Belize. *Economic Botany* 59(1):29–42.

Amiguet, Virginie. T., John T. Arnason, and Pedro Maquin

2006. A Regression Analysis of Q'eqchi' Maya Medicinal Plants from Southern Belize. *Economic Botany* 60(1):24–38.

Anderson, E. N.

2000. Maya Knowledge and "Science Wars." *Journal of Ethnobiology* 20(2):129–58.

Ankli, A.
2002. Yucatec Mayan Medicinal Plants: Evaluation Based on Indigenous Uses. *Journal of Ethnopharmacology* 79:43–52.

Ankli, Anna, Otto Sticher, and Michael Heinrich
1999. Medical Ethnobotany of the Yucatec Maya: Healer's Consensus and a Quantitative Criterion. *Economic Botany* 53(2):144–60.

Arvigo, R.
1994. *Sastun: My Apprenticeship with a Maya Healer.* New York: Harper Collins.

Astor-Aguilera Miguel Angel
2010. *The Maya World of Communicating Objects: Quadripartite Crosses, Trees, and Stones.* Albuquerque: University of New Mexico Press.

Atkinson, Jane M.
1992. Shamanisms Today. *Annual Review of Anthropology* 21:307–30.

Audet, Patrick, Brendan Walshe-Roussel, Victor Cal, Francisco Caal, Marco Otarola Rojas, Pablo Sanchez Vindas, Luis Poveda, Todd Pesek, and John T. Arnason
2013. Indigenous ex Situ Conservation of Q'eqchi' Maya Medicinal Plant Resources at the Itzamma Garden–Indian Creek, Belize, Central America. *Human Ecology* 41(2):313–24.

Awad, Rosalie, Fida Ahmed, Natalie Bourbonnais-Spear, Martha Mullally, Chieu Anh Ta, Andrew Tang, Zul Merali, Pedro Maquin, Francisco Caal, Victor Cal, Luis Poveda, Pablo Sanchez Vindas, Vance L. Trudeau, and John T. Arnason
2009. Ethnopharmacology of Q'eqchi' Maya Antiepileptic and Anxiolytic Plants: Effects on the GABergic System. *Journal of Ethnopharmacology* 125(2):257–64.

Ayora-Diaz, Steffan Igor
2000. Imagining Authenticities in the Local Medicines of Chiapas, Mexico. *Critique of Anthropology* 20(2):173–90.

Balick, Michael J., Jillian De Gezelle, and Rosita Arvigo
2008. Feeling the Pulse in Maya Medicine: An Endangered Traditional Tool for Diagnosis, Therapy, and Tracking Patients' Progress. *Explore* 4(2):113–19.

Bates, Don
1995. Scholarly Ways of Knowing. In *Knowledge and the Scholarly Medical Traditions.* Don Bates, ed. Pp. 1–22. Cambridge: Cambridge University Press.

Berg, Marc
1998. Order(s) and Disorder(s): Of Protocols and Medical Practices. In *Differences in Medicine: Unveiling Practices, Techniques, and Bodies.* Marc Berg and Annemarie Mol, eds. Pp. 226–46. Durham, NC: Duke University Press.

Belize National Institute of Culture and History (NICH)
2013. *National Culture Policy Draft*. Belmopan: National Institute of Culture and History.

Berlin, Elios Ann, and Brent Berlin
1966. *Medical Ethnobiology of the Highland Maya of Chiapas, Mexico: The Gastrointestinal Diseases*. Princeton, NJ: Princeton University Press.

Bird-David, Nurit
1999. "Animism" Revisited: Personhood, Environment, and Relational Epistemology. *Current Anthropology* 40(S1):S67–S91.

Boellstorff, Tom
2008. *Coming of Age in Second Life: An Anthropologist Explores the Virtually Human*. Princeton, NJ: Princeton University Press.

Bolland, Nigel
2003. *Colonialism and Resistance in Belize: Essays in Historical Sociology*. Barbados: University of the West Indies Press.

Borgatti, Stephen
1996. ANTHROPAC. Analytic Technologies. http://www.analytictech.com/anthropac/anthropac.htm.
1997. Multidimensional Scaling. Analytic Technologies. http://www.analytictech.com/borgatti/mds.htm.

Borgatti, Stephen., M. G. Everett, and L. C. Freeman
2002. Ucinet 6 for Windows: Software for Social Network Analysis. Harvard, MA: Analytic Technologies.

Borgatti, Stephen, and Daniel Halgin
2011. Consensus Analysis. In *A Companion to Cognitive Anthropology*. David B. Kronenfeld, Giovanni Bennardo, Victor C. de Munck, and Michael D. Fischer, eds. Pp. 171–90. Chichester: Wiley Blackwell.

Bourbonnais-Spear, Natalie, Rosalie Awad, Pedro Maquin, Victor Cal, Luis Poveda, and John T. Arnason
2005. Plant Use by the Q'eqchi' Maya of Belize in Ethnopsychiatry and Neurological Pathology. *Economic Botany* 59(4):326–36.

Bourbonnais-Spear, Natalie, Rosalie Awad, Zul Merali, Pedro Maquin, Victor Cal, and John T. Arnason
2007. Ethnopharmacological Investigation of Plants Used to Treat Susto, a Folk Illness. *Journal of Ethnopharmacology* 109:380–87.

Brady, Maggie
1995. Culture in Treatment, Culture as Treatment: A Critical Appraisal of

Developments in Addictions Programs for Indigenous North Americans and Australians. *Social Science and Medicine* 41(11):1487–98.

Cabarrús, Carlos
1979. *La Cosmovision K'ekchi' en Proceso de Cambio*. San Salvador: Universidad Centroamericana.

Cassell, Eric J.
1991. *The Nature of Suffering and the Goals of Medicine*. New York: Oxford University Press.
1997. *Doctoring: The Nature of Primary Care Medicine*. New York: Oxford University Press.

Chevalier, Jacques M., and Andrés Sánchez Bain
2003. *The Hot and the Cold: Ills of Humans and Maize in Native Mexico*. Toronto: University of Toronto Press.

Choco, Pedro
2015. A Preliminary Study of Ethnobotanical Use of Plant Species by the Q'eqchi' Maya Community in Toledo District. Bachelor of science thesis, University of Belize.

Clifford, James, and George E. Marcus
1986. *Writing Culture: The Poetics and Politics of Ethnography*. Berkeley: University of California Press.

Colson, Anthony C., and Karen E. Selby
1974. Medical Anthropology. *Annual Review of Anthropology* 3:245–62.

Consejo Mayor de Médicos Maya'ob' por Nacimiento
2016. *Raxnaq'il Nuk' Aslemal: Medicina Maya'ob' en Guatemala*. Guatemala City: Asociaciòn Ati't Alá.

Cook, Garrett W.
2000. *Renewing the Maya World: Expressive Culture in a Highland Town*. Austin: University of Texas Press.

Cooper, John M.
1935. Magic and Science. *Thought* 10:357.

Cosminsky, Sheila, and Mary Scrimshaw
1980. Medical Pluralism on a Guatemalan Plantation. *Social Science and Medicine* 14B:267–78.

Costandi, Mo
2011. Doctors Diagnose Disease as If Recognizing Objects. *Guardian*, December 20. https://www.theguardian.com/science/neurophilosophy/2011/dec/20/1.

Craig, Sienna R.
2012. *Healing Elements: Efficacy and the Social Ecologies of Tibetan Medicine*. Berkeley: University of California Press.

Cruikshank, Julie
2006. *Do Glaciers Listen? Local Knowledge, Colonial Encounters, and Social Imagination*. Vancouver: University of British Columbia Press.

Cumming, A. D., and S. I. R. Noble
2014. Good Medical Practice. In *Davidson's Principles and Practice of Medicine*. 22nd edition. Brian R. Walker, Nicki R. Colledge, Stuart Ralston, and Ian D. Penman, eds. Pp. 2–16. Edinburgh: Churchill Livingstone.

De Gezelle, Jillian
2014. *Q'eqchi' Maya Reproductive Ethnomedicine*. New York: Springer.

DeLanda, Manuel
2006. *A New Philosophy of Society: Assemblage Theory and Social Complexity*. London: Continuum.

Deleuze, Gilles
1991. *Bergsonism*. New York: Zone Books.
2004. *Difference and Repetition*. London: Continuum.

Deleuze, Gilles, and Félix Guattari
2004. *A Thousand Plateaus: Capitalism and Schizophrenia*. London: Continuum.

Desjarlais, Robert
1992. *Body and Emotion: The Aesthetics of Illness and Healing in the Nepal Himalayas*. Philadelphia: University of Pennsylvania Press.

Dickinson, D.
2008. Traditional Healers, HIV/AIDS and Company Programmes in South Africa. *African Journal of AIDS Research* 7(3):281–91.

Dow, James
1986. Universal Aspects of Symbolic Healing: A Theoretical Synthesis. *American Anthropologist* 88(1):56–69.

Eddy, David
1990a. The Challenge. *Journal of the American Medical Association* 263(2):287–90.
1990b. Anatomy of a Decision. *Journal of the American Medical Association* 263(3):441–43.
2011. The Origins of Evidence-Based Medicine: A Personal Perspective. *Virtual Mentor: American Medical Association Journal of Ethics* 13(1):55–60.

Eder, Karin, and Maria Manuela Garcia Pú
2002. *Model of Indigenous Maya Medicine in Guatemala*. Guatemala City: Asociacioń de Servicios Comunitarios de Salud.

Edgerton, Robert B.
1992. *Sick Societies: Challenging the Myth of Primitive Harmony*. New York: Free Press.

Eisenberg, Leon, and Arthur Kleinman

1981. Clinical Social Science. In *The Relevance of Social Science for Medicine*. Leon Eisenberg and Arthur Kleinman, eds. Pp. 1–23. Dordrecht: Reidel.

Erasmus, Charles John

1952. Changing Folk Beliefs and the Relativity of Empirical Knowledge. *Southwestern Journal of Anthropology* 8(4):411–28.

Erazo, Juliet, and Christopher Jarrett

2017. Managing Alterity from Within: The Ontological Turn in Anthropology and Indigenous Efforts to Shape Shamanism. *RAI: Journal of the Royal Anthropology Institute* (N.S.) 24:1–19.

Erickson, Pamela I.

2008. *Ethnomedicine*. Long Grove, IL: Waveland.

Evans-Pritchard, E. E.

1976 [1937]. *Witchcraft, Oracles, and Magic among the Azande*. Abridged. Oxford: Clarendon Press.

Fabrega, Horacio, Jr.

1970. Dynamics of Medical Practice in a Folk Community. *Milbank Memorial Fund Quarterly* 48(4):391–412.

1971. Medical Anthropology. *Biennial Review of Anthropology* 7:167–229.

Fabrega, Horacio, Jr., and Daniel Silver

1973. *Illness and Shamanistic Curing in Zinacantan*. Stanford, CA: Stanford University Press.

Fabrega, Horacio, Jr., Duane Metzger, and Gerald Williams

1970. Psychiatric Implications of Health and Illness in a Maya Indian Group: A Preliminary Statement. *Social Science and Medicine* 3:609–26.

Finkler, K.

1985. *Spiritualist Healers in Mexico: Success and Failures of Alternative Therapeutics*. South Hadley, MA: Bergen and Garvey.

1994. Sacred Healing and Biomedicine Compared. *Medical Anthropology Quarterly* 8:178–97.

Fischer, Edward F.

1999. Cultural Logic and Maya Identity: Rethinking Constructivism and Essentialism. *Current Anthropology* 40(4):473–99.

Foster, George M.

1976. Disease Etiologies in Non-Western Medical Systems. *American Anthropologist* 78:773–82.

1984a. Anthropological Research on Health Problems in Developing Countries. *Social Science and Medicine* 10:847–54.
1984b. How to Stay Well in Tzintzuntzan. *Social Science and Medicine* 19(5):523–33.
1985. How to Get Well in Tzintzuntzan. *Social Science and Medicine* 21(7):807–18.

Frank, Jerome
1961. *Persuasion and Healing: A Comparative Study of Psychotherapy.* Baltimore: Johns Hopkins University Press.

Frank, J., and J. Frank
1993. *Persuasion and Healing: A Comparative Study of Psychotherapy.* Baltimore: Johns Hopkins University Press.

Frazier, Jeffrey B.
2015. *Q'eqchi' Mayan Dictionary.* Self-published, Mayaglot.

Gaines, Atwood, and Robbie Davis-Floyd
2004. Biomedicine. In *Encyclopedia of Medical Anthropology.* Melvin Ember and Carol Ember, eds. Pp. 95–109. Dordrecht: Kluwer Academic Publishers.

García, Hernán, Antonio Sierra, and Gilberta Balám
1999. *Wind in the Blood: Mayan Healing and Chinese Medicine.* Berkeley: North Atlantic Books.

Garro, Linda C.
1990. Continuity and Change: The Interpretation of Illness in an Anishinaabe (Ojibway) Community. *Culture, Medicine, and Psychiatry* 14:417–54.

Gidrewicz, Dominica, and Chuck Wen
2005. The Peripheral Vascular Exam. In *Essentials of Clinical Examination Handbook.* 5th ed. Woganee Filate, Rico Leung, Dawn Ng, and Mark Sinyor, eds. Pp. 247–64. Toronto: Medical Society, Faculty of Medicine, University of Toronto.

Glik, Deborah
1988. Symbolic, Ritual and Social Dynamics of Spiritual Healing. *Social Science and Medicine* 27(11):1197–206.

Gonzales, Patrisia
2012. *Red Medicine: Traditional Indigenous Rites of Birthing and Healing.* Tucson: University of Arizona Press.

Good, Byron J.
1994. *Medicine, Rationality, and Experience: An Anthropological Perspective.* Cambridge: Cambridge University Press.

Gordon, Deborah R.
1988. Clinical Science and Clinical Expertise: Changing Boundaries between Art and

Science in Medicine. In *Biomedicine Examined*. Margaret Lock and Deborah R. Gordon, eds. Pp. 257–95. Dordrecht: Kluwer.

Government of Belize
2013. *National Culture Policy Draft*. Belmopan: National Institute of Culture and History.
2014. *Improving Quality Health Services: A Safer and Healthier Belize by 2024*. Belmopan: Ministry of Health.
2016. *Belize National Cultural Policy 2016–2026*. Belmopan: National Institute of Culture and History.

Green, Lawrence
2006. Public Health Asks of Systems Science: To Advance Our Evidence-Based Practice, Can You Help Us Get More Practice-Based Evidence? *American Journal of Public Health* 96(3):406–9.

Groark, Kevin
2005. Pathogenic Emotions: Sentiment, Sociality, and Sickness among the Tzotzil Maya of San Juan Chamula, Chiapas, Mexico. PhD dissertation, Department of Anthropology, University of California–Los Angeles.
2008. Social Opacity and the Dynamics of Empathic In-Sight among the Tzotzil Maya of Chiapas, Mexico. *Ethos* 36(4):427–48.

Grosz, Elizabeth
2017. *The Incorporeal: Ontology, Ethics, and the Limits of Materialism*. New York: Columbia University Press.

Guerra, Francisco
1964. Maya Medicine. *Medical History* 8(1):31–43.

Hahn, Robert A., and Arthur Kleinman
1983. Biomedical Practice and Anthropological Theory: Frameworks and Directions. *Annual Review of Anthropology* 12:305–33.

Hallowell, A. Irving
1955. *Culture and Experience*. Philadelphia: University of Pennsylvania Press.
1960. Ojibwa Ontology, Behavior, and World View. In *Essays in Honor of Paul Radin*, Stanley Diamond, ed. Pp. 19–52. New York: Columbia University Press.

Harris, Mark
2007. Ways of Knowing. In *Ways of Knowing: New Approaches in the Anthropology of Knowledge and Learning*, Mark Harris, ed. Pp 1–24. New York: Berghahn Books.

Harvey, Graham
2006. *Respecting the Living World*. New York: Columbia University Press.
2014. Introduction. In *The Handbook of Contemporary Animism*. Graham Harvey, ed. Pp.1–16. New York: Routledge.

Harvey, T. S.
2013. *Wellness beyond Words: Maya Compositions of Speech and Silence in Medical Care.* Albuquerque: University of New Mexico Press.

Harwood, Alan
1987 [1977]. *Rx: Spiritist as Needed: A Study of a Puerto Rican Community Mental Health Resource.* Ithaca, NY: Cornell University Press.

Hatala, Andrew R., James B. Waldram, and Tomas Caal
2015. Narrative Structures of Q'eqchi' Maya Mental Disorders. *Culture, Medicine, and Psychiatry* 39(3):449–86.

Hausmann-Muela, Susanna, and Joan Muela Ribera
2003. Recipe Knowledge: A Tool for Understanding Some Apparently Irrational Behaviour. *Anthropology and Medicine* 10(1):87–103.

Hazard, Sonia
2013. The Material Turn in the Study of Religion. *Religion and Society* 4:58–78.

Heinrich, Michael, Anita Ankli, Barbara Frel, Claudia Weiman, and Otto Sticher
1998. Medicinal Plants in Mexico: Healers' Consensus and Cultural Importance. *Social Science and Medicine* 47(11):1859–1871.

Herrera, César E. Giraldo
2018. *Microbes and Other Shamanic Beings.* Cham, Switzerland: Palgrave Macmillan.

Hinojosa, Servando Z.
2015. *In this Body: Kaqchikel Maya and the Grounding of Spirit.* Albuquerque: University of New Mexico Press.

Holbraad, Martin, and Morten Axel Pederson
2017. *The Ontological Turn: An Anthropological Exposition.* Cambridge: Cambridge University Press.

Holland, William R., and Roland G. Tharp
1964. Highland Maya Psychotherapy. *American Anthropologist* 66(1):41–52.

Horton, Robin
1967a. African Traditional Thought and Western Science. Part 1: From Tradition to Science. *Africa: Journal of the International African Institute* 37(1):50–71.
1967b. African Traditional Thought and Western Science. Part 2: The "Closed" and the "Open" Predicaments. *Africa: Journal of the International African Institute* 37(2):155–87.

Hughes, Charles C.
1968. Ethnomedicine. In *International Encyclopedia of the Social Sciences* 10:87–93.
1996. Ethnopsychiatry. In *Medical Anthropology: Contemporary Theory and Method.* Rev. ed. C. F. Sargent and T. M. Johnson, eds. Pp. 131–50. Westport, CT: Praeger.

Ingold, Tim
2006. Rethinking the Animate, Re-Animating Thought. *Ethnos* 71(1):9–20.
2007. Materials against Materiality. *Archaeological Dialogues* 14(1):1–16.
2014. Being Alive to a World without Objects. In *The Handbook of Contemporary Animism*. Graham Harvey, ed. Pp. 213–25. New York: Routledge.

Juárez, Miguel S., Ernesto C. Cao, Cristanto X. Tec, Domingo C. Chen, and Pedro T. Pop
2003. *Diccionario Q'eqchi'*. Antigua, Guatemala: Proyecto Lingüístico Francisco Marroquín.

Kahn, Hilary E.
2006. *Seeing and Being Seen: The Q'eqchi' Maya of Livingston, Guatemala, and Beyond.* Austin: University of Texas Press.

Kaiser, Bonnie N., Emily E. Haroz , Brandon A. Kohrt, Paul A. Bolton , Judith K. Bass, and Devon E. Hinton
2015. "Thinking Too Much": A Systematic Review of a Common Idiom of Distress. *Social Science and Medicine* 147:170–83.

Kiev, Ari
1962. The Psychotherapeutic Aspects of Primitive Medicine. *Human Organization* 21(1):25–29.

Kirmayer, Laurence J.
1993. Healing and the Invention of Metaphor: The Effectiveness of Symbols Revisited. *Culture, Medicine, and Psychiatry* 17:161–95.

Kleinman, Arthur
1980. *Patients and Healers in the Context of Culture*. Berkeley: University of California Press.

Kleinman, Arthur, and Lilias H. Sung
1979. Why Do Indigenous Practitioners Successfully Heal? *Social Science and Medicine* 13B:7–26.

Kohn, Eduardo
2013. *How Forests Think: Toward and Anthropology beyond the Human*. Berkeley: University of California Press.

Kohrt, Brandon A., and Ian Harper
2008. Navigating Diagnoses: Understanding Mind-Body Relations, Mental Health, and Stigma in Nepal. *Culture, Medicine, and Psychiatry* 32:462–91.

Konrad, Herman
1991. Pilgrimage as Cyclical Process: The Unending Pilgrimage of the Holy Cross of the Quintana Roo Maya. In *Pilgrimage in Latin America*. N. Ross Crumine and E. Alan Morinis, eds. Pp. 123–37. New York: Greenwood Press.

Kukul, Pedro

2013. Q'eqchi'. In *The Encyclopedia of Caribbean Religions*. Vol. 2. Patrick Taylor and Frederick J. Case, eds., Pp. 570–76. Urbana: University of Illinois Press.

Kunow, Marianna Appel

2003. *Maya Medicine: Traditional Healing in Yucatan*. Albuquerque: University of New Mexico Press.

Langford, Jean M.

1999. Medical Mimesis: Healing Signs of a Cosmopolitan "Quack." *American Ethnologist* 26(1):24–46.

Langwick, Stacey A.

2011. *Bodies, Politics, and African Healing: The Matter of Maladies in Tanzania*. Bloomington: Indiana University Press.

Lanzano, Cristiano

2013. What Kind of Knowledge Is "Indigenous Knowledge"? Critical Insights from a Case Study in Burkina Faso. *Transcience* 4(2):3–18.

Last, Murray

2007. The Importance of Knowing about Not Knowing. In *Knowing and Not Knowing in the Anthropology of Medicine*. Roland Littlewood, ed. Pp. 1–17. Walnut Creek, CA: Left Coast Press.

Lauer, Matthew

2012. Oral Traditions or Situated Practices? Understanding How Indigenous Communities Respond to Environmental Disasters. *Human Organization* 71(2):176–87.

Laughlin, William S.

1963. Primitive Theory of Medicine: Empirical Knowledge. In *Man's Image in Medicine and Anthropology*. Iago Galdston, ed. Pp. 116–40. New York: International Universities Press.

Lévi-Strauss, Claude

1966. *The Savage Mind*. London: Weidenfeld and Nicolson.

Lock, Margaret, and Nancy Scheper-Hughes

1996. A Critical-Interpretive Approach in Medical Anthropology: Rituals and Routines of Discipline and Dissent. In *Medical Anthropology: Contemporary Theory and Method*. Rev. ed. Carolyn F. Sargent and Thomas M. Johnson, eds. Pp. 41–70. Westport, CT: Praeger.

Lock, Margaret, and Vihn-Kim Nguyen

2010. *An Anthropology of Biomedicine*. Chichester: Wiley and Sons.

Lucas, Rodney H., and Robert J. Barrett
1995. Interpreting Culture and Psychopathology: Primitivist Themes in Cross-Cultural Debate. *Culture, Medicine, and Psychiatry* 19(3):287–326.

Marcus, George, and Michael Fischer
1986. *Anthropology as Cultural Critique: An Experimental Moment in the Human Sciences.* Chicago: University of Chicago Press.

Mattingly, Cheryl
1994. The Concept of Therapeutic "Emplotment." *Social Science and Medicine* 38(6):811–22.
1998a. In Search of the Good: Narrative Reasoning in Clinical Practice. *Medical Anthropology Quarterly* 12(3):273–97.
1998b. *Healing Dramas and Clinical Plots: The Narrative Structure of Experience.* Cambridge: Cambridge University Press.

McCabe, Mary S., William A. Wood, and Richard M. Goldberg
2010. When the Family Requests Withholding the Diagnosis: Who Owns the Truth? *Journal of Oncology Practice* 6(2):94–96. http://doi.org/10.1200/JOP.091086.

Mechanic, D., D. McAlpine, and M. Rosenthal
2001. Are Patients' Office Visits with Physicians Getting Shorter? *New England Journal of Medicine* 344:198–204.

Metzger, Duane, and Gerald Williams
1963. Tenejapa Medicine 1: The Curer. *Southwestern Journal of Anthropology* 19(2):216–34.

Michel, Joanna, Reinel Eduardo Duarte, Ping Yao, Judy L. Bolton, Yue Huang, Armando Cáceres, Mario Veliz, Djaja Doel Soejarto, and Gail B. Mahady
2007. Medical Potential of Plants Used by the Q'eqchi' Maya of Livingston, Guatemala, for the Treatment of Women's Health Complaints. *Journal of Ethnopharmacology* 114(1):92–101.

Moerman, Daniel E.
1983. Physiology and Symbols: The Anthropological Implications of the Placebo Effect. In *The Anthropology of Medicine: From Culture to Method.* Lola Romanucci-Ross, Daniel E. Moerman, and Laurence Tancredi, eds. Pp. 156–67. South Hadley, MA: Bergen and Garvey.
1979. Anthropology of Symbolic Healing. *Current Anthropology* 20(1):59–66.

Mol, Annemarie, and Marc Berg
1998. Differences in Medicine: An Introduction. In *Differences in Medicine: Unveiling Practices, Techniques, and Bodies.* Marc Berg and Annemarie Mol, eds. Pp. 1–12. Durham, NC: Duke University Press.

Montgomery, Kathryn
2006. *How Doctors Think: Clinical Judgement and the Practice of Medicine.* Oxford: Oxford University Press.

Moriarty, James Robert
1970. *A General Syllogy of Maya Medicine*. Museum of Anthropology Miscellaneous Series 15. Greeley: University of Northern Colorado, Museum of Anthropology.

Morley, Peter
1978. Culture and the Cognitive World of Traditional Medical Beliefs: Some Preliminary Considerations. In *Culture and Curing: Anthropological Perspectives on Traditional Medical Beliefs and Practices*. P. Morley and Roy R. Wallis, eds. Pp. 1–18. London: Peter Owen.

Morrison, Kenneth M.
2014. Animism and a Proposal for a Post-Cartesian Anthropology. In *The Handbook of Contemporary Animism*. Graham Harvey, ed. Pp. 38–52. New York: Routledge.

Murdock, George Peter
1980. *Theories of Illness: A World Survey*. Pittsburgh: University of Pittsburgh Press.

Nash, June
1967. The Logic of Behavior: Curing in a Maya Indian Town. *Human Organization* 26(3):132–40.

Nichter, Mark
1991. Ethnomedicine: Diverse Trends, Common Linkages. *Medical Anthropology* 13(1–2):137–71.

Oguamanam, Chidi
2006. *International Law and Indigenous Knowledge: Intellectual Property, Plant Biodiversity, and Traditional Medicine*. Toronto: University of Toronto Press.

O'Neill, John
1985. *Five Bodies: The Human Shape of Modern Society*. Ithaca, NY: Cornell University Press.

Orellana, Sandra L.
1987. *Indian Medicine in Highland Guatemala: The Pre-Hispanic and Colonial Periods*. Albuquerque: University of New Mexico Press.

Peckham, Carol
2016. Medscape Physician Compensation Report 2016. *Medscape*, April 1. http://www.medscape.com/features/slideshow/compensation/2016/public/overview?src=wnl_physrep_160401_mscpedit&uac=232148CZ&impID=1045700&faf=1#page=26.

Pedersen, Duncan, and Veronica Baruffati
1985. Health and Traditional Medicine Cultures in Latin America and the Caribbean. *Social Science and Medicine* 21(1):5–12.

Permanto, Stefan
2015. The Elders and the Hills: Animism and Cosmological Re-Creation among the Q'eqchi' Maya in Chisec, Guatemala. PhD thesis, University of Gothenburg.

Pesek, Todd, Marc Abramiuk, Nick Fini, Marco Otarola Rojas, Sean Collins, Victor Cal, Pablo Sanchez, Luis Poveda, and John Arnason
2010. Q'eqchi' Maya Healers' Traditional Knowledge in Prioritizing Conservation of Medicinal Plants: Culturally Relative Conservation in Sustaining Traditional Holistic Health Promotion. *Biodiversity and Conservation* 19:1–20.

Plumwood, Val
2014. Nature in the Active Voice. In *The Handbook of Contemporary Animism*. Graham Harvey, ed. Pp. 441–53. New York: Routledge.

Pollard, J.
2004. The Art of Decay and the Transformation of Substance. In *Substance, Memory, Display*. C. Renfrew, C. Gosden, and E. DeMarrais, eds. Pp. 47–62. Cambridge: McDonald Institute for Archaeological Research.

Porter, Roy
1997. *The Greatest Benefit to Mankind: A Medical History of Humanity*. New York: W. W. Norton.

Quah, Stella R.
2003. Traditional Healing Systems and the Ethos of Science. *Social Science and Medicine* 57:1997–2012.

Redfield, Robert
1950. *A Village That Chose Progress: Chan Kom Revisited*. Chicago: University of Chicago Press.

Redfield, Robert, and Margaret Park Redfield
1940. *Disease and Its Treatment in Dzitas, Yucatan*. Contributions to American Anthropology and History 32. Washington, DC: Carnegie Institute of Washington.

Redfield, Robert, and Alfonso Villa Rojas
1934. *Chan Kom: A Maya Village*. Chicago: University of Chicago Press.

Reeser, Douglas C.
2014. Medical Pluralism in a Neoliberal State: Health and Deservingness in Southern Belize. PhD dissertation, Department of Anthropology, University of South Florida.

Richter, Maurice N.
1972. *Science as a Cultural Process*. Morristown, NJ: Schenkman.

Rival, Laura
2014. The Materiality of Life: Revisiting the Anthropology of Nature in Amazonia. In *The Handbook of Contemporary Animism*. Graham Harvey, ed. Pp. 92–100. New York: Routledge.

Rivers, W. H. R.
2001 [1924]. *Medicine, Magic and Religion*. London: Routledge.

Robinson, Howard
1998. Materialism in the Philosophy of Mind. *Routledge Encyclopedia of Philosophy*. Abingdon, UK: Taylor and Francis.

Romney, A. Kimball, Susan C. Weller, and William H. Batchelder
1986. Culture as Consensus: A Theory of Culture and Informant Accuracy. *American Anthropologist* 88(2):313–38.

Rubel, Arthur
1964. The Epidemiology of a Folk Illness: Susto in Hispanic America. *Ethnology* 3(3):268–83.

Rubel, Arthur, and Michael J. Hass
1996. Ethnomedicine. In *Medical Anthropology: Contemporary Theory and Method*. Rev. ed. Carolyn F. Sargent and Thomas M. Johnson, eds. Pp. 113–30. Westport, CT: Praeger.

Salomon, Kristin, and Alvin Jin
2013. Diathesis-Stress Models. In *Encyclopedia of Behavioral Medicine*. Marc D. Gellman and J. Rick Turner, eds., Pp. 591–92. New York: Springer.

Saunders, John
2000. The Practice of Clinical Medicine as an Art and as a Science. *Journal of Medical Ethics: Medical Humanities* 26:18–22.

Scheper-Hughes, Nancy, and Margaret Lock
1987. The Mindful Body: A Prolegomenon to Future Work in Medical Anthropology. *Medical Anthropology Quarterly* 1(1):6–41.

Scotch, Norman
1963. Medical Anthropology. *Biennial Review of Anthropology* 3:30–68.

Segal, Robert A.
2014. Animism for Tylor. In *The Handbook of Contemporary Animism*. Graham Harvey, ed. Pp. 53–62. New York: Routledge.

Shields, Rob
2003. The Virtual. New York: Routledge.
2006. Virtualities. *Theory, Culture and Society* 23(2–3):284–86.

Shivola, Ari
2007. Metamaterials in Electromagnetics. *Metamaterials* 1:2–7.
2009. Metamaterials: A Personal View. *Radioengineering* 18(2):90–94.

Shweder, Richard
2003. *Why Do Men Barbecue?* Cambridge, MA: Harvard University Press.

Si-Qin, Timur
2011. Metamaterialism. Pool, July 11. http://pooool.info/metamaterialism.

Sillar, Bill
2009. The Social Agency of Things? Animism and Materiality in the Andes. *Cambridge Archaeological Journal* 19(3):369–79.

Sillitoe, Paul
1998. The Development of Indigenous Knowledge: A New Applied Anthropology. *Current Anthropology* 39(2):223–52.

Singer, Merrill, and Hans Baer
1995. *Critical Medical Anthropology*. Amityville, NY: Baywood.

Snyder, Lois
2012. *Ethics Manual*. 6th ed. Philadelphia: American College of Physicians.

Sontag, Susan
1978. *Illness as Metaphor*. New York: Farrer, Straus, and Giroux.

Stack, George J.
1998. Materialism. *Routledge Encyclopedia of Philosophy*. http://documents.routledge-interactive.s3.amazonaws.com/9781138936485/instr_philosophical/materialism.pdf.

Statistical Institute of Belize
2013. *Belize Population and Housing Census 2010, Country Report*. Belmopan City: Statistical Institute of Belize.

Sullivan, Mark D.
1993. Placebo Controls and Epistemic Control in Orthodox Medicine. *Journal of Medicine and Philosophy* 18:213–31.

Swisher, Anne K.
2010. Practice-Based Evidence. *Cardiopulmonary Physical Therapy Journal* 21(2):4.

Tax, Sol
1950. Animistic and Rational Thought. *Kroeber Anthropological Society Papers* 2:1–5.

Tedlock, Barbara
1987. An Interpretive Solution to the Problem of Humoral Medicine in Latin America. *Social Science and Medicine* 24(12):1069–83.
1992. The Role of Dreams and Visionary Narratives in Mayan Cultural Survival. *Ethos* 20(4):453–76.

Tenzel, James H.
1970. Shamanism and Concepts of Disease in a Mayan Indian Community. *Psychiatry* 33(3):372–80.

Thagard, Paul
2005. What Is a Medical Theory? In *Multidisciplinary Approaches to Theory in Medicine*. Vol. 3. Ray Paton and Laura McNamara, eds. Pp. 47–62. Amsterdam: Elsevier.

Thompson, J. Eric S.
1970. *Maya History and Religion*. Norman: University of Oklahoma Press.

Thornton, Robert
2015. Magical Empiricism and "Exposed Being" in Medicine and Traditional Healing. *Medical Anthropology* 34:353–70.

Tilley, C.
2007. Materiality in Materials. *Archaeological Dialogues* 14(1):16–20.

Turner, Victor
1967. *The Forest of Symbols*. Ithaca, NY: Cornell University Press.
1975. Symbolic Studies. *Annual Review of Anthropology* 4:145–61.

Tylor, E. B.
1913 [1871]. *Primitive Culture: Researches into the Development of Mythology, Philosophy, Religion, Art and Customs*. 2 vols. London: John Murray.

United Nations
2008. *Declaration on the Rights of Indigenous Peoples*. New York: United Nations.

Waldram, James B.
1997. *The Way of the Pipe: Aboriginal Spirituality and Symbolic Healing in Canadian Prisons*. Peterborough, ON: Broadview Press.
2000. The Efficacy of Traditional Medicine: Current Theoretical and Methodological Issues. *Medical Anthropology Quarterly* 14(4):603–25.
2004. *Revenge of the Windigo: The Construction of the Mind and Mental Health of North American Aboriginal Peoples*. Toronto: University of Toronto Press, Anthropological Horizons.
2012a. Healing History? Aboriginal Healing, Historical Trauma, and Personal Responsibility. *Transcultural Psychiatry* 51(3):370–86.
2012b. *Hound Pound Narrative: Sexual Offender Habilitation and the Anthropology of Therapeutic Intervention*. Berkeley: University of California Press.
2013. Transformative and Restorative Processes: Revisiting the Efficacy of Indigenous Healing. *Medical Anthropology* 32(3):191–207.
2015a. *Kawil Poyanam, Chaab'il Yu'am: Laj lilonel re B'elis (Healthy People, Beautiful Life: Maya Healers of Belize)*. Saskatoon: Anthro*In*Sight.
2015b. "I Don't Know the Words He Uses": Therapeutic Communication among Q'eqchi' Maya Healers and Their Patients. *Medical Anthropology Quarterly* 29(3):279–97.

Waldram, James B., Victor Cal, and Pedro Maquin
2009. The Q'eqchi' Healers Association of Belize: An Endogenous Movement in Heritage Preservation and Management. *Heritage Management* 2(1):35–54.

Waldram, James B., and Andrew R. Hatala
2015. Latent and Manifest Empiricism in Q'eqchi' Maya Healing: A Case Study of HIV/AIDS. *Social Science and Medicine* 126:9–16.

Walker, Brian R., Nicki R. Colledge, Stuart Ralston, and Ian D. Penman, eds.
2014. *Davidson's Principles and Practice of Medicine*. 22nd ed. Edinburgh: Churchill Livingstone.

Watanabe, John M.
1992. *Maya Saints and Souls in a Changing World*. Austin: University of Texas Press.

Weisner, Thomas S.
2009. Well-Being and Sustainability of Daily Routines: Families with Children with Disabilities in the United States. In *Pursuits of Happiness: Well-Being in Anthropological Perspective*. Gordon Matthews and Carolina Izquierdo, eds. Pp. 228–47. New York: Berghahn.

Wilk, Richard R.
1997. *Household Ecology: Economic Change and Domestic Life among the Kekchi Maya in Belize*. Tucson: University of Arizona Press.

Wilson, Richard
1993. Anchored Communities: Identity and History of the Maya-Q'eqchi'. *Man* (N.S.) 28(1):121–38.
1995. *Maya Resurgence in Guatemala: Q'eqchi' Experiences*. Norman: University of Oklahoma Press.

World Health Organization (WHO)
1946. Constitution of the World Health Organization. New York, New York. http://www.who.int/bulletin/archives/80(12)981.pdf. Accessed January 11 2017.
1984. Global Strategy for Health for All by the Year 2000: The Spiritual Dimension. 73rd Session of the Executive Board, Provisional Agenda Item 11. https://apps.who.int/iris/bitstream/handle/10665/160577/EB73_15_eng.pdf?sequence=1&isAllowed=y. Accessed July 19 2019.
2013. *WHO Traditional Medicine Strategy 2014–2023*. Geneva: World Health Organization, World Intellectual Property Organization, and World Trade Organization.
2012. *Promoting Access to Medical Technologies and Innovation: Intersections between Public Health, Intellectual Property, and Trade*. Geneva: World Health Organization.

Worsley, Peter
1982. Non-Western Medical Systems. *Annual Review of Anthropology* 11:315–48.

Yarris, Kristin E.
2011. The Pain of "Thinking Too Much": Dolor de Cerebro and the Embodiment of Social Hardship among Nicaraguan Women. *Ethos* 39(2):226–48.

Yim, O., and Ramdeen, K. T.
2015. Hierarchical Cluster Analysis: Comparison of Three Linkage Measures and Application to Psychological Data. *Quantitative Methods in Psychology* 11:8–21.

Young, Allan
1976a. Some Implications of Medical Beliefs and Practices for Social Anthropology. *American Anthropologist* 78(1):5–24.
1976b. Internalizing and Externalizing Medical Belief Systems: An Ethiopian Example. *Social Science and Medicine* 10:147–56.
1979. The Dimensions of Medical Rationality: A Problematic for the Psychosocial Study of Medicine. In *Toward a New Definition of Health: Psychosocial Dimensions.* Paul I. Ahmed and George V. Coelho, eds. Pp. 67–85. New York: Plenum.
1981. The Creation of Medical Knowledge: Some Problems in Interpretation. *Social Science and Medicine* 15B:379–86.
1982. The Anthropology of Illness and Sickness. *Annual Review of Anthropology* 11:257–85.
1983. The Relevance of Traditional Medical Cultures to Modern Primary Health Care. *Social Science and Medicine* 17(16):1205–11.

Young, James C.
1978. Illness Categories and Action Strategies in a Tarascan Town. *American Ethnologist* 5:81–97.

Index

Page numbers in italic text indicate illustrations. Page numbers in bold text indicate glossary entries.

www.ingramcontent.com/pod-product-compliance
Lightning Source LLC
Chambersburg PA
CBHW020842270326
41928CB00006B/515
* 9 7 8 0 8 2 6 3 6 4 4 4 9 *